Architectural Commercial Design
Using Autodesk® Revit® 2015

Daniel John Stine

Publications

SDC Publications
P.O. Box 1334
Mission, KS 66222
913-262-2664
www.SDCpublications.com
Publisher: Stephen Schroff

Examination Copies:
Books received as examination copies are for review purposes only and may not be made
available for student use. Resale of examination copies is prohibited.

Electronic Files:
Any electronic files associated with this book are licensed to the original user only. These
files may not be transferred to any other party.

Trademarks:
Autodesk®, AutoCAD®, Maya®, mental ray®, Revit®, 3ds Max® are registered
trademarks or trademarks of Autodesk, Inc., and/or its subsidiaries and/or affiliates in the
USA and/or other countries. All other trademarks are trademarks of their respective
holders.

Disclaimer:
The author and publisher of this book have used their best efforts in preparing this book.
These efforts include the development, research and testing of the material presented.
The author and publisher shall not be liable in any event for incidental or consequential
damages with, or arising out of, the furnishing, performance, or use of the material.

ISBN-13: 978-1-58503-881-7
ISBN-10: 1-58503-881-4

Printed and bound in the United States of America.

FOREWORD

To the Student:

This book has been written with the assumption that the reader has no prior experience using Autodesk® Revit®. The intent of this book is to provide the student with a well-rounded knowledge of architectural tools and techniques for use in both school and industry.

The book consists of a series of tutorials which primarily focus on the development of a single project. When you finish the book you will have learned how to document and model all of the major architectural aspects of a commercial project. This includes floor plans, interior and exterior elevations, wall and building sections, door and room finish schedules and organizing drawings on sheets for printing.

The CD has several videos that supplement the book. Studying these videos along with the book will help the reader to better understand Revit's architectural features. The book and videos will also help prepare for the Autodesk Revit Architecture Certification Exam, see Appendix A for more information.

Be sure to check out the additional material on the CD.

To the Instructor:

This book was designed for the architectural student using Revit 2015. *Note:* Students can successfully work through this book using Revit Architecture 2015 as well. Throughout the book, the student develops a two story commercial building. The drawings start with the floor plans and develop all the way to photo-realistic renderings similar to the one on the cover of this book.

Throughout the book many Revit tools and techniques are covered while creating the model. Also, in a way that is applicable to the current exercise, industry standards and conventions are covered. Access to the internet is required for some exercises.

Each chapter concludes with a self-exam and review questions. The answers to the self-exam questions are provided, but review question answers are not (they can only be found in the Instructor's Guide available from the publisher).

This text is updated every year for the latest version of Revit. The printed text has always been available for the fall term.

An Instructor's Resource Guide is available for this book. It contains:
- Answers to the questions at the end of each chapter
- Example images of each exercise to be turned in (can be used to grade students work)
- Outline of tools and topics to be covered in each lesson's lecture
- Suggestions for additional student work (for each lesson)
- Author's direct contact information

Errata:

Please check the publisher's website from time to time for any errors or typo's found in this book after it went to the printer. Simply browse to www.SDCpublications.com, and then navigate to the page for this book. Click the **View/Submit errata** link in the upper right corner of the page. If you find an error, please submit it so we can correct it in the next edition.

You may contact the publisher with comments or suggestions at **service@SDCpublications.com**.
Please do not email with Revit questions unless they relate to a problem with this book.

About the Author:

Dan Stine is a registered Architect with twenty years of experience in the architectural field. He currently works at LHB (a 200 person multidiscipline firm; www.LHBcorp.com) in Duluth Minnesota as the BIM Administrator, providing training, customization and support for two regional offices. Dan has worked in a total of four firms. While at these firms, he has participated in collaborative projects with several other firms on various projects (including Cesar Pelli, Weber Music Hall – University of Minnesota - Duluth). Dan is a member of the *Construction Specification Institute* (CSI) and the *Autodesk Developer Network* (ADN) and also teaches *AutoCAD* and *Revit Architecture* classes at Lake Superior College, for the Architectural Technology program; additionally, he is a Certified Construction Document Technician (CDT). He has presented at *Autodesk University* (http://au.autodesk.com), the *Revit Technology Conference* (http://www.revitconference.com) and Minnesota University (www.minn-u.com). Mr. Stine has written the following textbooks (published by SDC Publications):

- *Residential Design Using Autodesk Revit 2015*
- *Architectural Commercial Design Using Autodesk Revit 2015*
- *Design Integration Using Autodesk Revit 2015 (Architecture, Structure and MEP)*
- *Interior Design Using Autodesk Revit 2015 (with co-author Aaron Hansen)*
- *Residential Design Using AutoCAD 2015*
- *Commercial Design Using AutoCAD 2013*
- *Chapters in Architectural Drawing (with co-author Steven H. McNeill, AIA, LEED AP)*
- *Interior Design Using Hand Sketching, SketchUp and Photoshop (also with Steven H. McNeill)*
- *Google SketchUp 8 for Interior Designers; Just the Basics*

You may contact the publisher with comments or suggestions at **service@SDCpublications.com**

Thanks:

I could not have written this book without support from my family; Cheri, Kayla & Carter.

Many thanks go out to Stephen Schroff and *SDC Publications* for making this book possible!

Table of Contents

CD Content

Notes:

Lesson 1
Getting Started with Autodesk Revit 2015:

This chapter will introduce you to Autodesk® Revit® 2015. You will study the User Interface and learn how to open and exit a project and adjust the view of the drawing on the screen. It is recommended that you spend an ample amount of time learning this material, as it will greatly enhance your ability to progress smoothly through subsequent chapters.

Exercise 1-1:
What is Revit Architecture 2015?

What is Autodesk Revit used for?

Autodesk Revit (Architecture, Structure and MEP) is the world's first fully parametric building design software. This revolutionary software, for the first time, truly takes architectural computer aided design beyond simply being a high tech pencil. Revit is a product of Autodesk, makers of AutoCAD, Civil 3D, Inventor, 3DS Max, Maya and many other popular design programs.

Revit can be thought of as the foundation of a larger process called **Building Information Modeling** (BIM). The BIM process revolves around a virtual, information rich 3D model. In this model all the major building elements are represented and contain information such as manufacturer, model, cost, phase and much more. Once a model has been developed in Revit, third-party add-ins and applications can be used to further leverage the data. Some examples are Facilities Management, Analysis (Energy, Structural, Lighting), Construction Sequencing, Cost Estimating, Code Compliance and much more!

Revit can be an invaluable tool to designers when leveraged to its full potential. The iterative design process can be accomplished using special Revit features such as *Phasing* and *Design Options*. Material selections can be developed and attached to various elements in the model, where one simple change adjusts the wood from oak to maple throughout the project. The power of schedules may be used to determine quantities and document various parameters contained within content (this is the "I" in BIM, which stands for Information). Finally, the three-dimensional nature of a Revit-based model allows the designer to present compelling still images and animations. These graphics help to more clearly communicate the design intent to clients and other interested parties. This book will cover many of these tools and techniques to **assist** in the creative process.

What is a parametric building modeler?

Revit is a program designed from the ground up using state-of-the-art technology. The term parametric describes a process by which an element is modified and an adjacent element(s) is automatically modified to maintain a previously established relationship. For example, if a wall is moved, perpendicular walls will grow, or shrink, in length to remain attached to the related wall. Additionally, elements attached to the wall will move, such as wall cabinets, doors, windows, air grilles, etc.

Revit stands for **Rev**ise **In**stantly; a change made in one view is automatically updated in all other views and schedules. For example, if you move a door in an interior elevation view, the floor plan will automatically update. Or, if you delete a door, it will be deleted from all other views and schedules.

A major goal of Revit is to eliminate much of the repetitive and mundane tasks traditionally associated with CAD programs allowing more time for design, coordination and visualization. For example: all sheet numbers, elevation tags and reference bubbles are updated automatically when changed anywhere in the project. Therefore it is difficult to find a miss-referenced detail tag.

The best way to understand how a parametric model works is to describe the Revit project file. A single Revit file contains your entire building project. Even though you mostly draw in 2D views, you are actually drawing in 3D. In fact, the entire building project is a 3D model. From this 3D model you can generate 2D elevations, 2D sections and perspective views. Therefore, when you delete a door in an elevation view you are actually deleting the door from the 3D model from which all 2D views are generated and automatically updated.

Window model size controlled by parameters *Width* and *Height*

Another way in which Revit is a parametric building modeler is that **parameters** can be used to control the size and shape of geometry. For example, a window model can have two *parameters* set up which control the size of the window. Thus, from a window's properties it is possible to control the size of the window without using any of the drawing modify tools such as *Scale* or *Move*. Furthermore, the *parameter* settings (i.e., width and height in this example) can be saved within the window model (called a *Family*). You could have the 2' x 4' settings saved as "Type A" and the 2' x 6' as "Type B". Each saved list of values is called a *Type* within the *Family*. Thus, this one double-hung window *Family* could represent an unlimited number of window sizes! You will learn more about this later in the book.

What about the different "flavors" of Revit?

Revit comes in three different "flavors": **Revit Architecture**, **Revit Structure** and **Revit MEP** (which stands for Mechanical, Electrical and Plumbing). There is also a fourth option in which all disciplines are available in one application; this is just called **Revit**. The all-in-one version only comes with the *Autodesk Building Design Suite* Premium or Ultimate. Any "flavor" of Revit can open and edit the same Revit project file or content (aka, *Families*). The only requirement is that each "flavor" of Revit be the same version; for example, Autodesk Revit Architecture 2015, Autodesk Revit Structure 2015 and Autodesk Revit MEP 2015.

The tutorials in this textbook are based on Revit; you can also use Revit Architecture. You can download the free 30 day trial from autodesk.com. Students may download a free 13 month version of Revit, the all-in-one version, at www.students.autodesk.com.

Revit model of an existing building, with architecture, structural, mechanical, plumbing and electrical all modeled.

Image courteous of LHB, Inc.   www.LHBcorp.com

Now is as good a time as any to make sure the reader understands that Revit is not, nor has it ever been, backwards compatible. This means there is no *Save-As* back to a previous version of Revit. Also, an older version of Revit cannot open a file, project or content, saved in a newer format. So make sure you consider what version your school or employer is currently standardized on before upgrading any projects or content.

3D model of lunch room created in *Interior Design using Autodesk Revit 2015*

32bit versus 64bit?

One of the biggest advantages of the 64bit version of Revit is access to more than 3GB of RAM. Many BIM stations have 8 to 16GB of RAM to handle large projects. The 64bit version looks the same and creates a model identical to one created in the 32bit version of Revit. Either version of Revit will work fine for this textbook. You have no control over which version is installed, it is automatically based on whether you have a 32bit or 64bit operating system on your computer

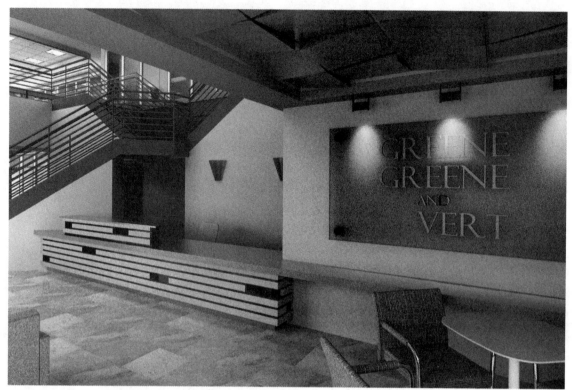

Lobby rendering from *Interior Design using Autodesk Revit 2015*

Why use Revit?

Many people ask the question, why use Revit versus other programs? The answer can certainly vary depending on the situation and particular needs of an individual or organization.

Generally speaking, this is why most companies use Revit:

- Many designers and drafters are using Revit to streamline repetitive drafting tasks and focus more on designing and detailing a project.
- Revit is a very progressive program and offers many features for designing buildings. Revit is constantly being developed and Autodesk provides incremental upgrades and patches on a regular basis; Revit 2015 was released about a year after the previous version.
- Revit was designed specifically for architectural design and includes features like:
  - Mental Ray's Photo Realistic Renderer
  - Phasing (existing, new construction, future construction, etc.)
  - Live schedules
  - Design Options
  - Cloud Rendering via *Autodesk 360*
  - Conceptual Energy Analysis via *Autodesk 360*

A few basic Revit concepts:

The following is meant to be a brief overview of the basic organization of Revit as a software application. You should not get too hung up on these concepts and terms as they will make more sense as you work through the tutorials in this book. This discussion is simply laying the groundwork so you have a general frame of reference on how Revit works.

The Revit platform has three fundamental types of elements:
- Model Elements
- Datum Elements
- View-Specific Elements

Model Elements

Think of *Model Elements* as things you can put your hands on once the building has been constructed. They are typically 3D, but can sometimes be 2D. There are two types of *Model Elements*:

- **Host Elements** (walls, floors, slabs, roofs, ceilings) – Tools are the same for each "flavor" of Revit.

- **Model Components** (Stairs, Doors, Furniture, Beams, Columns, Pipes, Ducts, Light Fixtures, Model Lines) – Options vary depending on the "flavor" of Revit (e.g., Revit MEP has a Duct tool whereas Revit Architecture and Revit Structure do not).

  o Some *Model Components* require a host before they can be placed within a project. For example, a window can only be placed in a host, which could be a wall, roof or floor depending on how the element was created. If the host is deleted, all hosted or dependent elements are automatically deleted.

Model Elements
Windows & Doors; require a host

Host Elements
Roof, Wall & Floor

Model Elements
Stair & Washer/Dryer; do not require a host

Datum Elements

Datum Elements are reference planes within the building that graphically and parametrically define the location of various elements within the model. These features are available in all "flavors" of Revit. These are the three types of *Datum Elements*:

- **Grids**
  - o Typically laid out in a plan view to locate structural elements such as columns and beams, as well as walls. Grids show up in plan, elevation and section views. Moving a grid in one view moves it in all other views as it is the same element. (See the next page for an example of a grid in plan view.)

- **Levels**
  - o Used to define vertical relationships, mainly surfaces that you walk on. They only show up in elevation and section views. Many elements are placed relative to a *Level*; when the *Level* is moved those elements move with it (e.g., doors, windows, casework, ceilings). **WARNING:** *If a* Level *is deleted, those same "dependent" elements will also be deleted from the project!*

- **Reference Planes**
  - o These are similar to grids in that they show up in plan and elevation or sections. They do not have reference bubbles at the end like grids. Revit breaks many tasks down into simple 2D tasks which result in 3D geometry. *Reference Planes* are used to define 2D surfaces on which to work within the 3D model. They can be placed in any view, either horizontally or vertically.

View-Specific Elements

As the name implies, the items about to be discussed only show up in the specific view in which they are created. For example, notes and dimensions added in the architectural floor plans will not show up in the structural floor plans. These elements are all 2D and are mainly communication tools used to accurately document the building for construction or presentations.

- **Annotation elements** (text, tags, symbols, dimensions)
  - o Size automatically set and changed based on selected drawing scale

- **Details** (detail lines, filled regions, 2D detail components)

File Types (and extensions):
Revit has four primary types of files that you will work with as a Revit user. Each file type, as with any Microsoft Windows based program, has a specific three letter file name extension; that is, after the name of the file on your hard drive you will see a period and three letters. They are:

.RVT	Revit project files; the file most used (also for backup files)
.RFA	Revit family file; loadable content for your project
.RTE	Revit template; a project starter file with office standards preset
.RFT	Revit family template; a family starter file with parameters

The Revit platform has three fundamental ways in which to work with the elements (for display and manipulation):

- Views
- Schedules
- Sheets

The following is a cursory overview of the main ideas you need to know. This is not an exhaustive study on views, schedules and sheets.

Views

Views, accessible from the *Project Browser* (see Page 5-4), is where most of the work is done while using Revit. Think of views as slices through the building, both horizontal (plans) and vertical (elevations and sections).

- **Plans**
  - A *Plan View* is a horizontal slice through the building. You can specify the location of the **cut plane** which determines if certain windows show up or how much of the stair is seen. A few examples are: architectural floor plan, reflected ceiling plan, site plan, structural framing plan, HVAC floor plan, electrical floor plan, lighting [ceiling] plan, etc. The images below show this concept; the image on the left is the 3D BIM. The middle image shows the portion of building above the cut plane removed. Finally, the last image on the right shows the plan view in which you work and place on a sheet.

- **Elevations**
  - Elevations are vertical slices, but where the slice lies outside the floor plan as in the middle image below. Each elevation created is listed in the *Project Browser*. The image on the right is an example of a South exterior elevation view, which is a "live" view of the 3D model. If you select a window here and delete it, the floor plans will update instantly.

- **Sections**
  - Similar to elevations, sections are also vertical slices. However, these slices cut through the building. A section view can be cropped down to become a wall section or even look just like an elevation. The images below show the slice, the portion of building in the foreground removed, and then the actual view created by the slice. A setting exists, for each section view, to control how far into that view you can see. The example on the right is "seeing" deep enough to show the doors on the interior walls.

- **3D and Camera**
  - In addition to the traditional "flattened" 2D views that you will typically work in, you are able to see your designs more naturally via 3D and Camera views. A 3D view is simply a non-perspective 3D view of the project viewed from the exterior. A Camera view is a true perspective view; cameras can be created both in and outside of the building. Like the 2D views, these 3D/Camera views can be placed on a sheet to be printed. Revit provides a number of tools to help explore the 3D view, such as Section Box, Steering Wheel, Temporary Hide and Isolate, and Render.

    The image on the left is a 3D view set to "shade mode" and has shadows turned on. The image on the right is a camera view set up inside the building; the view is set to "hidden line" rather than shaded, and the camera is at eyelevel.

Schedules

Schedules are lists of information generated based on content that has been placed, or modeled, within the project. A schedule can be created, such as the door schedule example shown below, that lists any of the data associated with each door that exists in the project. Revit allows you to work directly in the schedule views. Any change within a schedule view, is a change directly to the element being scheduled. Again, if a door were to be deleted from this schedule, that door would be instantly deleted from the project.

DOOR AND FRAME SCHEDULE												
DOOR NUMBER	DOOR				FRAME		DETAIL				FIRE RATING	HDWR GROUP	
	WIDTH	HEIGHT	MATL	TYPE	MATL	TYPE	HEAD	JAMB	SILL	GLAZING			
1000A	3' - 8"	7' - 2"	WD		HM		11/A8.01	11/A8.01					
1046	3' - 0"	7' - 2"	WD	D10	HM	F10	11/A8.01	11/A8.01 SIM				34	
1047A	6' - 0"	7' - 10"	ALUM	D15	ALUM	SF4	6/A8.01	6/A8.01	1/A8.01 SIM	1" INSUL		2	CARD READER N. LEAF
1047B	8' - 0"	7' - 2"	WD	D10	HM	F13	12/A8.01	11/A8.01 SIM			60 MIN	85	MAG HOLD OPENS
1050	3' - 0"	7' - 2"	WD	D10	HM	F21	8/A8.01	11/A8.01		1/4" TEMP		33	
1051	3' - 0"	7' - 2"	WD	D10	HM	F21	8/A8.01	11/A8.01		1/4" TEMP		33	
1052	3' - 0"	7' - 2"	WD	D10	HM	F21	8/A8.01	11/A8.01		1/4" TEMP		33	
1053	3' - 0"	7' - 2"	WD	D10	HM	F21	8/A8.01	11/A8.01		1/4" TEMP		33	
1054A	3' - 0"	7' - 2"	WD	D10	HM	F10	8/A8.01	11/A8.01		1/4" TEMP	-	34	
1054B	3' - 0"	7' - 2"	WD	D10	HM	F21	8/A8.01	11/A8.01		1/4" TEMP	-	33	
1055	3' - 0"	7' - 2"	WD	D10	HM	F21	8/A8.01	11/A8.01		1/4" TEMP	-	33	
1056A	3' - 0"	7' - 2"	WD	D10	HM	F10	9/A8.01	9/A8.01			20 MIN	33	
1056B	3' - 0"	7' - 2"	WD	D10	HM	F10	11/A8.01	11/A8.01			20 MIN	34	
1056C	3' - 0"	7' - 2"	WD	D10	HM	F10	20/A8.01	20/A8.01			20 MIN	33	
1057A	3' - 0"	7' - 2"	WD	D10	HM	F10	8/A8.01	11/A8.01			20 MIN	34	
1057B	3' - 0"	7' - 2"	WD	D10	HM	F30	9/A8.01	9/A8.01		1/4" TEMP	20 MIN	33	
1058A	3' - 0"	7' - 2"	WD	D10	HM	F10	9/A8.01	9/A8.01			-	33	

Sheets

You can think of sheets as the pieces of paper on which your views and schedules will be printed. Views and schedules are placed on sheets and then arranged. Once a view has been placed on a sheet, its reference bubble is automatically filled out and that view cannot be placed on any other sheet. The setting for each view, called "view scale," controls the size of the drawing on each sheet; view scale also controls the size of the text and dimensions.

Quick Access Toolbar:

Referred to as *QAT* in this book, this single toolbar provides access to often used tools (*Open*, *Save*, *Undo*, *Redo*, *Measure*, *Tag*, etc.). It is always visible regardless of what part of the *Ribbon* is active.

The *QAT* can be positioned above or below the *Ribbon* and any command from the *Ribbon* can be placed on it; simply right-click on any tool on the *Ribbon* and select *Add to Quick Access Toolbar*. Moving the *QAT* below the *Ribbon* gives you a lot more room for your favorite commands to be added from the *Ribbon*. Clicking the larger down-arrow to the far right reveals a list of common tools which can be toggled on and off.

Some of the icons on the *QAT* have a down-arrow on the right. Clicking this arrow reveals a list of related tools. In the case of *Undo* and *Redo*, you have the ability to undo (or redo) several actions at once.

Ribbon – Architecture Tab:

The *Architecture* tab on the *Ribbon* contains most of the tools the architect needs to model a building, essentially the things you can put your hands on when the building is done. The specific discipline versions of Revit omit some of the other discipline tabs.

Each tab starts with the *Modify* tool, i.e., the first button on the left. This tool puts you into "selection mode" so you can select elements to modify. Clicking this tool cancels the current tool and unselects elements. With the *Modify* tool selected you may select elements to view their properties or edit them. Note that the *Modify* tool, which is a button, is different than the *Modify* tab on the *Ribbon*.

The *Ribbon* has three types of buttons, *button*, *drop-down button* and *split*, as covered on the previous page. In the image above you can see the *Wall* tool is a **split button**. Most of the time you would simply click the top part of the button to draw a wall. Clicking the down-arrow part of the button, for the *Wall* tool example, gives you the option to draw a *Wall*, *Structural Wall*, *Wall by Face*, *Wall Sweep*, and a *Reveal*.

TIP: The Model Text tool is only for placing 3D text in your model, not for adding notes!

Ribbon – Annotate Tab:

To view this tab, simply click the label "Annotate" near the top of the *Ribbon*. This tab presents a series of tools which allow you to add notes, dimensions and 2D "embellishments" to your model in a specific view, such as a floor plan, elevation, or section. All of these tools are **view specific**, meaning a note added in the first floor plan will not show up anywhere else, not even another first floor plan: for instance, a first floor electrical plan.

Notice, in the image above, that the *Dimension* panel label has a down-arrow next to it. Clicking the down-arrow will reveal an **extended panel** with additional related tools.

Finally, notice the *Component* tool in the image above; it is a **split button** rather than a *drop-down button*. Clicking the top part of this button will initiate the *Detail Component* tool. Clicking the bottom part of the button opens the fly-out menu revealing related tools. Once you select an option from the fly-out, that tool becomes the default for the top part of the split button for the current session of Revit (see image to right).

Ribbon – Modify Tab:

Several tools which manipulate and derive information from the current model are available on the *Modify* tab. Additional *Modify* tools are automatically appended to this tab when elements are selected in the model (see *Modify Contextual Tab* on the next page).

TIP: Do not confuse the Modify tab with the Modify tool when following instructions in this book.

Ribbon – View Tab:

The tools on the *View* tab allow you to create new views of your 3D model; this includes views that look 2D (e.g., floor plans, elevations and sections) as well as 3D views (e.g., isometric and perspective views).

The *View* tab also gives you tools to control how views look, everything from what types of elements are seen (e.g., Plumbing Fixture, Furniture or Section Marks) as well as line weights.

> NOTE: *Line weights are controlled at a project wide level, but may be overridden on a view by view basis.*

Finally, notice the little arrow in the lower-right corner of the *Graphics* panel. When you see an arrow like this you can click on it to open a dialog box with settings that relate to the panel's tool set (*Graphics* in this example). Hovering over the arrow reveals a tooltip which will tell you what dialog box will be opened.

Ribbon – Modify Contextual Tab:

The *Modify* tab is appended when certain tools are active or elements are selected in the model; this is referred to as a *contextual tab*. The first image, below, shows the *Place Wall* tab which presents various options while adding walls. The next example shows the *Modify Walls* contextual tab which is accessible when one or more walls are selected.

Place Wall contextual tab – visible when the Wall tool is active.

Modify Walls contextual tab – visible when a wall is selected.

Ribbon – Customization:

There is not too much customization that can be done to the *Ribbon*. One of the only things you can do is pull a panel off the *Ribbon* by clicking and holding down the left mouse button on the titles listed across the bottom. This panel can be placed within the *drawing window* or on another screen if you have a dual monitor setup.

The image above shows the *Build* panel, from the *Architecture* tab, detached from the *Ribbon* and floating within the drawing window. Notice that the *Insert* tab is active. Thus, you have constant access to the *Build* tools while accessing other tools. Note that the *Build* panel is not available on the *Architecture* tab as it is literally moved, not just copied.

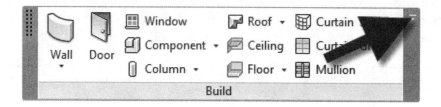

When you need to move a detached panel back to the *Ribbon* you do the following: hover over the detached panel until the sidebars show up and then click the "Return panels to ribbon" icon in the upper right (identified in the image above).

FYI: Whenever the resolution of your monitor is too low or you don't have the Revit application maximized on the screen the buttons may be modified to take up less room on the Ribbon; typically the words are removed. Compare the image to the right with the Build panel above.

Ribbon – States:

The *Ribbon* can be displayed in one of four states:

- Full Ribbon (default)
- Minimize to Tabs
- Minimize to Panel Tiles
- Minimize to Panel Buttons

The intent of this feature is to increase the size of the available drawing window. It is recommended, however, that you leave the *Ribbon* fully expanded while learning to use the program. The images in this book show the fully expanded state. The images below show the other three options. When using one of the minimized options you simply hover (or click) your cursor over the Tab or Panel to temporarily reveal the tools.

FYI: Double-clicking on a Ribbon tab will also toggle the states.

Minimize to Tabs

Minimize to Panel Tiles

Minimize to Panel Buttons

Ribbon – References in this Book:

When the exercises make reference to the tools in the *Ribbon* a consistent method is used to eliminate excessive wording and save space. Take a moment to understand this so that things go smoothly for you later.

Throughout the textbook you will see an instruction similar to the following:

> 23. Select **Architecture** → **Build** → **Wall**

This means, click the ***Architecture*** tab, and within the ***Build*** panel, select the ***Wall*** tool. Note that the *Wall* tool is actually a split button, but a subsequent tool was not listed so you are to click on the primary part of the button. Compare the above example to the one below:

> 23. Select **Architecture** → **Build** → **Wall** → **Structural Wall**

The above example indicates that you should click the down-arrow part of the *Wall* tool in order to select the *Structural Wall* option.

Thus the general pattern is this:

Tab → Panel → Tool → drop-down list item

#1 Tab: This will get you to the correct area within the *Ribbon*.

#2 Panel: This will narrow down your search for the desired tool.

#3 Tool: Specific tool to select and use.

Drop-down list item: This will only be specified for drop-down buttons and sometimes for split buttons.

The image below shows the order in which the instructions are given to select a tool; note that you do not actually click the panel title.

Options Bar:

This area dynamically changes to show options that complement the current operation. The *Options Bar* is located directly below the *Ribbon*. When you are learning to use Revit you should keep your eye on this area and watch for features and options appearing at specific times. The image below shows the *Options Bar* example with the *Wall* tool active.

Properties Palette – Element Type Selector:

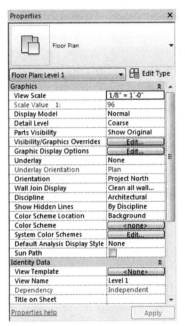

The *Properties Palette* provides instant access to settings related to the element selected or about to be created. When nothing is selected, it shows information about the current view. When multiple elements are selected, the common parameters are displayed.

The *Element Type Selector* is an important part of the *Properties Palette*. Whenever you are adding elements or have them selected, you can select from this list to determine how a wall to be drawn will look, or how a wall previously drawn should look (see image to right). If a wall type needs to change, you never delete it and redraw it; you simply select it and pick a new type from the *Type Selector*.

Type Selector; Wall tool active or a Wall is selected

The **Selection Filter** drop-down list below the *Type Selector* lets you know the type and quantity of the elements currently selected. When multiple elements are selected you can narrow down the properties for just one element type, such as *wall*. Notice the image to the right shows four walls are in the current selection set. Selecting **Walls (4)** will cause the *Palette* to only show *Wall* properties even though many other elements are selected (and remain selected).

The width of the *Properties Palette* and the center column position can be adjusted by dragging the cursor over that area. You may need to do this at times to see all the information. However, making the *Palette* too wide will reduce the useable drawing area.

Selection Filter; multiple elements selected

The *Properties Palette* should be left open; if you accidentally close it you can reopen it by **View → Window → User Interface → Properties**; or by typing **PP** on the keyboard.

Project Browser:

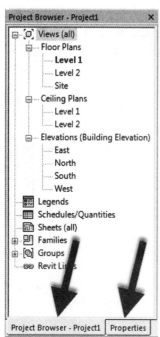

The *Project Browser* is the "Grand Central Station" of the Revit project database. All the views, schedules, sheets and content are accessible through this hierarchical list. The first image to the left shows the seven major categories; any item with a "plus" next to it contains sub-categories or items.

Double-clicking on a View, Legend, Schedule or Sheet will open it for editing; the current item open for editing is bold (**Level 1** in the example to the left). Right-clicking will display a pop-up menu with a few options such as *Delete* and *Copy*.

Right-click on *Views (all)*, at the top of the *Project Browser*, and you will find a **Search** option in the pop-up menu. This can be used to search for a *View, Family*, etc., a very useful tool when working on a large project with 100's of items to sift through.

Like the *Properties Palette*, the width of the *Project Browser* can be adjusted. When the two are stacked above each other, they both move together. You can also stack the two directly on top of each other; in this case you will see a tab for each at the bottom as shown in the second image to the left.

The *Project Browser* should be left open; if you accidentally close it, by clicking the "X" in the upper right, you can reopen it by: **View → Window → User Interface → Project Browser**.

The *Project Browser* and *Properties Palette* can be repositioned on a second monitor, if you have one, when you want more room to work in the drawing window.

Status Bar:

This area will display information, on the far left, about the current command or list information about a selected element. The right hand side of the *Status Bar* shows the number of elements selected. The small funnel icon to the left of the selection number can be clicked to open the *Filter* dialog box, which allows you to reduce your current selection to a specific category; for example, you could select the entire floor plan, and then filter it down to just the doors. This is different than the *Selection Filter* in the *Properties Palette* which keeps everything selected.

On the *Status Bar*, the five icons on the left in the image below control how elements are selected. From left to right these are:

- Select Links
- Select Underlay Elements
- Select Pinned Elements
- Select Elements by Face
- Drag Elements on Selection

Hover your cursor over an icon for the name and for a brief description of what it does. These are toggles that are on or off; **the red 'X' in the upper right of each icon means you cannot select that type of element within the model**. These controls help prevent accidentally moving or deleting things. Keep these toggles in mind if you are having trouble selecting something; you may have accidentally toggled one of these on.

Finally, the two drop-down lists towards the center of the *Status Bar* control **Design Options** and **Worksets** (see image on previous page). The latter is not covered in this book but *Design Options* are. *Worksets* relate to the ability for more than one designer to be in the model at a time.

View Control Bar:

This is a feature which gives you convenient access to tools which control each view's display settings (i.e., scale, shadows, detail level, graphics style, etc.). The options vary slightly between view types: 2D View, 3D view, Sheet and Schedule. The important thing to know is that these settings only affect the current view, the one listed on the *Application Title Bar*. All of these settings are available in the *Properties Palette*, but this toolbar cannot be turned off like the *Properties Palette* can.

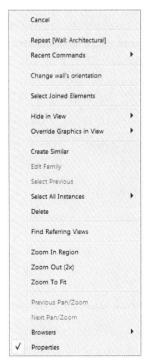

Context Menu:

The *context menu* appears near the cursor whenever you right-click on the mouse (see image at right). The options on that menu will vary depending on what tool is active or what element is selected.

Drawing Window:

This is where you manipulate the Building Information Model (BIM). Here you will see the current view (plan, elevation or section), schedule or sheet. Any changes made are instantly propagated to the entire database.

Context menu example with a wall selected

Elevation Marker:

This item is not really part of the Revit UI, but is visible in the drawing window by default via the various templates you can start with, so it is worth mentioning at this point. The four elevation markers point at each side of your project and ultimately indicate the drawing sheet on which you would find an elevation drawing of each side of the building. All you need to know right now is that you should draw your floor plan generally in the middle of the four elevation markers that you will see in each plan view; DO NOT delete them as this will remove the related view from the *Project Browser*.

Revit Options:

There are several settings, related to the *User Interface*, which are not tied to the current model. That is, these settings apply to the installation of Revit on your computer, rather than applying to just one model or file on your computer. A few of these settings will be briefly discussed here. It is recommended that you don't make any changes here right now.

Click on **Options** in the *Application Menu* (the purple "R"). The options in the <u>User Interface</u> section are fairly self-explanatory. In the <u>Graphics</u> section you can verify your display driver is approved (i.e., tested) by Autodesk. If Revit is crashing or exhibits strange behavior, it likely relates to your graphics driver. You can bypass this problem by turning off *Use Hardware Acceleration*, but this will make Revit run slower.

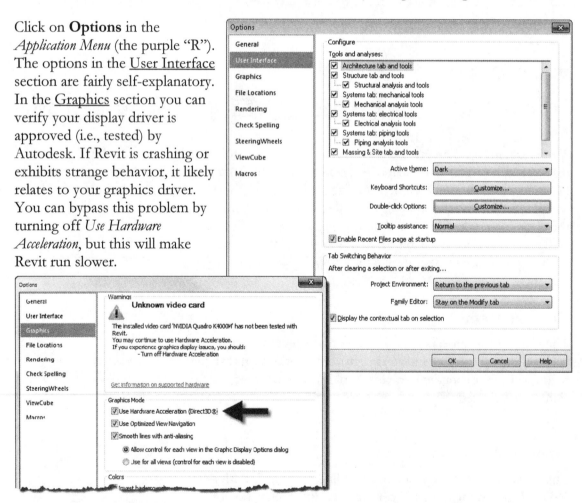

This concludes your brief overview of the Revit user interface. Many of these tools and operations will be covered in more detail throughout the book.

Efficient Practices

The *Ribbon* and menus are really helpful when learning a program like Revit; however, most experienced users rarely use them! The process of moving the mouse to the edge of the screen to select a command and then back to where you were is very inefficient, especially for those who do this all day long, five days a week. Here are a few ways experienced BIM operators work:

- Use the wheel on the mouse to Zoom (spin the wheel), Pan (press and hold the wheel button while moving the mouse) and Zoom Extents (double-clicking the wheel button). All this can be done while in another command; so, if you are in the middle of drawing walls and need to zoom in to see which point you are about to Snap to, you can do it without canceling the Line command and without losing focus on the area you are designing by having to click an icon near the edge of the screen.

- Revit conforms to many of the Microsoft Windows operating system standards. Most programs, including Revit, have several standard commands that can be accessed via keyboard shortcuts. Here are a few examples (press both keys at the same time):

  - Ctrl + S   Save   *(saves the current model)*
  - Ctrl + A   Select All   *(selects everything in text editor)*
  - Ctrl + Z   Undo   *(undoes the previous action)*
  - Ctrl + X   Cut   *(Cut to Windows clipboard)*
  - Ctrl + C   Copy   *(does not replace Revit's Copy tool)*
  - Ctrl + V   Paste   *(used to copy between models/views/levels)*
  - Ctrl + Tab   Change View   *(toggles between open views)*
  - Ctrl + P   Print   *(opens print dialog)*
  - Ctrl + N   New   *(create new project file)*
  - F7   Spelling   *(launch spell check feature)*
  - ENTER   Previous Command   *(repeat previous command)*

- If you recall, the *Open Documents* area in the *Application* menu lists all the views that are currently open on your computer. By clicking one of the names in the list you "switch" to that view. A shortcut is to press **Ctrl + Tab** to quickly cycle through the open drawings.

- Many Revit commands also have keyboard shortcuts. So, with your right hand on the mouse (and not moving from the "design" area), your left hand can type **WA** when you want to draw a Wall for example. You can see all the preloaded shortcuts and add new ones by clicking *View (tab)* → *User Interface (drop-down)* → *Keyboard Shortcuts*.

It should be noted that any customized keyboard shortcuts are specific to the computer you are working on, not the project. You can use the *Export* button (see image to right) to save the entire keyboard shortcuts list to a file, and then *Import* it into another computer's copy of Revit.

This concludes your brief overview of the Revit user interface. Many of these tools and operations will be covered in more detail throughout the book.

Keyboard shortcuts dialog

Exterior rendering from Design Integration using Autodesk Revit 2015

Exercise 1-3:
Open, Save and Close a Revit Project

To *Open* **Revit 2015**:

Start → All Programs → Autodesk → Autodesk Revit 2015

Revit 2015

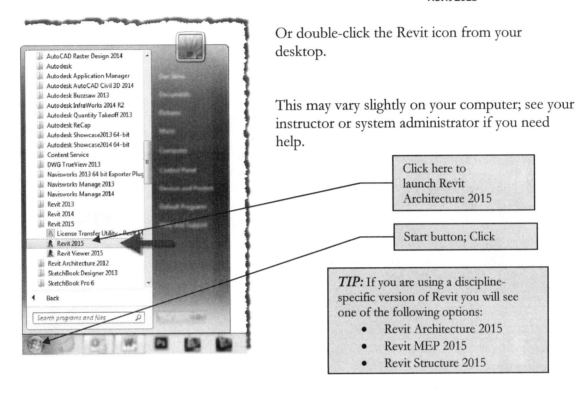

Or double-click the Revit icon from your desktop.

This may vary slightly on your computer; see your instructor or system administrator if you need help.

Click here to launch Revit Architecture 2015

Start button; Click

TIP: If you are using a discipline-specific version of Revit you will see one of the following options:
- Revit Architecture 2015
- Revit MEP 2015
- Revit Structure 2015

How to Open a Revit Project:

By default, Revit will open in the *Recent Files* window, which will display thumbnails of recent projects you have worked on. Clicking on the preview will open the project.

1. Click the **Open** link (see the image to the right).

FIGURE 1-3.1 *Recent Files startup screen*

You may click open under *Project* or on the *Quick Access Toolbar*.

Next you will open an existing Revit project file. You will select a sample file provided on the DVD that came with this book.

2.   Click the drop-down box at the top of the *Open* dialog (Figure 1-3.2). Browse to your DVD drive; the drive letter will vary from computer to computer.

> *TIP: If you cannot locate the DVD that came with this textbook, you can substitute any Revit file you can find. Some sample files may be found here on your computer's hard drive:*
> *C:\Program Files\Autodesk\Revit 2015\Samples*

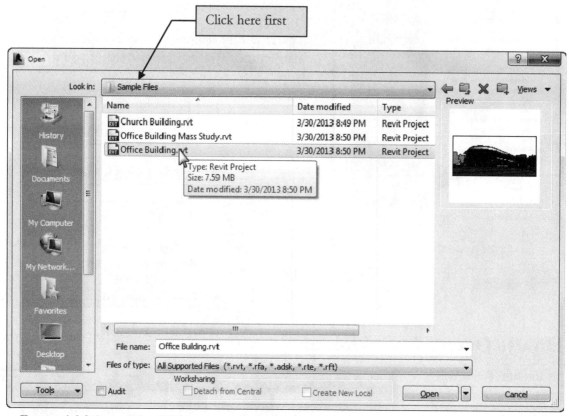

FIGURE 1-3.2 Open dialog; DVD contents shown

3.   Select the file named **Office Building.rvt** and click **Open**.

FYI: Notice the preview of the selected file. This will help you select the correct file before taking the time to open it.

The *Office Building.rvt* file is now open and the last saved view is displayed in the drawing window (Figure 1-3.3).

FIGURE 1-3.3 Sample file "Office Building.rvt"

The *Application Menu* lists the projects and views currently open on your computer (Figure 1-3.4).

4. Click **Application Menu →**
   Open Documents (icon)
   (Figure 1-3.4).

Notice that the *Office Building.rvt* project file is listed. Next to the project name is the name of a view open on your computer (e.g., floor plan, elevation).

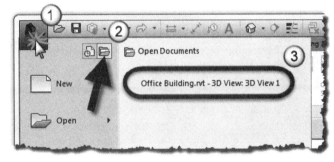

Figure 1-3.4 Application Menu: Open Documents view

Additional views will be added to the list as you open them. Each view has the project name as a prefix. The current view, the view you are working in, is always at the top of the list. You can quickly toggle between opened views from this menu by clicking on them.

You can also use the *Switch Windows* tool on the *View* tab; both do essentially the same thing.

Switch
Windows

Opening Another Revit Project:

Revit allows you to have more than one project open at a time.

5. Click **Open** from the *Quick Access Toolbar*.

6. Per the instructions previously covered, browse to the **DVD**.

7. Select the file named **Church Building.rvt** and click **Open** (Figure 1-3.5).

> *TIP: If you cannot locate the DVD that came with this textbook, substitute one of the sample files.*

FIGURE 1-3.5 Sample file "Church Building.rvt"

8. Click **Open Documents** from the *Application* menu (Figure 1-3.6).

Notice that the *Church Building.rvt* project is now listed along with a view: Floor Plan: Level 1.

Try toggling between projects by clicking on *Office Building.rvt – 3D View: 3D View 1*.

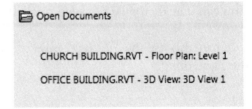

FIGURE 1-3.6 Open Documents

Close a Revit Project:

9. Select **Application menu → Close**; click **No** if prompted to save.

This will close the current project/view. If more than one view is open for a project, only the current view will close. The project and the other opened views will not close until you get to the last open view.

10. Repeat the previous step to close the other project file.

If you made changes and have not saved your project yet, you will be prompted to do so before Revit closes the view. **Do not save at this time**. When all open project files are closed, you find yourself back in the *Recent Files* screen – which is where you started.

Saving a Revit Project:

At this time we will not actually save a project.

To save a project file, simply select *Save* from the *Quick Access Toolbar*. You can also select *Save* from the *Application* menu or press *Ctrl + S* on the keyboard.

You should get in the habit of saving often to avoid losing work due to a power outage or program crash.

You can also save a copy of the current project by selecting **Save As** from the Application Menu. Once you have used the *Save As* command you are in the new project file and the file you started in is then closed.

Closing the Revit Program:

Finally, from the *Application* menu select **Exit Revit**. This will close any open projects/views and shut down Revit. Again you will be prompted to save, if needed, before Revit closes the view. **Do not save at this time**.

You can also click the "X" in the upper right corner of the *Revit Application* window.

Exercise 1-4:
Creating a New Project

Open **Autodesk Revit Architecture**.

Creating a New Project File:

The steps required to set up a new Revit Architecture model project file are very simple. As mentioned earlier, simply opening the Revit program starts you in the *Recent Files* window.

To manually create a new project (maybe you just finished working on a previous assignment and want to start the next one):

1.   Select **Application menu → New → Project**.

   FYI: You can also select the New *link in the* Recent Files *startup screen.*

After clicking *New → Project* you will get the **New Project** dialog box (Figure 1-4.1).

FIGURE 1-4.1 New Project dialog box

The *New Project* dialog box lets you specify the template file you want to use, or not use a template at all. You can also specify whether you want to create a new project or template file.

2. Select the **Architectural Template** *template file*. Leave *Create new* set to **Project** (Figure 1-4.1).

3. Click **OK**. You now have a new unnamed project file.

To name an unnamed project file you simply *Save*. The first time an unnamed project file is saved you will be prompted to specify the name and location for the project file.

4. Select **Application menu → Save** from the *Menu Bar*.

5. Specify a **name** and **location** for your new project file.
   Your instructor may specify a location or folder for your files if in a classroom setting.

What is a Template File?

A template file allows you to start your project with specific content and certain settings preset the way you like or need them.

For example, you can have the units set to *Imperial* or *Metric*. You can have the door, window and wall families you use most loaded and eliminate other less often used content. Also, you can have your company's title block preloaded and even have all the sheets for a project set up.

A custom template is a must for design firms using Revit and will prove useful to the student as he or she becomes more proficient with the program.

Be Aware:
It will be assumed from this point forward that the reader understands how to create, open and save project files. Please refer back to this section as needed. If you still need further assistance, ask your instructor for help.

Exercise 1-5:
Using Zoom and Pan to View Your Drawings

Learning to *Pan* and *Zoom* in and out of a drawing is essential for accurate and efficient drafting and visualization. We will review these commands now so you are ready to use them with the first design exercise.

Open **Revit Architecture**.

You will select a sample file from the DVD that came with this textbook.

1. Select **Open** from the *Quick Access Toolbar*.

2. Browse to the **DVD** (usually the D drive, but this can vary).

3. Select the file named **Church Building.rvt** and click **Open** (Figure 1-5.1).

> **TIP:** *If you cannot locate the DVD that came with this textbook, substitute any of the training files that come with Revit, found at C:\Program Files\Autodesk\Revit 2015\Samples.*

FIGURE 1-5.1 Church Building.rvt project

If the default view that is loaded is not **Floor Plan: Level 1**, double-click on **Level 1** under **Views\Floor Plans** in the *Project Browser*. Level 1 will be bold when it is the active or current view in the drawing window.

Using Zoom and Pan Tools:

You can access the zoom tools from the *Navigation Bar*, or the *scroll wheel* on your mouse.

The *Zoom* icon contains several *Zoom* related tools:
- The default (i.e., visible) icon is *Zoom in Region*, which allows you to window an area to zoom into.
- The *Zoom* icon is a **split button**.
- Clicking the down-arrow part of the button reveals a list of related *Zoom* tools.
- You will see the drop-down list on the next page.

Zoom In

4. Select the top portion of the *Zoom* icon (see image to right).

5. Drag a window over your plan view (Figure 1-5.2).

Selection window: Pick two diagonal points, that is, two opposite corners to define the window.

FIGURE 1-5.2 Zoom In window

You should now be zoomed in to the specified area (Figure 1-5.3).

FIGURE 1-5.3 Zoom In results

Zoom Out

6. Click the down-arrow next to the zoom icon (Figure 1-5.4). Select **Previous Pan/Zoom**.

You should now be back where you started. Each time you select this icon you are resorting to a previous view state. Sometimes you have to select this option multiple times if you did some panning and multiple zooms.

Take a minute and try the other *Zoom* tools to see how they work. When finished, click **Zoom to Fit** before moving on.

FIGURE 1-5.4 Zoom Icon drop-down

TIP: You can double-click the wheel button on your mouse to Zoom Extents *in the current view.*

Default 3D View

Clicking on the *Default 3D View* icon, on the *QAT*, loads a 3D View. This allows you to quickly switch to a 3D view.

7. Click on the **Default 3D View** icon.

8. Go to the **Open Documents** listing in the *Application Menu* and notice the *3D View* and the *Floor Plan* view are both listed at the bottom.

    REMEMBER: You can toggle between views here.

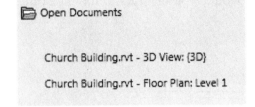

9. Click the **Esc** key to close the *Application* menu.

ViewCube

The *ViewCube* gives you convenient view control over the 3D view. This technology has been implemented in many of Autodesk's programs to make the process seamless for the user.

10. You should notice the ***ViewCube*** in the upper right corner of the drawing window (Figure 1-5.5). If not, you can turn it on by clicking *View → Windows → User Interface → ViewCube.*

    TIP: The ViewCube only shows up in 3D views.

Hovering your cursor over the *ViewCube* activates it. As you move about the *Cube* you see various areas highlight. If you click, you will be taken to that highlighted area in the drawing window. You can also click and drag your cursor on the *Cube* to "roll" the model in an unconstrained fashion. Clicking and dragging the mouse on the disk below the *Cube* allows you to spin the model without rolling. Finally, you have a few options in a right-click menu, and the **Home** icon, just above the *Cube*, gets you back to where you started if things get disoriented!

FIGURE 1-5.5 ViewCube

11. Give the *ViewCube* a try, then click the **Home** icon when you are done.

    REMEMBER: The Home icon only shows up when your cursor is over the ViewCube.

Navigation Wheel

Similar to the *ViewCube*, the *Navigation Wheel* aids in navigating your model. With the *Navigation Wheel* you can walk through your model, going down hallways and turning into rooms. Revit has not advanced to the point where the doors will open for you; thus, you walk through closed doors or walls as if you were a ghost!

The *Navigation Wheel* is activated by clicking the upper icon on the *Navigation Bar*.

Unfortunately, it is way too early in your Revit endeavors to learn to use the *Navigation Wheel*. You can try this in the chapter on creating photorealistic renderings and camera views. You would typically use this tool in a camera view.

Figure 1-5.6 Navigation Wheel

12.   **Close** the *Church Building* project **without** saving.

Using the Scroll Wheel on the Mouse

The scroll wheel on the mouse is a must for those using BIM software. In Revit you can *Pan* and *Zoom* without even clicking a zoom icon. You simply **scroll the wheel to zoom** and **hold the wheel button down to pan**. This can be done while in another command (e.g., while drawing walls). Another nice feature is that the drawing zooms into the area near your cursor, rather than zooming only at the center of the drawing window. Give this a try before moving on. Once you get the hang of it, you will not want to use the icons. Also, double-clicking the wheel button does a *Zoom to Fit* so everything is visible on the screen.

Exercise 1-6:
Using Revit's Help System

This section of your introductory chapter will provide a quick overview of Revit's *Help System*. This will allow you to study topics in more detail if you want to know how something works beyond the introductory scope of this textbook.

1. Click the **round question mark** icon in the upper-right corner of the screen.

You are now in Revit's *WikiHelp site* (Figure 1-6.1). This is a website which opened in your web browser. This window can be positioned side by side with Revit, which is especially nice if you have a dual-screen computer system. This interface requires a connection to the internet. As a website, Autodesk has the ability to add and revise information at any time, unlike files stored on your hard drive. This also means that the site can change quite a bit, potentially making the following overview out of date. If the site has changed, just follow along as best you can for the next three pages.

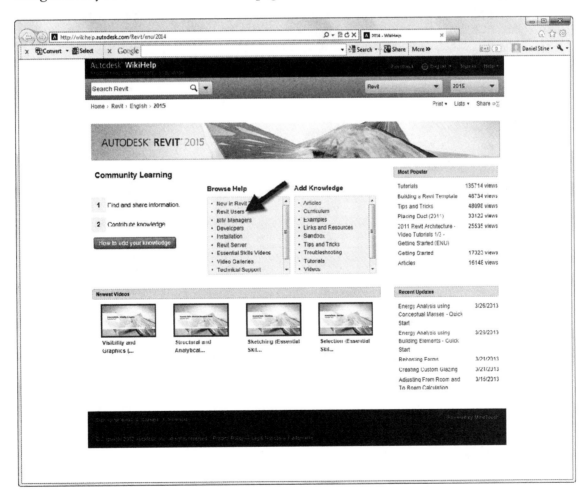

FIGURE 1-6.1 Autodesk WikiHelp site

In the upper left you can search the *Help System* for a word or phrase. You may also click any one of the links to learn more about the topic listed. The next few steps will show you how to access the *Help System's* content on the Revit user interface, a topic you have just studied.

2. In the *Browse Help* section, select **Revit Users**.

3. Expand the tree outline on the left; click the plus next to *Help* (Figure 1-6.2).

Notice the tree structure on the left. You can use this to quickly navigate the User's Guide.

4. On the left, click the plus symbols for: **Revit Users → Introduction to Revit → User Interface** and then click directly on **Ribbon**.

You now see information about the *Ribbon* as shown in the image below. Notice additional links are provided below on the current topic. You can use the browser's *Back* and *Forward* buttons to move around in the *Help System*.

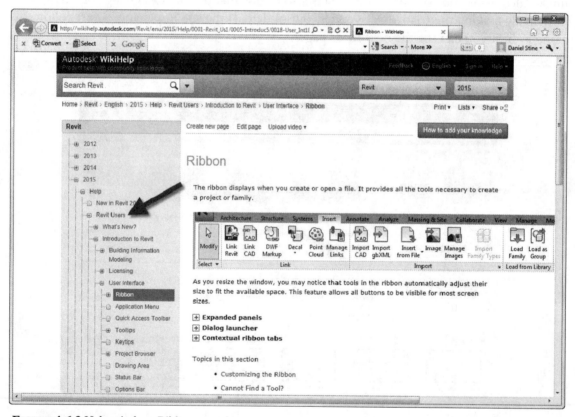

FIGURE 1-6.2 Help window; Ribbon overview

Next, you will try searching the Revit *Help System* for a specific Revit feature. This is a quick way to find information if you have an idea of what it is you are looking for.

5. In the upper-left corner of the current *Help System* web page, click in the *Search* textbox and enter **gutter**.

6. Press **Enter** on the keyboard.

The search results are shown in Figure 1-6.3. Each item is a link which will take you to information on that topic.

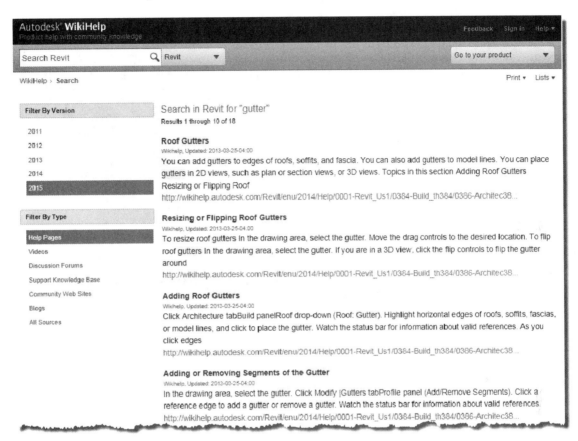

FIGURE 1-6.3 Help search results

The *Help System* can be used to complement this textbook. It is a reference resource, not a tutorial. As you are working though the tutorials in this book, you may want to use the *Help System* to fill in the blanks if you are having trouble or want more information on a topic.

What is a Wiki?

The Revit *Help System* is set up on a Wiki website. A Wiki site is a special type of website where anyone can add information to the site. This makes the potential knowledgebase very large. Anyone who sees a mistake in the steps or instructions provided can make a change. Additionally, a person with specific expertise can add additional information which will help other users. This is similar to the popular information website *Wikipedia*. For more information about Autodesk's *WikiHelp* site and how users such as you may add to and edit the content, visit: http://wikihelp.autodesk.com/training/enu/wiki_guidelines.

Exercise 1-7:
Introduction to Autodesk 360

We will finish this chapter with a look at Autodesk 360, which is "ground zero" for all of Autodesk's **Cloud services**. It is important that the student read this information in order to follow along in the book when specific steps related to using these *Cloud* services are covered. The reader does not necessarily need to use Autodesk's *Cloud* services to successfully complete this book.

The main features employed in the book are:

- Saving your work to *Autodesk 360* so you can access the data anywhere and know that the files are in a secure, backed up location. This feature is free to anyone, with some limitations to be discussed later.

- Sending your photorealistic rendering project to the *Cloud* to dramatically reduce the overall processing time. This feature is free to students and a free trail is available to everyone else.

Here is how Autodesk describes *Autodesk 360* on their website:

> The Autodesk® 360 cloud-based framework provides tools and services to extend design beyond the desktop. Streamline your workflows, effectively collaborate, and quickly access and share your work anytime, from anywhere. With virtually infinite computing power in the cloud, Autodesk 360 scales up or down to meet business needs without the infrastructure or upfront investment required for traditional desktop software.

Before we discuss *Autodesk 360* with more specificity, let's define what the *Cloud* is. **The Cloud is a service, or collection of services, which exists partially or completely online.** This is different from the *Internet*, which mostly involves downloading static information, in that you are creating and manipulating data. Most of this happens outside of your laptop or desktop computer. This gives the average user access to massive amounts of storage space, computing power and software they could not otherwise afford if they had to actually own, install and maintain these resources in their office, school or home. In one sense, this is similar to a *Tool Rental Center*, in that the average person could not afford, nor would it be cost-effective to own, a jackhammer. However, for a fraction of the cost of ownership and maintenance, we can rent it for a few hours. In this case, everyone wins!

Creating a Free Autodesk 360 Account

The first thing an individual needs to do in order to gain access to Autodesk 360 is create a free account at https://360.autodesk.com (students: see *TIP* below); the specific steps will be covered later in this section, so you don't need to do this now. This account is for an individual person, not a computer, not an installation of Revit or AutoCAD, nor does it come from your employer or school. Each person who wishes to access Autodesk 360 services must create an account, which will give them a unique username and password.

> *TIP: Students should first create an account at* http://students.autodesk.com. *This is the same place you go to download free Autodesk software. Be sure to use your school email address as this is what identifies you as a qualifying student. Once you create an account there, you can use this same user name and password to access Autodesk 360. Following these steps will give you access to more storage space and unlimited Cloud rendering!*

Generally speaking, there are three ways you can access *Autodesk 360 Cloud* services:

- Autodesk 360 website
- Within Revit or AutoCAD; local computer
- Mobile device; smart phone or tablet

Autodesk 360 Website

When you have documents stored in the *Cloud* you may access them via your web browser. Here you can manage your files, view them without the full application (some file formats not supported) and share them. These features use some advanced browser technology, so you need to make sure your browser is up to date; specifically:

To view most 2D documents, use these browsers:

- Mozilla® Firefox® 10 and later

- Google Chrome™ 16 and later

- Microsoft® Internet Explorer® 8 and later

- Apple® Safari® 5.1 and later

To view both 2D and 3D documents, use these browsers:

- Mozilla® Firefox® 10 and later

- Google Chrome™ 16 and later

IMPORTANT: Depending on your browser, the Adobe® Flash® Player may be required to upload files and view video.

Using the website, you can upload files from your computer to store in the *Cloud*. To do this, you switch to the **Folders and Categories** section and click the **Upload** option (Figure 1-7.1).

TIP: If using Firefox or Chrome, you can drag and drop documents into the Upload Documents *window. This is a great way to create a secure backup of your documents.*

FIGURE 1-7.1 Viewing files stored in the *Cloud*

You can share files stored in the *Cloud* with others. Private sharing is with others who have an *Autodesk 360* account and is very easy. Another option is public sharing, which allows you to send someone a link and they can access the file, even if they don't have a 360 account. Simply right-click on a file within *Autodesk 360* to see the sharing options (Figure 1-7.2).

FIGURE 1-7.2 Sharing files stored in the *Cloud*

Autodesk 360 within Revit or AutoCAD; local computer

Another way in which you can access you data, stored in the *Cloud*, is from with-in your Autodesk application; for example, Revit or AutoCAD. This is typically the most convenient as you can open, view and modify your drawings. Once logged in, you will also have access to any *Cloud Services* available to you from within the application, such as rendering or *Green Building Studio*.

To sign in to *Autodesk 360* within your application, simply click the **Sign In** option in the notification area in the upper right corner of the window. You will need to enter your student email address and password (or personal email if not a student) as discussed in the previous section. When properly logged in, you will see your username or email address listed as shown in Figure 1-7.3 below. You will try this later in this section.

FIGURE 1-7.3 Example of user logged into Autodesk 360

Once you are logged in, and if *Autodesk 360* is installed on your computer, you can manually browse to the Autodesk 360 cloud files synced on your computer, as shown in Fig. 1-7.4. *The path is:* **C:\Users\WindowsLoginName\AppData\Local\Autodesk\Autodesk Sync\Cloud\A360LoginName**

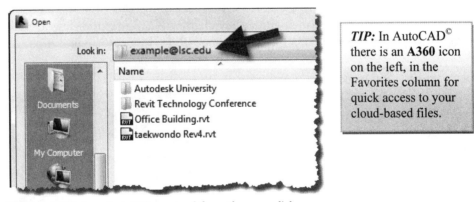

FIGURE 1-7.4 Autodesk 360 accessed from the open dialog

Keep in mind that ALL files stored in *Autodesk 360* are saved on the hard drive of ANY computer you are using; this is ONLY true if you log into *Autodesk 360*. The files are not easy to find manually; recall the path listed above. **The files are NOT deleted off of the local computer when you log out either**. This should not be a problem for working through this book, but you will want to be careful when working with design files from your firm or office (if you work in one).

When you are logged into *Autodesk 360* from within your application, you can also view your files using *Windows Explorer*. Notice in the image below (Figure 1-7.5), that *Autodesk 360* is listed as a *Favorite*. When you click the Autodesk 360 link, your files and folders are shown to the right. Using this view, you can more easily add folders and copy files.

FIGURE 1-7.5 Autodesk 360 files accessed from windows explorer

Using Revit or AutoCAD on your computer, it is possible to work on files directly in the *Cloud* – kind of. You actually work on the local version of your files, which are automatically synched with the online version anytime they change. Keep in mind this does not work for the multi-user environment, called work-sharing, which Revit is capable of.

When *Autodesk 360* is installed on your local computer system, you will have an icon for it in the *Windows* system tray as shown in Figure 1-7.6. If you right-click on this icon you will be presented with a few options, such as: open the local folder, open the website view, sync now, pause sync and preferences.

FIGURE 1-7.6
Autodesk 360 in the system tray

Clicking preferences presents the dialog box shown in Figure 1-7.7. Here you can see how much space you have available, enable automatic log-in upon system start up and specify what to do with linked files. You can also force a *Sign Out* to manually break the connection to the *Cloud*. Your local version of the files will still be on your computer, but the Autodesk 360 links will not reveal them.

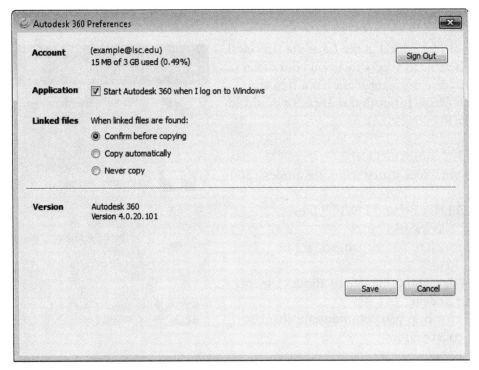

FIGURE 1-7.7 Autodesk 360 preferences for your computer

When using the **Render in Cloud** feature (Figure 1-7.8) or **Run Energy Simulation** (Figure 1-7.9), you must be logged into *Autodesk 360* within the application. If you are not logged in when you click this tool, Revit will prompt you to log in. This is how the *Cloud Service* validates your job request. You either need to be a student, have an account associated with Autodesk Subscription, or have pre-paid Autodesk *Cloud* credits.

FIGURE 1-7.8 Cloud-based tools within the application; View tab

FIGURE 1-7.9 *Cloud*-based tools within the application; Analyze tab

Autodesk 360 Mobile

Once you have your files stored in the *Cloud* via Autodesk 360, you will also be able to access them on your tablet or smart phone if you have one. Autodesk has a free app called *Autodesk 360 Mobile* for both the Apple or Android phones and tablets.

Some of the mobile features include:
- Open and view files stored in your Autodesk 360 account
- 2D and 3D DWG™ and DWF™ files
- Revit® and Navisworks® files
- Use multi-touch to zoom, pan, and rotate drawings
- View meta data and other details about elements within your drawing
- Find tools that help you communicate changes with your collaborators

The Android app is installed via *Google Play* and the Apple app comes from *iTunes*.

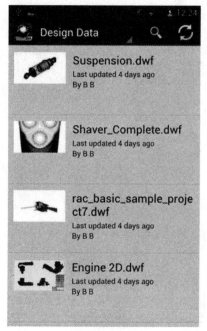

FIGURE 1-7.10
Viewing files on smart phone

Setting up your Autodesk 360 account

The next few steps will walk you through the process of setting up your free online account at *Autodesk 360*. These steps are not absolutely critical to completing this book, so if you have any reservations about creating an *Autodesk 360* account – don't do it.

1. To create a free Autodesk 360 account, do one of the following:

    a. If you are a **student**: create an account at http://students.autodesk.com.

    b. If you work for a company who has their Autodesk software on **subscription**: ask your *Contract Administrator* (this is a person in your office) to create an account for you and send you an invitation via http://subscription.autodesk.com.

    c. **Everyone else**: create an account at: https://360.autodesk.com

    FYI: The "s" at the end of "http" in the Autodesk 360 URL means this is a secure website.

2. Open your application: AutoCAD or Revit.

3. Click the **Sign In** option in the upper-right corner of the application window (Figure 1-7.11).

FIGURE 1-7.11 Signing in to Autodesk 360

It is recommended, as you work through this book, that you save all of your work in the *Cloud*, via Autodesk 360, so you will have a safe and secure location for your files. These files can then be accessed from several locations via the three methods discussed here. It is still important to maintain a separate copy of your files on a flash drive, portable hard drive or in another *Cloud*-type location such as *Dropbox*. This will be important if your main files ever become corrupt. You should manually backup your files to your backup location so a corrupt file does not automatically corrupt your backup file.

TIP: If you have a file that will not open try one of the following:

- In AutoCAD: *Open AutoCAD and then, from the Application Menu, select Drawing Utilities → Recover → Recover. Then browse to your file and open it. AutoCAD will try to recover the drawing file. This may require some things to be deleted, but is better than losing the entire file.*

- In Revit: *Open Revit and, from the Application Menu, select Open; browse to your file, then select it. Click the Audit check box, and then click Open. Revit will attempt to repair any problems with the project database. Some elements may need to be deleted, but this is better than losing the entire file.*

Be sure to check out the Autodesk website to learn more about Autodesk 360 and the growing number of *Cloud* services Autodesk offers.

Self-Exam:

The following questions can be used as a way to check your knowledge of this lesson. The answers can be found at the bottom of this page.

1. The *View* tab allows you to save your project file. (T/F)

2. You can zoom in and out using the wheel on a wheel mouse. (T/F)

3. Revit is a parametric architectural design program. (T/F)

4. A _____ file allows you to start your project with specific content and certain settings preset the way you like or need them.

5. Autodesk 360 allows you to save your files safely in the _____ .

Review Questions:

The following questions may be assigned by your instructor as a way to assess your knowledge of this section. Your instructor has the answers to the review questions.

1. The *Options Bar* dynamically changes to show options that complement the current operation. (T/F)

2. Revit is strictly a 2D drafting program. (T/F)

3. The Projects/Views listed in the *Open Documents* list allow you to see which Projects/Views are currently open. (T/F)

4. When you use the *Pan* tool you are actually moving the drawing, not just changing what part of the drawing you can see on the screen. (T/F)

5. Revit was not originally created for architecture. (T/F)

6. The icon with the floppy disk picture (💾) allows you to _____ a project file.

7. Clicking on the _____ next to the *Zoom* icon will list additional zoom tools not currently shown in the *View* toolbar.

8. You do not see the *ViewCube* unless you are in a _____ view.

9. Creating an *Autodesk 360* account is free. (T/F)

10. Synched files are deleted from your hard drive when you log out of *Autodesk 360*. (T/F)

Lesson 2
Quick Start: Small Office:

In this lesson you will get a down and dirty overview of the functionality of Autodesk Revit. The very basics of creating the primary components of a floor plan: Walls, Doors, Windows, Roof, Annotation and Dimensioning will be covered. This lesson will show you the amazing "out-of-the-box" powerful, yet easy to use, features in Revit. It should get you very excited about learning this software program. Future lessons will cover these features in more detail while learning other editing tools and such along the way.

Exercise 2-1:
Walls, Grids and Dimensions

In this exercise you will draw the walls, starting with the exterior. Read the directions carefully, everything you need to do is clearly listed.

Exterior Walls:

1. Start a new project named **Small Office** per the following instructions:

    a. **Application Menu → New → Project**

    b. Click **Browse...** (Figure 2-1.1)

    c. Select the template file named **Commercial-Default.rte**. *(You should be brought to the correct folder automatically.)*

    FIGURE 2-1.1 New Project

    d. Click **Open**.

    e. With the template file just selected and *Create new* "Project" selected, click **OK** (Figure 2-1.1).

    See Lesson 1 for more information on creating a new project.

2. Select **Architecture → Build → Wall** on the *Ribbon*. (See Figure 2-1.2.)

    FIGURE 2-1.2 Wall tool

Notice that the *Ribbon*, *Options Bar* and *Properties Palette* have changed to show settings related to walls. Next you will modify those settings.

FYI: By default, the bottoms of new walls will be at the current floor level and the tops of the walls are set via the Options Bar as shown in the next step.

FIGURE 2-1.3 Ribbon and Options Bar

3. Modify the *Ribbon*, *Options Bar* and *Type Selector* to the following (Figure 2-1.3):

    a. *Element Type Selector:* Click the down-arrow and select *Basic Wall:* **Generic – 12″**.

    b. *Height:* Change the height from 14′-0″ to **9′-0″**.

    c. *Location Line:* Set this to **Finish Face : Exterior**.

    d. Click the Rectangle icon. *(This allows you to draw four walls at once [i.e., a rectangle], rather than one wall at a time.)*

You are now ready to draw the exterior walls.

4. In the *Drawing Window*, click in the upper left corner.

    TIP: Make sure to draw within the four elevation markers (see image to right).

5. Start moving the mouse down and to the right. **Click** when the two temporary on-screen listening dimensions are approximately **100′** (East to West) and **60′** (front to back).

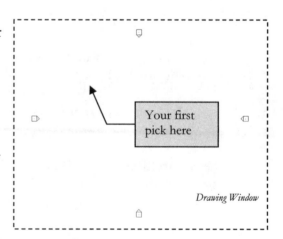

Getting the dimensions exact is not important as they will be revised later on.

Your drawing should look similar to Figure 2-1.4; similar in that the dimensions do not have to be exact right now and the building's location relative to the four elevation tags may vary slightly.

The *Temporary Dimensions* are displayed until the next action is invoked by the user. While the dimensions are displayed, you can click on the dimension text and adjust the wall dimensions. Also, by default the *Temporary Dimensions* reference the center of the wall – you can change this by simply clicking on the grips located on each *Witness Line*; each click toggles the witness line location between center, exterior face and interior face.

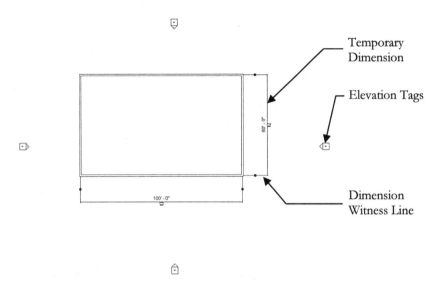

Temporary Dimension

Elevation Tags

Dimension Witness Line

FIGURE 2-1.4 Exterior walls

In the next few steps you will create grid lines and establish a relationship between the walls and the grids such that moving a grid causes the wall to move with it.

Grids:

Grids are used to position structural columns and beams in a building. Adding a grid involves selecting the *Grid* tool and then picking two points in the drawing window.

6. Click **Modify** on the *Ribbon* (to finish using the *Wall* tool) and then select the **Architecture → Datum → Grid**.

   FYI: The same Grid *tool is also found on the* Structure *tab.*

Next you will draw a vertical grid off to the left of your building. Once you have drawn all the grids you will use a special tool to align the grid with the walls and lock that relationship.

7. [*first pick*] **Click** down and to the left of your building as shown in Figure 2.1-5.

    FYI: 'Click' always means left-click, unless a right-click is specifically called for.

8. [*second pick*] Move the cursor straight up (i.e., vertically) making sure you see a dashed cyan line, which indicates you are snapped to the vertical plane, and the angle dimension reads 90 degrees. Just past the North edge of the building (as shown in Figure 2.1-5), click.

FIGURE 2-1.5 Drawing a grid

You have now drawn your first grid line. Next you will quickly draw four more grid lines; two horizontal and two vertical.

> **NOTE:** *The Grid tool will remain active until you select another tool or select Modify (selecting Modify allows you to select other elements in the drawing window).*

9. Draw another vertical grid approximately centered on your building. BEFORE YOU PICK THE FIRST POINT, make sure you see a dashed cyan reference line indicating the grid line will align with the previous grid line (you will see this before clicking the mouse at each end of the grid line), then go ahead and pick both points (Figure 2-1.6).

10. Draw the remaining grid lines shown in Figure 2-1.6. Again, do not worry about the exact location of the grid lines, just make sure the ends align with each other.

FIGURE 2-1.6 Grids added

Next you will change the two horizontal grid lines to have letters instead of numbers.

11. Zoom in on the grid bubble for the upper horizontal grid line.

12. Click *Modify* and then click on the grid line to select it.

13. With the grid line selected, click on the dark blue text within the bubble.

14. Type **A** and press *Enter* on the keyboard. (Figure 2-1.7)

15. Click **Modify** again.

16. Change the other horizontal grid to **B**.

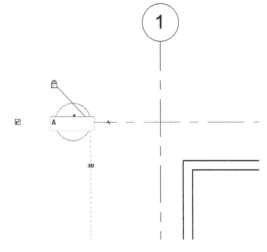

FIGURE 2-1.7 Grid edit

Align:

Next you will use the *Align* tool to reposition the grid lines so they "align" with the exterior face of the adjacent walls. The steps are simple: select the *Align* tool from the *Ribbon*; pick the reference line (i.e., the exterior wall face); and then you select the item to move (i.e., the grid line). This tool works on many Revit objects!

17. Select **Modify** → **Modify** → **Align** from the *Ribbon*.

    REMINDER: Ribbon instructions are Tab → Panel → Tool

18. [*Align: first pick*] With the *Align* tool active notice the prompt on the *Status Bar*, select **Wall faces** on the *Options Bar*, next to Prefer, and then select the exterior face of the wall adjacent to grid line 1.

19. [*Align: second pick*] Select **grid line 1**. Be sure to see the next step before doing anything else!

The grid line should now be aligned with the exterior face of the wall. Immediately after using the *Align* tool you have the option of "locking" that relationship; you will do that next. The ability to lock this relationship is only available until the next tool is activated. After that you would need to use the *Align* tool again.

20. Click the un-locked **padlock** symbol to "lock" the relationship between the grid line and the wall (see Figure 2-1.8).

21. Use the steps just outlined to **Align** and **Lock** the remaining grid lines with their adjacent walls. Do not worry about the location of grid line 2 (i.e., the vertical grid in the center).

FIGURE 2-1.8 Align "lock"

Dimensions:

Next you will add dimensions to the grid lines and use them to drive the location of the walls and grids and learn how to lock them.

22. Select **Modify** and then **right-click** anywhere within the *Drawing Window*, click **Zoom To Fit**.

23. Select **Annotate → Dimensions → Aligned** tool.

Aligned

At this point you are in the *Dimension* tool. Notice the various controls available on the *Ribbon* and *Options Bar*. You can set things like the dimension style (via the *Element Type Selector*) and the kind of dimension (linear, angle, radius, etc.) and which portion of the wall to *Prefer* (e.g., face, center, core face).

24. With the *Ribbon*, *Options Bar* and *Properties Palette* as shown above, which should be the default settings, **select grid line 1**.

> *FYI: The grid line will pre-highlight before you select it, which helps make sure you select the correct item (e.g., the grid line versus the wall). Be careful not to select the wall.*

25. Now **select grid line 2** and then **select grid line 3**.

Your last pick point is to decide where the dimension line should be.

26. Click in the location shown in Figure 2-1.9 to position the dimension line.

> *TIP: Do not click near any other objects or Revit will continue the dimension string to that item.*

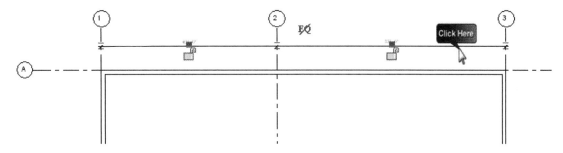

FIGURE 2-1.9 Adding dimensions

Notice that while the dimension string is selected, you see an EQ symbol with a slash through it. This symbol indicates that the individual components of the dimension string are not equal in length. The next step will show you how easy it is to make these dimensions equal!

27. With the dimension string selected, click the EQ symbol located near the middle of the dimension.

The grid lines are now equally spaced (Figure 2-1.10) and this relationship will be maintained until the EQ symbol is selected again to toggle the "dimension equality" feature off.

> NOTE: *When dimension equality is turned off or the dimension is deleted the grid line* **will not** *move back to its original location; Revit does not remember where the grid was.*

Typically, you would not want to click the padlock icons here because that would lock the current dimension and make it so the grid lines could not be moved at all.

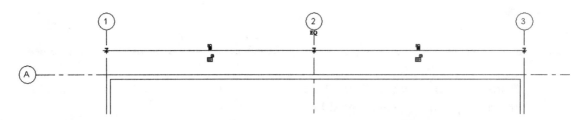

FIGURE 2-1.10 Toggling dimension equality

Next you will add an "overall building" dimension from grid line 1 to grid line 3. This dimension can be used to drive the overall size of your building (all the time, keeping grid line 2 equally spaced).

28. Using the **Aligned** *Dimension* tool, add a dimension from grid line 1 to grid line 3 and then pick to position the dimension line (Figure 2-1.11).

FIGURE 2-1.11 Overall building dimension added

When using a dimension to drive the location of geometry, you need to select the item you want to move and then select the dimension text to enter the new value. You cannot just select the dimension because Revit does not know whether you want the left, right or both grid lines to move. The only thing you can do, graphically, by selecting the dimension directly is "lock" that dimension by clicking on the padlock symbol and then click the blue dimension text to add a suffix if desired. Next you will adjust the overall building size.

29. Click **Modify** (or press the *Esc* key twice) to make sure you cancel or finish the *Dimension* tool and that nothing is selected.

30. **Select grid line 3.**

31. With grid line 3 selected, click the dimension text and type **101** and then press *Enter*.

    FYI: *Notice that Revit assumes feet if you do not provide a foot or inch symbol.*

32. Repeating the previous steps, add a dimension between grid lines A and B, and then adjust the model so the dimension reads **68'-0"**.

FIGURE 2-1.12 Building size established

Your project should now look similar to Figure 2-1.12. You should notice that dimensions must "touch" two or more items (the grid lines in this case). Also, because the walls where aligned and locked to the grids, moving the grids caused the walls to move.

The last thing you will do before moving on to the interior walls is to swap out the generic walls with a more specific wall. This would be a common situation in a design firm; a generic wall is added as a "place holder" until the design is refined to the point where the exterior wall system is selected.

The process for swapping a wall is very simple: select the wall and pick a different type from the *Type Selector*. The next steps will do this, but will also show you how to quickly select all the exterior walls so you can change them all at once!

33. Click **Modify** and then hover your cursor over one of the exterior walls so it pre-highlights. (Do not click yet.)

34. *With an exterior wall pre-highlighted,* take your hand off the mouse and tap the **Tab** key until all four walls pre-highlight.

    FYI: The Tab *key cycles through the various items below your cursor. The current options should include: one wall, a chain of walls, and a grid line.*

35. *With all four walls pre-highlighted:* **click** to select them.

36. *With all four walls selected:* pick *Basic Wall:* **Exterior – Brick on CMU** from the *Type Selector* on the *Properties Palette.*

Type Selector with the four exterior walls selected.

Detail Level:

Revit allows you to control how much
detail is shown in the walls.

37. On the *View Control Bar*, located
    in the lower left corner of the
    Drawing Window on the *View
    Control Bar*, set the *Detail Level* to
    Fine.

As you can see in the two images below, *Coarse* simply shows the outline of a wall type and
Fine shows the individual components of the wall (i.e., brick, insulation, concrete block, etc.).

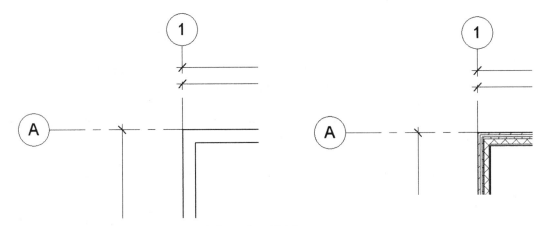

FIGURE 2-1.13 Detail level – coarse (left) vs. fine (right)

Now that you have the exterior walls established, the grid lines properly placed, and their
relationships locked in the project, you can now proceed with the layout of the interior
spaces.

Interior Walls:

38. With the **Wall** tool selected, modify the *Ribbon*, *Options Bar* and *Properties Palette* to the
    following (also, see image on the following page):

    a. *Type Selector:* set to *Basic Wall:* **Interior – 4 7/8″ Partition (1-hr)**.

    b. *Height:* **Roof**

    c. *Location Line:* Set this to **Wall Centerline.**

    d. *Turn off Chair.*

39. Draw a wall from the West wall (i.e., "vertical" wall on the left) to the East wall (on the right). See Figure 2-1.14.

    a. Make sure your cursor "snaps" to the wall before clicking.

    b. Before clicking the second point of the wall, make sure the dashed cyan line is visible so you know the wall will be truly horizontal.

    c. The exact position of the wall is not important at this point as you will adjust it in the next step.

    d. With the temporary dimensions still active, proceed to the next step.

FIGURE 2-1.14 Adding interior walls – North indicator added for reference only

40. Click the **witness line grips** (see Figure 2-1.14) until the "clear" space of the room is listed (see Figure 2-1.15).

41. Now click the blue text of the temporary dimension, type **22**, and then press *Enter* (Figure 2-1.15).

42. Click **Modify** to finish the current task.

FIGURE 2-1.15 Repositioning interior wall via temporary dimensions

The clear space between the interior wall and the north wall is now 22'-0". Next you will add additional interior walls to create equally spaced rooms in this area.

43. Using the same settings as the interior wall just added, draw five (5) vertical walls as shown in Figure 2-1.16.

   a. Make sure they are orthogonal (i.e., the dashed cyan line is visible before picking the walls endpoint).

   b. Make sure you "snap" to the perpendicular walls (at the start and endpoint of the walls you are adding).

   c. Do not worry about the exact position of the walls.

   TIP: Uncheck Chain on the Options Bar.

FIGURE 2-1.16 Adding additional interior walls

In the next step you will use a dimension string to reposition the walls so they are equally spaced. This process is similar to what you did to reposition grid line 2. However, you have to specify which part of the wall you want to dimension to (center, face, core center, core face).

FYI: The "core" portion of a wall system typically consists of the structural element(s) such as the concrete block (in your exterior walls) or the metal studs (in your interior walls).

44. Select **Annotate → Dimension → Aligned** tool on the *Ribbon*.

45. On the *Options Bar*, select **Wall Faces**.

This setting will force Revit to only look for the face of a wall system. You can select either face depending on which side of the wall you favor with your cursor. This feature lets you confidently pick specific references without needing to continually zoom in and out all over the floor plan.

46. Select the interior face of the West wall to start your dimension string.

The next several picks will need to reference the wall centerlines. Revit allows you to toggle the wall position option on the fly via the *Options Bar*.

47. Change the setting to **Wall Centerlines**.

48. The next five picks will be on the five "vertical" interior walls. Make sure you see the dashed reference line centered on the wall to let you know you are about to select the correct reference plane.

49. Change the wall location setting back to **Wall Faces** and select the interior face of the East wall (the wall at grid line 3).

50. Your last pick should be away from any elements to position the dimension string somewhere within the rooms (Figure 2-1.17).

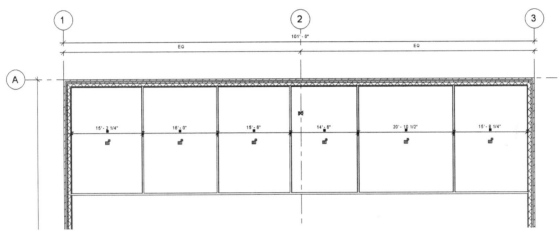

FIGURE 2-1.17 Adding a dimension string

51. Click the EQ symbol to reposition the interior walls.

52. Click **Modify**.

The interior walls are now equally spaced (Figure 2-1.18)!

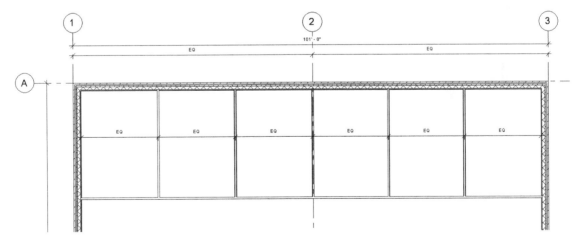

FIGURE 2-1.18 Enabling dimension equality

53. Add a vertical "clear" dimension to indicate the depth of the rooms. Set *Prefer* to **Wall Faces** for both ends of the dimension line. See Figure 2-1.19.

54. Click the **padlock** symbol (🔒) to tell Revit this dimension should not change (Figure 2-1.19).

55. Click **Modify**.

Next you will adjust the overall building dimensions and notice how the various parametric relationships you established cause the model to update!

FIGURE 2-1.19
Locking dimensions

56. Click grid line 3 and change the overall dimension from 101 to **40**, by clicking on the dimension text and then press *Enter*.

TIP: When adjusting the building footprint via the dimensions, you need to select the grid line, not the east wall, because the dimension references the grid line.

Notice the interior walls have adjusted to remain equal, and grid line 2 is still centered between grids 1 and 3 (Figure 2-1.20).

FIGURE 2-1.20 Adjusting dimensions

57. Change the 40'-0" dimension to **110'-0"**.

58. Select grid line A and change the 68'-0" dimension to **38'-0"**.

Your model should now look similar to Figure 2-1.21. Notice the interior wall maintained its 22'-0" clear dimension because the interior wall has a dimension which is locked to the exterior wall, and the exterior wall has an alignment which is locked to grid line A.

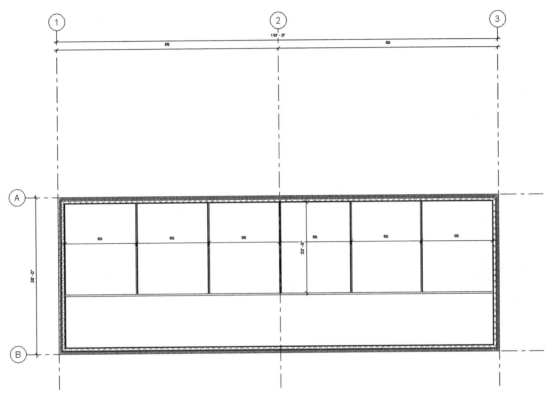

FIGURE 2-1.21 Adjusting dimensions

59. Click **Undo** icon on the *QAT* to restore the 68' dimension.

Your building should now be 110'-0" x 68'-0".

60. **Save** your project (*Small Office.rvt*).

TIP: You can use the Measure tool to list the distance between two points. This is helpful when you want to quickly verify the clear dimension between walls. Simply click the icon and snap to two points and Revit will temporarily display the distance. You can also click "chain" on the Options Bar and have Revit add up the total length of several picks.

Exercise 2-2:
Doors

In this exercise you will add doors to your small office building.

1.   Open **Small Office.rvt** created in Exercise 2-1.

Placing Doors:

2.   Select **Architecture → Build → Door** tool on the *Ribbon* (Figure 2-2.1).

Notice that the *Ribbon, Options Bar & Properties Palette* have changed to show options related to Doors. Next you will modify those settings.

The *Type Selector* indicates the door style, width and height. Clicking the down arrow to the right lists all the doors pre-loaded into the current project.

FIGURE 2-2.1 Door tool

FIGURE 2-2.2 Type selector: Doors

The default template project that you started from has several sizes for a single flush door. Notice, in Figure 2-2.2, that there are two standard heights in the list. The 80″ (6′-8″) doors are the standard residential height and the 84″ (7′-0″) doors are the standard commercial door height.

3.   Change the *Element Type Selector* to:
     Single-Flush: **36″ x 84″**, and click **Tag on Placement** on the *Ribbon.*

4.   Move your cursor over a wall and position the door as shown in **Figure 2-2.3**. (Do <u>not</u> click yet.)

Notice that the swing of the door changes depending on what side of the wall your cursor is favoring.

Also notice Revit displays listening dimensions to help you place the door in the correct location.

5. Click to place the door. Revit automatically trims the wall and adds a door tag.

   TIP: Press the spacebar before clicking to flip the door swing if needed.

6. While the door is still selected, click on the *change swing (control arrows)* symbol to make the door swing against the wall if it is not already (Figure 2-2.4).

FIGURE 2-2.3 Adding door

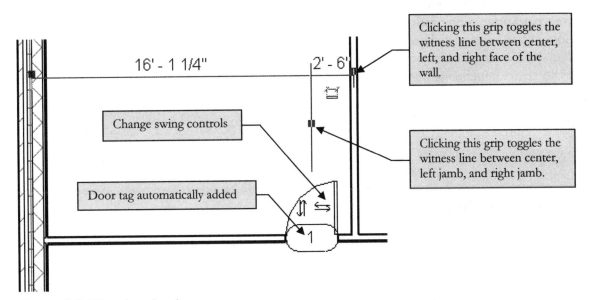

FIGURE 2-2.4 Door just placed

Next you will reposition the door relative to the adjacent wall.

7. Click **Modify** to finish the *Door* tool.

8. Click the door, (not the door tag) you just placed, to select it.

9. Click the **witness line grips** so the temporary dimension references the right door jamb and the wall face as shown in Figure 2-2.5.

TIP: *You can also click and drag the witness line grip to another wall or line if the default location was not what you are concerned with.*

10. Click on the dimension text, type **4″** and press *Enter*. Make sure you add the inch symbol or you will get feet rather than inches (Figure 2-2.5).

FIGURE 2-2.5 Edit door location

Unfortunately, the door *Families* loaded in the commercial template do not have frames. So the 4″ dimension just entered provides for a 2″ fame and 2″ of wall. The library installed on your hard drive, along with the Revit "web library", do provide some doors with frames. It is possible to create just about any door and frame combination via the *Family Editor*. The *Family Editor* is a special mode within Autodesk Revit that allows custom parametric content to be created, including doors with sidelights, transoms and more!

Mirroring Doors:

The *Mirror* command will now be used to quickly create another door opposite the adjacent perpendicular wall.

11. With the door selected, click the **Mirror → Pick Mirror Axis** on the *Contextual Tab*.

12. On the *Options Bar*, click **Copy**. If copy was not selected, then the door would be relocated rather than copied.

Modify | Doors   ☑ Copy

13. With the door selected and the *Mirror* command active: hover the cursor over the adjacent wall until the dashed reference line appears centered on the wall, keep moving the mouse until you see this, and then click. (Figure 2-2.6)

FIGURE 2-2.6 Mirroring a door

As you can see in Figure 2-2.7, the door has been mirrored into the correct location.

Revit does not automatically add door tags to mirrored or copied doors. These will be added later.

TIP: The size of the door tag is controlled by the view's scale.

FIGURE 2-2.7 Door mirrored

Copying Doors:

Now you will copy the two doors so the other rooms have access.

14. Click to select the first door (not the door tag) and then press and hold the **Ctrl** key. *While holding the Ctrl key,* click to add the second door to the selection set.

15. With the two doors selected, click the **Copy** tool.

16. On the *Options Bar*, select **Multiple**.

At this point you need to pick two points: a "copy from here" point and a "copy to there" point. The first point does not have to be directly on the elements(s) to be copied. The next step will demonstrate this; you will pick the midpoint of the wall adjacent to the two doors (first pick) and then you will pick the midpoint of the wall where you want a set of doors (second pick). With "multiple" checked, you can continue picking "second points" until you are finished making copies (pressing *Esc* or *Modify* to end the command).

17. Pick three points:

    a. *First pick:* midpoint/centerline of wall (see Figure 2-2.8);

    b. *Second pick:* midpoint/centerline of wall shown in Figure 2-2.9;

    c. *Third pick:* midpoint/centerline of wall shown in Figure 2-2.9.

18. Pick **Modify** to end *Copy*.

The doors are now copied.

FIGURE 2-2.8 Copy – first point with midpoint symbol visible

FIGURE 2-2.9 Numbers indicate pick-points listed in step #17

You will now add two exterior doors using the same door type.

19. Using the **Door** tool, add two exterior doors approximately located per Figure 2-2.10. Match the swing and hand shown.

FIGURE 2-2.10 Adding exterior doors

Tag All (Not Tagged):

Revit provides a command to quickly add a tag (e.g., a door tag) to any door that does not currently have one in the current view. The tag might have to be moved or rotated once placed, but this still saves time and the possibility of missing a door tag.

20. Select **Annotate → Tag → Tag All**.

21. In the *Tag All Not Tagged* dialog box, select **Door Tags** under *Category* and set *Orientation* to **Vertical**. Click **OK** (see image on next page).

All the doors should now be tagged in your floor plan.

FYI: Door tags can be deleted at any time and added again later at any time. Tags simply display information in the element being tagged – thus, no information about the element is being deleted; the building information integrity remains intact.

Deleting Doors:

Next you will learn how to delete a door when needed. This process will work for most elements (i.e., walls, windows, text, etc.) in Revit.

22. Click **Modify**.

23. Click on door number 7 (the door on the left, not the door tag) and press the **Delete key** on your keyboard.

As you can see, the door is deleted and the wall is automatically filled back in. Also, a door tag can only exist by being attached to a door; therefore the door tag was also deleted.

One last thing to observe: Revit numbers the doors in the order in which they have been placed (regardless of level). Doors are not automatically renumbered when one is deleted. Also, doors can be renumbered to just about anything you want.

24. **Save** your project *(Small Office.rvt)*.

Exercise 2-3:
Windows

In this exercise you will add windows to your small office building.

1. Open **Small Office.rvt** created in Exercise 2-2.

Placing Windows:

2. Select **Architecture → Build → Window**.

Notice that the *Ribbon, Options Bar* and *Properties Palette* have changed to show options related to windows. Next you will modify those settings.

The *Type Selector* indicates the window style, width and height. Clicking the down arrow to the right lists all the windows loaded in the current project.

3. With the *Window* tool active, do the following (Figure 2-3.1):

    a. Change the *Type Selector* to *Fixed:* **36″ x 48″**.

    b. Verify *Tag on Placement* is toggled off on the *Ribbon*.

    c. Note the **Sill Height** value in the *Properties Palette*.

FIGURE 2-3.1 Ribbon and Options Bar: Window tool active

4. Move your cursor over a wall and place **two windows** as shown in **Figure 2-3.2**. *Notice that the position of the window changes depending on what side of the wall your cursor favors.*

FYI: *The window sill height is controlled by Properties Palette which you will study later in this book. For now, the default dimension was used.*

5. Adjust the **temporary dimensions** per the following:

    a. Dimensions per Figure 2-3.2.

    b. Use the witness line grip to adjust the witness line position.

    REMEMBER: *The selected item moves when temporary dimensions are adjusted. Pick the left window to set the 6'-0" dimension and the right for the 8'-0" dimension.*

6. Using the **Copy** command, in a way similar to copying the doors in the previous exercise, copy the two windows into each office as shown in Figure 2-3.3. (Do not worry about exact dimensions.)

7. **Save** your project *(Small Office.rvt)*.

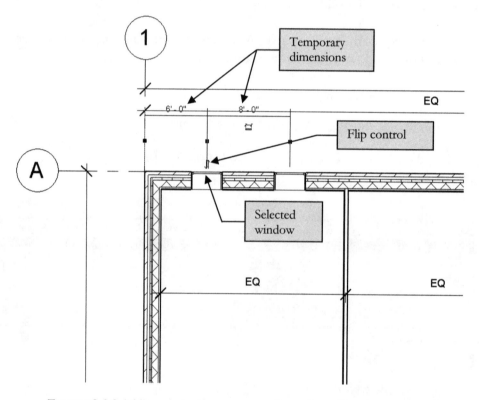

FIGURE 2-3.2 Adding windows – temporary dimensions still active

FIGURE 2-3.3 Windows added to north wall

The windows will not adjust with the grid lines and interior walls; it is possible to add dimensions and get this to work. If you tried to change the overall dimension from 110′ to 40′ again, Revit would let you know it needed to delete some windows before the change could be made. Like doors, windows need their host to exist.

The windows can all be adjusted via the temporary dimensions. The window selected is the largest width available in the project (based on the template file from which the project was started), but it is not a masonry dimension. However, additional window sizes can be added on the fly at any time. Additionally, you can create your own template file that has the doors, windows, walls, etc. that you typically need for the kind of design work you do.

In addition to the preloaded windows, several window styles are available via the family library loaded on your hard drive and the *Autodesk Web Library* (e.g., dbl-hung, casement, etc.). It is also possible to create just about any window design in the *Family Editor*.

Object Snap Symbols:
By now you should be well aware of the snaps that Revit suggests as you move your cursor about the drawing window.

If you hold your cursor still for a moment while a snap symbol is displayed, a tooltip will appear on the screen. However, when you become familiar with the snap symbols you can pick sooner (Figure 2-3.4).

The TAB key cycles through the available snaps near your cursor.

The keyboard shortcut turns off the other snaps for one pick. For example, if you type SE on the keyboard while in the Wall command, Revit will only look for an endpoint for the next pick.

Finally, typing SO (snaps off) turns all snaps off for one pick.

Symbol	Position	Keyboard Shortcut
✕	Intersection	SI
☐	Endpoint	SE
△	Midpoint	SM
○	Center	SC
✕	Nearest	SN
⌐	Perpendicular	SP
◯	Tangent	ST

FIGURE 2-3.4 Snap Reference Chart

Exercise 2-4:
Roof

You will now add a simple roof to your building.

1.   Open **Small Office.rvt** created in Exercise 2-3.

The first thing you will do is take a quick look at a 3D view of your building and notice an adjustment that needs to be made to the exterior walls.

2.   Click the **Default 3D View** icon on the *QAT*.

The 3D icon switches you to the default 3D view in the current project. Your view should look similar to Figure 2-4.1. Notice the exterior walls are not high enough, which is due to a previous decision to set the wall height to 9'-0". Next you will change this, which can be done in the plan view or the current 3D view.

FIGURE 2-4.1 3D view of small office

3.   In the 3D view, hover your cursor over one of the exterior walls to pre-highlight it, then (before clicking) press the **Tab** key to pre-highlight a "chain of walls" (i.e., all the exterior walls), and then click to select them.

Next you will access the properties of the selected walls so you can adjust the wall height. In Revit, most any design decisions that are made can be adjusted at any time.

4. Change the following in the *Properties Palette*:

    a. *Top Constraint:* **Up to level: Roof**

    b. *Top Offset:* **2'-0"**

    c. Click **Apply** (Figure 2-4.2B).

FIGURE 2-4.2A Exterior wall heights adjusted

Figure 2-4.2B Selected wall properties

Setting the top of wall to be associated with a *Level* establishes a parametric relationship that causes the wall height to automatically adjust if the level datum is adjusted (e.g., from 12'-0" to 14'-0").

Plus, the *Top Offset* at 2'-0" creates a 2'-0" parapet, which will always be 2'-0" high no matter what the roof elevation is set to. There are instances when you would want the height to be fixed.

All of the settings related to the selected wall show up here, these are called instance parameters.

Sketching a Roof:

Now that the exterior walls are the correct height, you will now add the roof. This building will have a flat roof located at the roof level.

5. Double-click **Level 1** in the *Project Browser* to switch back to that view.

6. Click **Architecture → Build → Roof** (Figure 2-4.3).

The fly-out prompts you to choose the method you want to use to create the roof.

7. Click **Roof by Footprint**.

At this point you have entered *Sketch Mode* where the Revit model is grayed out so the perimeter you are about to sketch stands out.

Also notice the *Ribbon, Options Bar* and *Properties Palette* have temporarily been replaced with Sketch options relative to the roof (Figure 2-4.4).

FIGURE 2-4.3 Roof tool

8. Click **Extend to Core** on the *Options Bar;* and make sure **Defines Slope** is not checked (Figure 2-4.4).

FIGURE 2-4.4 Roof sketch tools

9. Select all the exterior walls:

    a. Hover your cursor over one of the exterior walls to pre-highlight the wall.

    b. Press **Tab** to select a "Chain of Walls" (i.e., all the exterior walls).

    c. **Click** to select the exterior walls.

At this point you should have four magenta lines, one on each wall, which represent the perimeter of the roof you are creating. When sketching a roof footprint, you need to make sure that lines do not overlap and corners are cleaned up with the *Trim* command if required. Your sketch lines require no additional edits because of the way you added them (i.e., Pick walls and Tab select).

Before you finish the roof sketch you need to adjust the level on which the roof will be created. By default, the top surface of the roof element will be parametrically aligned with the current level (i.e., Level 1 in this case). You will change this to the roof level.

FIGURE 2-4.5 Roof instance properties

10. In the *Properties Palette*, set *Base Level* to **Roof** (Figure 2-4.5).

Now you are ready to finish the roof and exit sketch mode.

11. Click the **green check mark** on the *Ribbon*.

12. Click **Yes** to the join geometry prompt (Figure 2-4.6).

The join geometry option will make the line work look correct in sections. If you clicked "No," the wall and floor lines would just overlap each other and look messy.

FIGURE 2-4.6 Join geometry prompt

The roof is now created and, in section, will extend through the finishes to the concrete block because "extend to core" was selected when the sketch lines were added. Also, because you used the "Pick Walls" option on the *Ribbon* (which was the default), the roof edge will move with the exterior walls.

13. To see the roof, click the **Default 3D View** icon.

14. To adjust the 3D view: press and hold the **Shift** key while pressing the **wheel button** and dragging the mouse around.

FIGURE 2-4.7 Default 3D View

15. Click the **X** in the upper right corner of the *Drawing Window* to close the current view (3D). This will close the 3D view but not the project or the Level 1 view.

    REMEMBER: *Clicking the X in the upper right of the application title bar will close Revit, but it will prompt you to save first if needed.*

16. **Save** your project.

Exercise 2-5:
Annotation, Room Tags & Schedules

Adding text is very simple in Revit. In this exercise you will add a title below the floor plan. You will also place room tags.

Placing Text:

1. Open **Small Office.rvt** created in Exercise 2-4.

2. Make sure your current view is **Level 1**. The word "Level 1" will be bold under the *Floor Plans* heading in your *Project Browser*. If Level 1 is not current, simply double-click on the Level 1 text in the *Project Browser*.

3. Select **Annotate → Text → Text** tool on the *Ribbon*.

Once again, notice the *Ribbon* has changed to display some options related to the active tool (Figure 2-5.1).

FIGURE **2-5.1** Ribbon with Text tool active

The *Type Selector* indicates the text style (which determines the font style, height and more); users can create additional text styles. From this *Contextual Tab*, on the Ribbon, your alignment (i.e., Left justified, Centered or Right justified) can also be set.

4. Set the *Ribbon* settings to match those shown above, **Click** below the floor plan to place the text (Figure 2-5.2).

5. Type **OFFICE BUILDING – Option A**, then click somewhere in the plan view to finish the text (do not press *Enter*).

The text height, in the *Type Selector*, refers to the size of the text on a printed piece of paper. For example, if you print your plan you should be able to place a ruler on the text and read ¼″ when the text is set to ¼″ in the *Type Selector*.

Text size can be a complicated process in CAD programs; Revit makes it very simple. All you need to do is change the **view scale** for **Level 1** and Revit automatically adjusts the text and annotation to match that scale – so it always prints ¼″ tall on the paper.

FIGURE 2-5.2 Placing text

You will not change the scale now, but it can be done via the *View Control Bar* (Figure 2-5.3). If you want to try changing it, just make sure it is set back to ⅛″ = 1′-0″ when done.

You should now notice that your text and even your door and window symbols are half the size they used to be when changing from ⅛″ to ¼″.

You should understand that this scale adjustment will only affect the current view (i.e., Level 1). If you switched to Level 2 (if you had one) you would notice it is still set to ⅛″=1′-0″. This is nice because you may, on occasion, want one plan at a larger scale to show more detail.

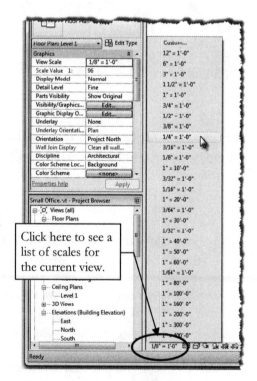

FIGURE 2-5.3 Set View Scale

Placing Room Tags:

Placing *Room Tags* must be preceded by placing a *Room*. A *Room* element is used to define a space and hold information about a space (e.g., floor finish, area, department, etc.). See this author's article in the AUGI AEC-Edge magazine for a detailed discussion on this topic (www.AUGI.com). Like a *Door Tag*, a *Room Tag* simply lists information contained within the element being tagged.

The *Room* feature searches for areas enclosed by walls; a valid area is pre-highlighted before you click to create it.

By default, Revit will automatically place a *Room Tag* at the cursor location when you click to add the *Room* element.

6. Select **Architecture → Room & Area → Room**.

7. Set the *Type Selector* to **Room Tag: Room Tag With Area** and make sure **Tag on placement** is selected on the *Ribbon*.

8. Click within each room in the order shown in Figure 2-5.4; watch for the dashed reference line to align the tags.

FIGURE 2-5.4 Placing rooms and room tags

While the *Room* tool is active, the placed rooms in the model are shaded light blue so you can see which spaces already have rooms placed. The large "X" is also part of the room. When the *Room* tool is not active, you can hover the cursor over the approximate location of the "X" until it pre-highlights, then you can click to select the room. With the *Room* object selected you can add information or delete it via the *Properties Palette*.

9. Click **Modify** to end the current tool.

Notice the rooms are not visible and the "X" is gone. Also notice, the *Room Tag* selected shows the following information stored within the *Room* object: Name, Number and Area.

> *FYI:* *The area updates automatically when the walls move. Next you will change the room names.*

10. Click on the *Room Tag* for **room number 1** to select it.

When a *Room Tag* is selected the "dark blue" text is editable and the "lighter blue" text is not. An example of text that cannot be edited would be the actual text "Sheet Number" next to the sheet number on a sheet border.

11. Click on the room name text, type **OFFICE**, and then press **Enter** on the keyboard.

12. Change rooms 2-4 to also be named **OFFICE**.

13. Change the large room name to **LOBBY**.

14. Leave two rooms (5 and 6) as "Room" for now.

Schedules:

The template you started your project from had room and door schedules set up. So from the first door and room you placed, these schedules started filling themselves out! You will take a quick look at this to finish out this section.

15. In the *Project Browser*, click the "+" symbol next to *Schedules/Quantities* to expand that section (if required) and then double-click on **Room Schedule** to open that view.

The room schedule is a tabular view of the Revit model. This information is "live" and can be changed (Figure 2-5.5).

<Room Schedule>							
A	B	C	D	E	F	G	H
Room Number	Room Name	Floor Finish	Base Finish	Wall Finish	Ceiling Finish	Ceiling Height	Comments
1	OFFICE						
2	OFFICE						
3	OFFICE						
4	OFFICE						
5	Room						
6	Room						
7	LOBBY						

FIGURE 2-5.5 Room Schedule

Next you will change the two rooms named "room", and see that the floor plan is automatically updated!

16. Click in the *Room Name* column for room number 5 and change the text to read **MEN'S TOILET RM**.

17. Click in the *Room Name* column for room number 6 and change the text to read **WOMEN'S TOILET RM**.

Room Number	Room Name
1	OFFICE
2	OFFICE
3	OFFICE
4	OFFICE
5	MEN'S TOILET R
6	WOMEN'S TOILE
7	LOBBY

18. Click the lower "X" in the upper right of the drawing window to close the room schedule view.

19. Switch to *Level 1* (if required) and **zoom in** on rooms 5 and 6 (Figure 2-5.6).

Notice that the room names have been updated because the two views (floor plan and schedule) are listing information from the same "parameter value" in the project database.

FIGURE 2-5.6 Room names updated

20. Open and Close the door schedule to view its current status.

21. **Save** your project.

Exercise 2-6:
Printing

The last thing you need to know to round off your basic knowledge of Revit is how to print the current view.

Printing the current view:

1. In *Level 1* view, right-click anywhere and select **Zoom to Fit**.

2. Select **Application Menu → Print**.

3. Adjust your settings to match those shown in **Figure 2-6.1**.

    - Select a printer from the list that you have access to.
    - Set *Print Range* to: **Visible portion of current window**.

FIGURE 2-6.1 Print dialog

4. Click on the **Setup** button to adjust additional print settings.

5. Adjust your settings to match those shown in **Figure 2-6.2**.

    - *Set Zoom to:* **Fit to page**

FIGURE 2-6.2 Print Setup dialog

6. Click **OK** to close the *Print Setup* dialog and return to *Print*.

7. Click the **Preview** button in the lower left corner. This will save paper and time by verifying the drawing will be correctly positioned on the page (Figure 2-6.3).

8. Click the **Print** button at the top of the preview window.

9. Click **OK** to print to the selected printer.

FYI: Notice you do not have the option to set the scale (i.e., ⅛″ = 1′-0″). If you recall from our previous exercise, the scale is set in the properties for each view. If you want a quick half-scale print you can change the zoom factor to 50%. You could also select "Fit to page" to get the largest image possible but not to scale.

FIGURE 2-6.3 Print Preview

Printer versus Plotter?

Revit can print to any printer or plotter installed on your computer.

A <u>Printer</u> is an output device that uses smaller paper (e.g., 8½"x11" or 11"x17"). A <u>Plotter</u> is an output device that uses larger paper; plotters typically have one or more rolls of paper ranging in size from 18" wide to 36" wide. A roll feed plotter has a built-in cutter that can – for example – cut paper from a 36" wide roll to make a 24"x36" sheet.

Plotter with three paper rolls

Color **printer** / copier

Self-Exam:

The following questions can be used as a way to check your knowledge of this lesson. The answers can be found at the bottom of this page.

1. The *Measure* tool is used to dimension drawings. (T/F)

2. Revit will automatically trim the wall lines when you place a door. (T/F)

3. Snap will help you to draw faster and more accurately. (T/F)

4. A 6'-8" door is a standard door height in _____ construction.

5. While using the wall tool, the height can be quickly adjusted on the

   _____ *Bar.*

Review Questions:

The following questions may be assigned by your instructor as a way to assess your knowledge of this section. Your instructor has the answers to the review questions.

1. The *View Scale* for a view is set by clicking the scale listed on the *View Control Bar.* (T/F)

2. Dimensions are placed with only two clicks of the mouse. (T/F)

3. The relative size of text in a drawing is controlled by the *View Scale.* (T/F)

4. You can quickly switch to a different view by double-clicking on that view's label in the *Project Browser.* (T/F)

5. You cannot select which side of the wall a window is offset to. (T/F)

6. The _____ key cycles through the available snaps near your cursor.

7. The _____ tool can be used to list the distance between two walls without drawing a dimension.

8. While in the *Door* tool you can change the door style and size via the

   _____ _____ within the *Properties Palette.*

Notes:

Lesson 3
Office Building: FLOOR PLAN (First Floor):

In this lesson you will draw the first floor plan of an office building. The office building will be further developed in subsequent chapters. It is recommended that you spend adequate time on this lesson as later lessons build on this one.

Exercise 3-1:
Project Overview

A program statement is created in the pre-design phase of a project. Working with the client (or user group), the architect gathers as much information as possible about the project before starting to design.

The information gathered includes:
- Rooms: What rooms are required?
- Size: How big the rooms need to be? (E.g., toilets for a convention center are much bigger than for a dentist's office.)
- Adjacencies: This room needs to be next to that room. (E.g., the public toilets need to be accessible from the public lobby.)

With the project statement in hand, the architect can begin the design process. Although modifications may (and will) need to be made to the program statement, it is used as a goal to meet the client's needs.

You will not have a program statement, per se, with this project. However, the same information will be provided via step-by-step instructions in this book.

Project Overview:

You will model a three-story office building located in a rural setting. Just to the North of the building site is a medium-sized lake. For the sake of simplicity, the property is virtually flat.

The main entry and parking is from the south side of the building. You enter the building into a three-story atrium. Levels 2 and 3 have guard railings that look down into Level 1 in the atrium. The atrium is enclosed on three sides by full height curtain walls (glass walls). See the image on the front cover.

This building is not meant to meet any particular building code. It is strictly a tool to learn how to use Revit. Having said that, however, there are several general comments as to how codes may impact a particular part of the design.

The floor plans are mostly open office areas with a few smaller rooms for toilets, private offices, work and break rooms, etc. These areas have several "punched" window openings on the exterior walls (punched as opposed to ribbon windows).

FIGURE 3-1.1 Level 1 floor plan sketch

FIGURE 3-1.2 South elevation sketch

Exercise 3-2:
Exterior Walls

You will begin the first floor plan by drawing the exterior walls. Like many projects, early on you might not be certain what the exterior walls are going to be. So, we will start out using the generic wall styles. Then we will change them to a custom wall style (that you will create) once we have decided what the wall construction is.

Adjust Wall Settings:

1. Start a new project using the **Architectural Template**. _Warning:_ Be sure to select the correct template as this is the basis for the remained of the book.

The previous chapter started with a more complete template. This chapter starts from the default template so you have the opportunity to learn how to create things such as the room finish schedule so you better understand how Revit work.

2. Select the **Wall** tool from the _Ribbon_ and then make the following changes to the wall options (Figure 3-2.1):

   - Wall style: _Basic Wall:_ **Generic – 12″**
   - _Height:_ **Unconnected**
   - _Height:_ **36′ 0″**
   - _Location Line:_ **Finish Face: Exterior**
   - _Chain:_ **Checked**

FIGURE 3-2.1 Ribbon, Options Bar and Type Selector: Wall tool active

Draw the Exterior Walls:

3. Draw the walls shown in Figure 3-2.2. Make sure your dimensions are correct. Use the _Measure_ tool to verify your dimensions. Do not add the dimensions.

   NOTE: If you draw in a clockwise fashion, your walls will have the exterior side of the wall correctly positioned. You can also use the spacebar to toggle which side the exterior face is on.

FIGURE 3-2.2 Exterior walls

Create a Custom Wall Style:

Revit provides several predefined wall styles, from metal studs with gypsum board to concrete block and brick cavity walls. However, you will occasionally need a wall style that has not yet been predefined by Revit. You will study this feature next.

First, you will take a quick look at a more complex wall type that Revit provides so you can see how they are set up.

4. With the *Wall* tool selected, pick the wall type: *Basic Wall:* **Exterior – Brick on CMU**, from the *Type Selector* drop-down list. (See image at right.)

5. Click the **Edit Type** button on the Properties Palette (Fig. 3-2.3).

6. You should be in the *Type Properties* dialog box. Click the **Edit** button next to the *Structure* parameter (Figure 3-2.4).

FIGURE 3-2.3 Properties Palette

FIGURE 3-2.4 Type Properties

7. Finally, you are in the *Edit Assembly* dialog box. This is where you can modify existing wall types or create new ones. Click **<<Preview** to display a preview of the selected wall type. (Figure 3-2.5)

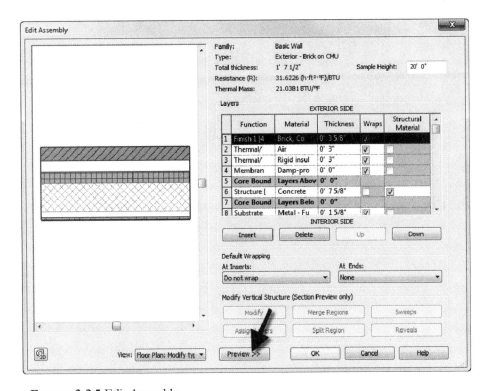

FIGURE 3-2.5 Edit Assembly

Here, the *Edit Assembly* dialog box allows you to change the composition of an existing wall or to create a new wall.

Things to notice in the *Edit Assembly* dialog box (Figure 3-2.5):
- The exterior side is labeled at the top and interior side at the bottom.

- You will see horizontal rows (i.e., Core Boundary) identifying the core material. The core material can be used to place walls and dimension walls. For example: the *Wall* tool will let you draw a wall with the interior or exterior core face as the reference line. On an interior wall you would typically dimension to the face of CMU rather than to the finished face of gypsum board. This is to work out coursing and give the contractor the information needed for the part of the wall he will build first.

- Each row is called a layer. By clicking on a layer and picking the **Up** or **Down** buttons, you can reposition materials, or layer, within the wall assembly.

8. Click **Cancel** in each open dialog box to close them.

9. Set the wall style back to *Basic Wall:* **Generic – 12″** in the *Type Selector*.

10. Click the **Edit Type** button again on the *Properties Palette*.

11. Click **Duplicate**.

12. Enter **Brick & CMU cavity wall** for the new wall type name, and then click **OK** (Figure 3-2.6).

FIGURE 3-2.6 New wall type name

13. Click the **Edit** button next to the *Structure* parameter.

Using the **Insert** button and the **Up** and **Down** buttons, add the *layers* to your new wall style as shown below in **Figure 3-2.7**.

Function	Material	Thickness
Finish 1 [4]	Brick, Common	4″
Thermal/Air Layer [3]	Air	2″
Thermal/Air Layer [3]	Rigid insulation	2″
Membrane Layer	Damp-proofing	0″
Core Boundary	*Layers above wrap*	*0″*
Structure [1]	Concrete Masonry Units	8″
Core Boundary	*Layers below wrap*	*0″*
Substrate [2]	Metal – Furring	2 1/2″
Finish 2 [5]	Gypsum Wall Board	5/8″

FIGURE 3-2.7 New wall layers

Masonry is typically drawn nominally in plans and smaller scaled details. This helps to figure out coursing for both drawing and dimensioning. For example, 8″ concrete block is actually 7⅝″.

Also, notice that the CMU, Rigid Insulation, Air Space and Brick add up to 16″ in thickness. This portion of the wall would sit on a 16″ concrete block (CMU) foundation wall directly below.

14. Your dialog should look like **Figure 3-2.8**. Click **OK** to close all dialog boxes.

FIGURE 3-2.8 Edit Assembly for new wall type

The next step is to change the wall type for the walls previously drawn.

15. Select the **Modify** button on the *Ribbon*; this allows you to select elements in your drawing.

16. **Zoom out** so you can see the entire plan. Dragging your mouse from one corner to the other, make a window over the plan to select all the walls.

17. With the walls selected, pick *Basic Wall:* **Brick & CMU cavity wall** from the *Type Selector* drop down.

TIP: If, after selecting all the walls, the Type Selector is not active and does not show any wall types, you probably have some other elements selected such as text or dimensions. Try to find those elements and delete them (except the elevation tags). You can also click on the Filter button (located on the Ribbon when objects are selected) and uncheck the types of elements to exclude from the current selection.

You should notice the wall thickness change, but the wall cavity lines and hatch are not showing yet. This is controlled by the *Detail Level* option for each view.

18. Click on **Detail Level** icon in the lower-left corner of the *Drawing Window*, on the *View Control Bar*.

Detail Level; Set to Medium

19. Select **Medium**.

You should now see the brick and CMU thicknesses with hatching. If you did not pay attention when drawing the walls originally, some of your walls may show the brick to the inside of the building.

20. Select **Modify** (or press **Esc**); select a wall. You will see a symbol appear that allows you to flip the wall orientation by clicking on that symbol (Figure 3-2.9).

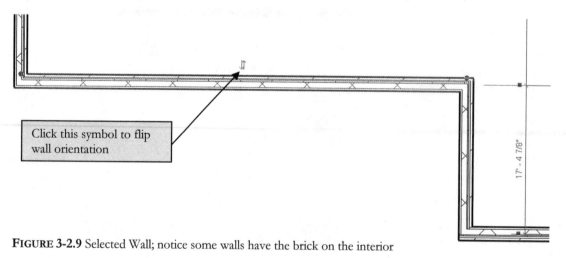

Click this symbol to flip wall orientation

FIGURE 3-2.9 Selected Wall; notice some walls have the brick on the interior

21. Whether you need to adjust walls or not, click on the flip symbol to experiment with its operation.

   TIP: The Flip symbol is always on the exterior side (or what Revit thinks is the exterior side) of the wall.

22. If some walls do need to be adjusted so the brick is to the exterior, do it now. You will probably have to select the wall(s) and use the *Move* tool to reposition the walls to match the required dimensions.

   TIP: If you set the "location line", via the Properties Palette, to "Wall Centerline" the wall will not move and mess up the overall dimensions when flipping it. You will want to set the "location line" back to Finish Face: Exterior when done.

23. **Save** your Project as ex3-2.rvt.

TIP: You can use the MOVE tool Move *on the Ribbon (when a wall is selected) to accurately move walls.*

Follow these steps to move an object:
- *Select the wall*
- *Click the Move tool*
- *Pick any point on the wall*
- *Start your cursor in the desired direction (don't click)*
- *Start typing the distance you want to move the wall and press Enter.*

Finally, you will change the three walls at the atrium to be curtain walls (full glass). This will let lots of light into the atrium and better identify the main entry of the building.

24. Drag a selection window (from left to right) to select the three walls around the atrium, or hold the Ctrl key on the keyboard and select them.

25. With the walls selected, select *Curtain Wall:* **Curtain Wall 1** from the *Type Selector* drop-down.

Your atrium is now surrounded by curtain walls (Figure 3-2.10). In a later lesson we will add horizontal and vertical mullions to the curtain wall.

You can see your progress nicely with a 3D view. Click the **3D View** button on the *QAT*. Notice that Revit shows the curtain wall as transparent because it knows the curtain wall is glass. The other walls are shaded on the exterior side due to the brick pattern that is applied.

26. Save your project as **ex3-2.rvt**.

Revit automatically sets the hatch intensity and line weights.

FIGURE 3-2.10 Completed exercise

FIGURE 3-2.11 Completed exercise

Exercise 3-3:
Interior Walls

In this lesson you will draw the interior walls for the first floor.

Adjust Wall Settings:

1. Select **Architecture → Build → Wall** from the *Ribbon*.

2. Make the following changes to the wall options on the *Ribbon, Options Bar* and *Type Selector* (Figure 3-2.1):
    *   Wall style: *Basic Wall:* **Interior – 4 7/8″ partition (1-hr)**
    *   *Height:* **Level 2**
    *   *Location Line:* **Wall Centerline**

Draw the Interior Walls:

3. Draw a "vertical" wall approximately as shown in Figure 3-3.1. You will adjust its exact position in step #4.

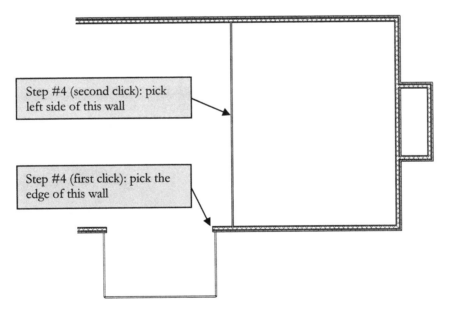

FIGURE 3-3.1 First interior wall

4. Select **Modify → Modify → Align** tool to align it with the edge of the exterior wall in the atrium (Figure 3-3.1). When you are done, the wall should look like Figure 3-3.2.

5. Create the same wall for the West side of the atrium repeating the above steps.

Modify an Existing Wall Type:

Next you will add some additional interior walls. You will be drawing 8″ CMU walls. Revit does have an 8″ Masonry wall type available in the default template file that you started your project from. However, the thickness for this wall type is 7⅝″, which is the actual size of a block. Floor plans are usually drawn nominally (i.e., 8″) not actual (7⅝″). This is done so you can figure out coursing so minimal cutting is required. Therefore, rather than creating a new wall type you can simply modify the existing wall type.

Note: some may disagree with this approach. However, these changes should still be made to this project so you learn more about how walls work and so all the tasks in this book work as expected or intended.

FIGURE 3-3.2

6. Select the wall type: _Basic Wall:_ **Generic – 8″ Masonry**.

7. Select the **Edit Type** button on the _Properties Palette_ to view the wall's _Type Parameters_, and then click **Edit** next to the _Structure_ parameter.

8. Change the masonry thickness from 7⅝″ to **8″** in the _Edit Assembly_ dialog box, and then select **OK** to close each dialog (do not close the _Properties Palette_).

Occasionally Revit will not list dimensions, relative to the walls you want to draw new walls from, while in the create wall mode. One way to deal with this is to draw temporary _Detail Lines_ to use as a reference. After using the temporary line as a reference you can delete it.

9. Select **Annotate → Detail → Detail Line** from the _Ribbon_; the line type does not really matter, but select a continuous one via the _Type Selector._

10. Draw the "vertical" line shown in Figure 3-3.3; be sure to snap to the _Midpoint_ of the atrium wall as your first point.

Next you will draw an elevator shaft, centered on the atrium and 35′-0″ back (thus the temp. line).

The <u>inside</u> dimensions of the elevator are: **7′-4″ x 6′-10″**. Because you know the inside dimension you will want to adjust the location line to match the known info.

11. Use the _Wall_ tool to draw _Basic Wall:_ **Generic – 8″ Masonry**.

12. Set the *Location Line* to: **Finish Face: Interior**.

13. Draw the elevator shaft. Make sure the location line is to the <u>inside</u> so your shaft is the correct dimension. Draw the shaft anywhere in the *Drawing Window*; you will adjust the exact position next.

    FYI: *The inside dimensions are listed above.*

14. Select the 4 walls that represent the elevator shaft, and then pick the **Move** tool.

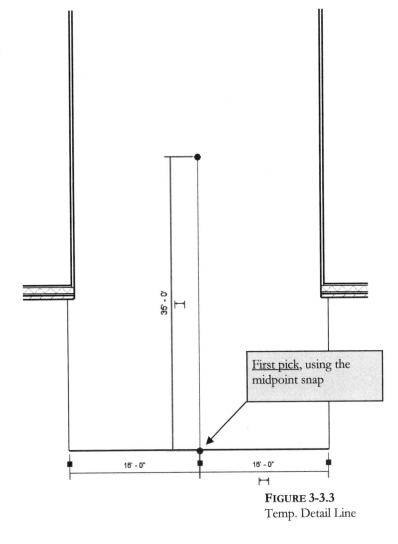

First pick, using the midpoint snap

35' - 0"

16' - 0"   16' - 0"

FIGURE 3-3.3
Temp. Detail Line

TIP: *Concrete blocks come in various widths, and most are 16″ long and 8″ high. When drawing plans there is a simple rule to keep in mind to make sure you are designing walls to coursing. This applies to wall lengths and openings within CMU walls.*

Dimension rules for CMU coursing in floor plans:
- *e'-0″ or e'8″*   *where e is any even number (e.g., 6'-0″ or 24'-8″)*
- *o'4″*   *where o is any odd number (e.g., 5'-4″)*

15. Snap to the *Midpoint* of the shaft as your first point, and then snap to the *Middle Endpoint* of your temporary detail line (Figure 3-3.4). You should zoom in to verify your snaps. Do not draw the dimensions, they are for reference only.

The elevator shaft is now perfectly centered in the atrium and exactly 35'-0" back from the South curtain wall.

16. At this point you can **delete** the temporary line. Select the line and then right-click and select delete or press the Delete key on the keyboard.

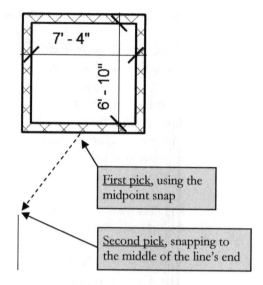

First pick, using the midpoint snap

Second pick, snapping to the middle of the line's end

FIGURE 3-3.4 Move elevator shaft into place

FYI: When a wall is selected, you can see that wall's properties via the Properties Palette *(Type "PP" to open the Palette if it is not visible). Click one of the elevator shaft walls and verify that it is 36'-0" tall.*

Modify an Existing Wall:

Next we want to change the portion of wall between the building and the East and West stair shafts. To do this you will need to split the current wall, trim the corners and then draw an 8" masonry wall.

17. **Zoom** in on the West stair shaft and select the **Split Element** tool (*Modify* tab on the *Ribbon*).

18. Pick somewhere in the middle of the wall (Figure 3-3.5).

19. Select **Modify → Modify → Trim** to trim the corners so the exterior wall only occurs at exterior conditions (Figure 3-3.6).

TIP: Select the portion of wall you wish to retain.

FIGURE 3-3.5 Split tool   **FIGURE 3-3.6** Trim tool

Additional Custom Wall Types:

We decide that the stair shafts are mostly utilitarian and do not require gypsum board on the walls. In the next steps you will create a new exterior wall type just like the one previously created less the gypsum board and metal studs. Also, you will create a custom wall type to close the open side we created in the previous steps. This wall type will have gypsum board and metal studs on one side.

20. Using wall type: _Basic Wall: Brick & CMU cavity wall_ as a starting point, create a new wall type named **Brick & CMU cavity wall (no GWB)**. Remove the gypsum board and metal studs and save the new wall type. *(Remember to click Duplicate.)*

21. Change the three exterior walls around the west stair shaft to the new wall type created in the previous step.

22. Using wall type: _Basic Wall: Brick & CMU cavity wall_ as a starting point, create a new wall type named **8" Masonry with GWB 1S**. Remove the brick, air space, rigid insulation and membrane layer and save the new wall type (Figure 3-3.7).

> **FYI:** _It will be useful to come up with a standard naming system for your custom wall types. If the names get to long they are hard to read. The example above has:_
> - _GWB = Gypsum Wall Board (and would imply studs)_
> - _1S = finish only occurs on one side of the wall._

Function	Material	Thickness
_n/a_	_n/a_	_n/a_
Core Boundary	_Layers above wrap_	_0"_
Structure [1]	Concrete Masonry Units	8"
Core Boundary	_Layers below wrap_	_0"_
Substrate [2]	Metal – Furring	2½"
Finish 2 [5]	Gypsum Wall Board	⅝"

FIGURE 3-3.7 New wall layers

23. Draw a wall so the gypsum finish continues on the office side, using the _Align_ tool if necessary (Figure 3-3.8).
    Use the Measure tool to make sure the stair shaft is the correct size; don't draw the dimensions.

Next you will use the _Mirror_ tool to update the east stair, but first you will draw a _Reference Plane_ to use as the _Axis of Reflection_ (more on this later while using the Mirror tool).

24. Select **Architecture → Work Plane → Ref Plane** from the _Ribbon_.

25. Draw a Reference Plane snapped to the vertical, centered on the South atrium wall (See Figure 3-3.9).

26. Erase the four walls of the East stair shaft; this will include the main east wall of the office building (Figure 3-3.9).

27. Select the six walls at the West stair (Figure 3-3.9).

FIGURE 3-3.8 Revised west stair

> **TIP:** _Make sure the count is correct on the Status Bar._

28. Select the **Mirror - Draw Axis** tool (on the *Ribbon*) and then select the Reference Plane (Figure 3-3.9).

Pick the
Reference Plane
as the axis of
reflection

FIGURE 3-3.9 Mirror west stair

29. Use the **Measure** tool to verify the overall length of the building is 140'-0". Adjust as necessary (see Fig. 3-2.2).

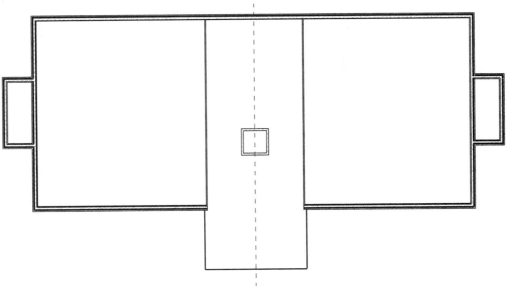

FIGURE 3-3.10 Mirrored west stair

Finally, you will draw a few more interior walls to compete the first floor plan. **Do not delete the *Reference Plane*** (note: the reference line may not show up in every image in this text).

30. Using the *Wall* tool, set the wall type to: *Basic Wall:* **Interior – 4 7/8" partition (1-hr)**

31. Draw the additional walls shown in Figure 3-3.11. Make sure to position the walls per the dimensions shown. Use the *Measure* tool to verify accuracy. Also, modify the *Location Line* as required.

DRAWING TIPS: *Copy the existing atrium wall 6'-4⅞" over (6'-0" plus one wall thickness), draw a wall from the midpoint of the elevator shaft with centerline reference (Location Line), and use the Trim and Mirror tools. Do not draw the dimensions.* **SAVE YOUR PROJECT** *as ex3-3.rvt.*

FIGURE 3-3.11 Remaining interior walls

Exercise 3-4:
Elevator

This lesson will show you how to insert an elevator into your elevator shaft.

Insert Elevator:

Revit provides many *Families*, which are predefined elements ready to insert into your project. However, many elements are not readily available, like elevators for example. You will get an elevator family online in this exercise. The online library is where you will acquire an elevator family for use in your project.

1. Open project ex3-3.rvt and *Save As* ex3-4.rvt.

You will have to download the elevator from the web. *Of course you will need to be connected to the Internet.*

2. Click on the **Insert** tab on the *Ribbon*.

3. Type in **Elevator-Electric** and then press **Enter** (Figure 3-4.1).

FIGURE 3-4.1 Insert tab; Autodesk Seek panel

Your browser will open and you will be looking at the contents of Revit's Seek.Autodesk.com website (Figure 3-4.2).

The family you searched for is generic content provided by Autodesk. However, manufacturer created content can also be found here. It is ideal to use actual manufacturer content as they should be the correct size and have good information stored in them.

FIGURE 3-4.2 Seek.Autodesk.com

4. Click the **2 RFA** icon highlighted in Figure 3-4.2.

You now see a larger preview of the family, in the plan view in this case (Figure 3-4.3). Next you need to select which version of content you want to download. Revit is not backwards compatible so you cannot download a newer version of content than the version of Revit you have. However, you can download older content and Revit will automatically upgrade it anytime you try using it. *NOTE: When a newer version is not available, just use the newest version posted. Revit will automatically upgrade the family upon insertion into your model.*

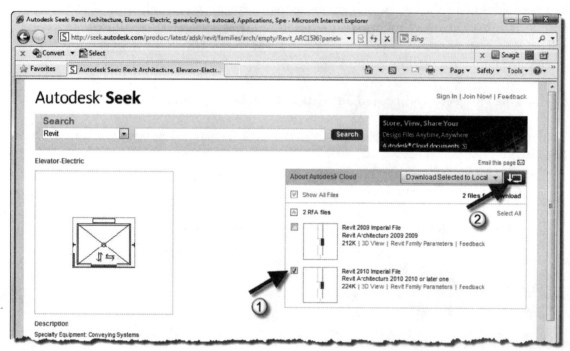

FIGURE 3-4.3 Web content

5. Click the box next to **Revit 2010 Imperial File**.

6. Click the **Download** button just up and to the right of the selected content.

7. If you wish to proceed, you need to check the box and click *Accept* for the *Terms and Conditions* of Autodesk Seek participation (Figure 3-4.5).

8. Select **Save** (Figure 3-4.4).

FIGURE 3-4.4 Web browser prompt

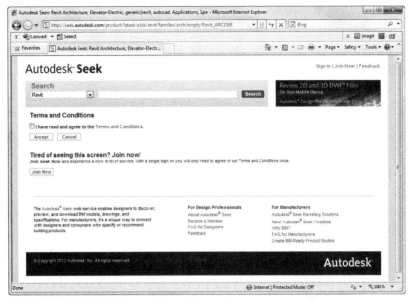

FIGURE 3-4.5 Seek.com terms and conditions

9. Save the file to the *Desktop* using the default name provided.

Now that you have saved the elevator family file to the hard drive, you need to load it into your current project.

10. Select **Insert → Load from Library → Load Family** from the *Ribbon*.

    Load Family

11. Browse to the *Desktop* and select the **Elevator-Electric.RFA**, and then click **Open**.

12. In the *Project Browser*, click the plus next to **Families** to expand the list (Figure 3-4.6).

13. Expand the **Specialty Equipment** list, and then **Elevator-Electric**.

As you can see, four elevator types were loaded into your project. Similar to wall types, you can add one of these types as-is, or you can modify or create a new type. Next, you will add information in the *Type Properties* dialog to better document the elevator specified.

14. Right-click on the elevator type: **2000 lbs**, and then select **Type Properties** from the pop-up menu.

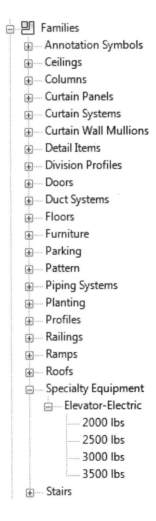

FIGURE 3-4.6 Elevator family: Project Browser

You will now see a listing of the type properties for the selected elevator type.

15. Click the **Preview** button (if necessary) to see the graphical review of the elevator type. Set the *View* to 3D View: View 1.

16. Add the following information (Figure 3-4.7):

- *Model:* **MadeUp 8864**
- *Manufacturer:* **ThyssenKrupp Elevator**
- *URL:* **www.thyssenelevator.com**

The three entries in step 16 are optional (although not for this exercise), but this is a great way to better document the project. This is the **I** in **BIM** (Building Information Modeling).

FIGURE 3-4.7 Elevator properties

17. Click **OK** to close the open dialog box.

18. Drag the **2000 lbs** elevator type from the *Project Browser* into the first floor plan.

   FYI: You can also use the Component tool from the Architecture tab to place the elevator.

The elevator type will be attached to your cursor, ready for insertion.

19. Move your cursor within the elevator shaft and adjust it until the elevator "snaps" in place; then click (Figure 3-4.10).

20. Press **Esc** twice to tell Revit you are finished placing elevators.

Now you have to add an elevator door in the shaft walls at each level; this is similar to a regular door in a wall. Like the elevator, the elevator door has to be downloaded from the internet. You will do that next.

21. Similar to the steps previously covered, load the **Elevator Door – Center** family from the Seek.Autodesk.com website (Figure 3-4.8).

FIGURE 3-4.8 Elevator door from Seek.Autodesk.com

22. Drag the **36″ x 84″** elevator door type from the project browser into the first floor plan (Figure 3-4.9).

23. Place the elevator door at the center of the wall, aligned with the elevator door on the cab (Figure 3-4.10).

> *TIP: If the door is inserted on the wrong side of the wall, select the door and click the Control Arrows to flip it within the wall.*

⊞···· Roofs
⊟···· Specialty Equipment
    ⊟···· Elevator Door-Center
        ···· 32″ x 84″
        ···· **36″ x 84″**
        ···· 42″ x 84″
        ···· 48″ x 84″
        ···· 900 x 2100mm
    ⊟···· Elevator-Electric
        ···· 2000 lbs
        ···· 2500 lbs
        ···· 3000 lbs
        ···· 3500 lbs
⊞···· Stairs
⊞···· Structural Columns

FIGURE 3-4.9 Elevator doors in Project Browser

FIGURE 3-4.10 Elevator door added to plan

Notice when the elevator is selected, the flip icon (control arrow) is displayed. Similar to the doors and walls, you can click this icon to flip the orientation of the elevator within the shaft.

24. Save your project as **ex3-4.rvt**.

Exercise 3-5:
Doors and Windows

This lesson will take a closer look at inserting doors and windows.

Insert Doors:

Revit has done an excellent job providing several different door families. This makes sense seeing as doors are an important part of an architectural project. Some of the provided families include bi-fold, double, pocket, sectional (garage), and vertical rolling, to name a few. In addition to the families found on your local hard drive, many more are available via Seek.Autodesk.com as well as other internet sites (some free some not).

The default template you started with only provides the **Sgl Flush** (Single Flush) group in the *Doors* category. If you want to insert other styles you will need to load them from the library. The reason for this step is that, when you load a family, Revit actually copies the data into your project file. If every possible family was loaded into your project at the beginning, not only would it be hard to find what you want in a large list of doors, but also the files would be several megabytes in size before you even drew the first wall.

You will begin this section by loading a few additional families into your project.

1. Open project ex3-4.rvt and **Save-As ex3-5.rvt**.

2. From the Insert tab, select the **Load Family** button on the *Ribbon* (Figure 3-5.1).

3. Browse through the **US Imperial** library folder for a moment.

FIGURE 3-5.1 Load Family

Each file represents a *Family*; next you will load four door *Families* into your project.

FIGURE 3-5.2 Door families on hard drive

4. Open the **Doors** folder and then select **Curtain Wall Dbl Glass.rfa**, and then click **Open**. (Figure 3-5.2)

5. Repeat steps 2 – 4 to load the following door families:

   a. **Double-Glass 1**
   b. **Sidelights 1**
   c. **Single-Glass 1**

6. In the *Project Browser*, expand *Families* and *Doors* to see the loaded door families (Figure 3-5.3).

If you expand a door family itself in the *Project Browser* you see the predefined door sizes associated with that family. Right-clicking on a door size allows you to rename, delete or duplicate it. To add a door size you duplicate and then modify properties for the new item.

Next you will insert the doors into the stair shafts.

FIGURE 3-5.3 Loaded door families

7. Select the *Door* tool from the *Architecture* tab and then pick **Sgl Flush: 36″ x 84″** from the *Type Selector* on the *Properties Palette*.

8. Insert two doors in the West stair shaft as shown in Figure 3-5.4. Remember you are inserting a door into a masonry wall so your door position and size need to work with coursing. Thus the 8″ dimension (however, you would also need to include the door frame into the equation).

9. Repeat the previous step to insert doors into the East stair shaft.

10. Finish inserting doors for the first floor (Figure 3-5.5).
    Use the following guidelines:

    a. All doors should be 36″ wide and 7′-0″ tall.
    b. You will not insert doors into the curtain wall for now. You will do that in a later lesson when you design the curtain wall.
    c. Use the style and approximate location shown in Figure 3-5.5.
    d. Doors across from each other in the two atrium walls should align with each other.

    TIP: While inserting the second set of doors, watch/wait for the reference line to show up, indicating alignment.

    e. Place doors approximately as shown, exact location not given.

FIGURE 3-5.4 Doors in West stair shaft

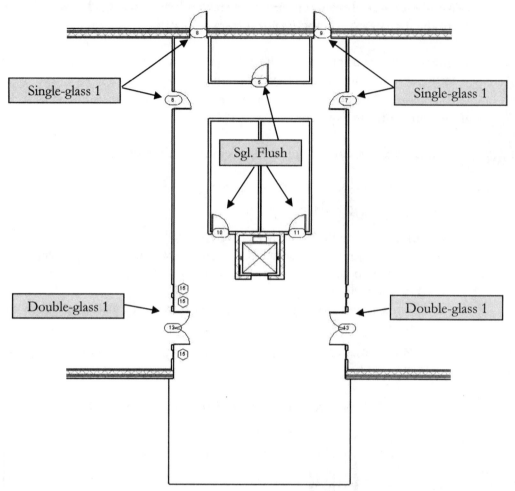

FIGURE 3-5.5 First floor with doors

FIGURE 3-5.6 Door properties

Door Properties:

If you select *Edit Type* while the Door tool is active (selected), you can modify various properties related to the door.

You can easily add another standard door size to the *Family* as required. Click "Duplicate," type a name (Figure 3-5.6).

Standard doors sizes (and *Families*) can be added to your template file, so you don't have to load them for every new project.

Insert Windows:

Adding windows to your project is very similar to adding doors. Like the doors, the template file you started from has one family preloaded into your project, the FIXED family. Looking at the *Type Selector* drop-down you will see the various sizes available for insertion. At this point you should also see the SIDELIGHT family that you loaded in the previous exercise. First, you will add a few interior borrowed lights using the sidelight family.

Interior Windows (Borrowed Lights):

11. With the *Window* tool selected, pick: *Sidelights 1* : **18″ x 84″** from the *Type Selector.*

12. On the West side of the atrium, insert the borrowed lights as shown in Figure 3-5.7; do not add the dimensions.

Make sure the borrowed light frames are flush with the atrium side of the wall. You can control that option by moving your cursor to the side of the wall you want the frame flush with before clicking to insert. After drawing the window, you can select the frame and use the flip icon (similar to doors and walls).

13. Repeat the previous steps to insert the borrowed lights on the East side of the atrium.

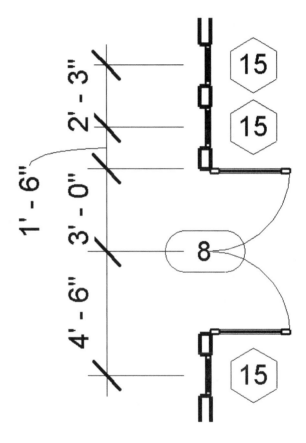

FIGURE 3-5.7 Sidelights added

Exterior Windows:

14. Using the methods previously covered in this book; create a new window size in the *FIXED* family. Create: <u>*Fixed:*</u> **32" x 48"**. You are creating this new size to fit coursing in the plan view. The largest window (preloaded) that fits coursing in the plan view is 24".

15. Adjust the sill height for your new window size to fit within coursing as well. Set the sill height for <u>*Fixed:*</u> **32" x 48"** to be **3'-4"** (Figure 3-5.8).

FIGURE 3-5.8 Added window size

16. Insert the window as shown in **Figure 3-5.9**. The window should be inserted with masonry coursing in mind.

> *NOTE: The dimensions displayed while inserting the window will not work as displayed for coursing because Revit is measuring from the center of the adjacent exterior wall. Thus, you will have to insert the window as close as possible and adjust its location, verifying with the* Measure *tool.*

Array Window:

The *Array* tool allows you to quickly copy several objects that have the same distance between them. You will use *Array* to copy the windows:

17. Click the *Modify* tool and then select your window.

18. With the window selected, pick the **Array** tool from the *Modify* tab.

19. In the *Options Bar*, type **6** for the *Number* field.

20. Click the left mouse button at the midpoint of the window and move your mouse to the East until the dimension displayed is **8'-6"**.

21. You should now see the windows arrayed in the wall. 8'-6" is not coursing, so select the **Activate Dimensions** button on the *Options Bar* and then enter **8'-8"** in the displayed dimension to adjust the window openings. This allows you to more accurately adjust the dimensions.

FIGURE 3-5.9 Exterior window

FIGURE 3-5.10 Window to be arrayed

FIGURE 3-5.11 Window after array

22. Set the windows up on the three remaining walls of the first floor (Figure 3-5.12). Consider the following:

    a. This would be a good use for the *Mirror* tool.

    b. If you need to create a temporary wall for a mirror reflection axis, make sure the temporary wall is set to centerline.

    c. You can use the *Reference Plane* to mirror the windows in the East West direction.

    d. Use the *Measure* tool to verify accuracy.

    e. Use the Ctrl key to select multiple windows.

FIGURE 3-5.12 Completed window layout

Cleaning House:

As previously mentioned, you can view the various Families and types loaded into your project. The more Families and Types you have loaded the larger your project file is, whether or not you are using them in your project. Therefore, it is a good idea to get rid of any door, window, etc., that you know you will not need in the current project.

23. In the *Project Browser*, navigate to Families → Windows → Fixed. Right click on **36″ x 48″** and select **Delete**.

FIGURE 3-5.13 Project Browser

Self-Exam:

The following questions can be used as a way to check your knowledge of this lesson. The answers can be found at the bottom of this page.

1. The *Options Bar* allows you to set the height of a wall when first drawing it. (T/F)

2. It is not possible to draw a wall with the interior or exterior face of the core as the reference point. (T/F)

3. Elements cannot be moved accurately with the **Move** tool. (T/F)

4. The _____ tool, in the *Ribbon*, has to be selected in order to select an element in your project.

5. A wall has to be _____ to see its flip icons.

Review Questions:

The following questions may be assigned by your instructor as a way to assess your knowledge of this section. Your instructor has the answers to the review questions.

1. Revit comes with many predefined doors and windows. (T/F)

2. The length 3'-8" is a masonry dimension. (T/F)

3. You can delete unused families and types in the *Project Browser*. (T/F)

4. It is not possible to load families and types from the internet. (T/F)

5. It is not possible to select which side of the wall a window should be on while you are inserting it. (T/F)

6. What tool will break a wall into two smaller pieces? _____

7. The _____ tool allows you to match the surface of two adjacent walls.

8. Occasionally you have to draw _____ lines (or walls) to use as a reference point for another object or as a reflection mirror.

9. You can use the _____ tool to copy an element multiple times in one step.

10. The _____ file has a few doors, windows and walls preloaded in it.

Notes:

Lesson 4
Office Building: FLOOR PLAN (2nd and 3rd Floors):

In this lesson you will setup the upper two floors. This will mostly involve copying elements from the first floor with some modifications along the way. You will also adjust the floor-to-floor height and insert stairs into the stair shafts.

Exercise 4-1:
Copy Common Walls from First Floor

Setting Up the Second (and Third) Floor View:

The first thing you need to do is make a few adjustments to the second (and third) floor settings. The default template you started your project from already has a second floor view setup in the project. The third floor has not been set up, so you will do that.

1. Open Exercise ex3-5.rvt and Save-As **ex4-1.rvt**.

2. In the *Project Browser*, double-click on the **Level 2** view under Floor Plans (Figure 4-1.1).

The current view is always bold in the *Project Browser*.

You should now see the second floor plan. Notice that the dark wall lines, shown in this view, exist at this level. The light gray lines are walls for the floor below. (Figure 4-1.2)

You will turn off the view of the lower level and set the *Detail Level* to show more detail in the walls.

FIGURE 4-1.1 Project Browser; Level 2 view

3. Make sure nothing is selected and the *Properties Palette* is open (type PP to open it); when nothing is selected the *Properties Palette* shows the current view's properties.

FIGURE 4-1.2 Level 2 initial view

4. Make the following adjustments (*Instance Properties* dialog):
   a. *Detail Level:* **Medium**
   b. *Underlay:* **None**
   c. See image to right.

5. Click **Apply**. Your Level 2 floor plan should look like the plan shown below (Figure 4-1.3).

FIGURE 4-1.3 Level 2 with view properties modified

Because the walls and doors you will copy from the first floor are set up to extend to the floor above, you need to setup the third floor before you copy the walls from first to second (so the second floor walls have a floor to extend to).

Adding another floor is surprisingly simple. You switch to an elevation view and draw in a *Level* datum. By doing that Revit automatically sets up a Level 3 view in the *Project Browser*.

6. Double-click on one of the four elevation views listed under *Elevations* in the *Project Browser*. If you do not see your drawing in elevation, try another view and/or see the tip below.

7. With an elevation in the drawing window, select *Modify* and then select **Architecture → Datum → Level** on the *Ribbon*.

8. As you move your cursor near the Level 2 symbol you will see a dimension displayed, indicating the distance between Level 2 floor and Level 3 floor you are about to insert. For now, **set Level 3 to be 10'-0" above Level 2** (Figure 4-1.4).

    a. Pick two points (left to right) to draw the *Level* datum.

    b. Make sure you see the "alignment" reference lines before picking the two points, so it aligns with the other levels.

FIGURE 4-1.4 (Partial) South elevation

4-3

Notice that the Level 3 floor plan view was automatically added to the *Project Browser*. (See image to the right.)

> *TIP: The default template has four Elevation tags shown in the plan view. These tags represent what the four pre-setup views (under elevation) will see. Therefore, you should start drawing your plan in the approximate center of the four symbols. The symbols can be moved by dragging them with your mouse. This is covered more thoroughly in Lesson 7.*

Next you will copy walls and doors from the first floor.

9. Switch to the **Level 1** view (see step 2).

10. Select all the interior walls (except the elevator shaft), doors and interior windows.

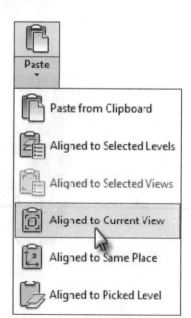

> *TIP: You will need to hold the Ctrl key to select multiple elements with multiple picks. You can drag a window(s) to select multiple objects at once.*

11. With the objects selected, pick **Modify | Walls → Clipboard → Copy to clipboard** from the *Contextual Tab* on the *Ribbon*, or **Ctrl + C** on the keyboard.

12. Click **Modify** on the *Ribbon* and then switch back to the **Level 2** view.

13. Select **Modify → Clipboard → Paste** (down-arrow) **→ Aligned to Current View**.

> *FYI: Paste aligned will make the new elements align with the original elements below, but on the current level.*

Notice the walls, doors and interior windows are now copied to Level 2 (Figure 4-1.5). We still need to copy the exterior windows and the elevator door.

Also, notice that the new doors have different numbers (note: you will only have tags on level 2 if they were selected in the copy / paste) while the interior windows have the same number. Why is this? It relates to industry standards for architectural documentation. Each interior window that is the same size and configuration has the same type number throughout the project (this is a *Type Parameter*). Each door has a unique number because doors have so many variables such as locks, hinges, closer, panic bar, material, and fire rating (this is an *Instance Parameter*). To make doors easier to find, many architectural firms will make the door number the same as the room number the door opens into. You can change the door number by selecting the door tag and then clicking on the text. The door schedule will be updated automatically.

14. Using the same techniques described in the previous steps, copy the exterior windows and elevator door to Level 2.

     TIP: You will need to ungroup your windows (grouped with array) before copying them. Select one of the windows and pick the ungroup button on the Ribbon.

Why not draw these interior walls 36'-0" high like the exterior walls and elevator shaft?

Simulating real-world construction is ideal for several reasons. Mostly, you can be sure shafts align from floor to floor when the shaft is one continuous wall. Although the toilet and atrium interior walls align, they do not necessarily have to because they are separated by floor construction, this allows one floor to be modified later easily.

FIGURE 4-1.5 (Partial) Level 2 – walls added

Finally, you will copy several elements to Level 3. But first you need to change the height setting for the walls (on Level 2) before you paste them to Level 3 because there is nothing above (yet) to extend the walls to (e.g., roof or floor).

15. In the Level 2 view, select all the interior walls, doors and windows (except the elevator shaft).

You need to narrow your selection down to just the walls.

16. Select the **Filter** button on the *Ribbon.*

17. **Uncheck** all the items listed except *Walls* (Figure 4-1.6).

The list varies depending on what elements are in the selection set. (Figure 4-1.6)

18. Click **OK**.

Now only the walls are selected.

FIGURE 4-1.6 Filter dialog

19. In the *Properties Palette*, change the *Top Constraint* to **Unconnected**, then **Apply**.

> **FYI:** *If you pasted the walls without changing the* Top Constraint *it would still be set to Level 3, but with a Top Offset of 10'-0".*

20. Select the elements again; now copy the selected elements to the *Clipboard.*

21. Switch to **Level 3** and make the *View Properties* changes listed in step 4 above (e.g., *Underlay* and *Detail Level*).

22. Paste (aligned to current view) the Level 2 elements to Level 3, including the exterior windows and elevator door.

23. Select all the Level 2 walls again and set the *Top Constraint* back to **Level 3**.

24. **Save your project**.

Exercise 4-2:
Additional Interior Walls

This short exercise will help reinforce the commands you have already learned. You will add walls and openings to your project.

Adding Walls:

1. Add the interior walls and doors to **Level 1** as shown in Figure 4-2.1. Use the stud wall you used previously. Use the *Align* tool to align the walls, which are not dimensioned, with the adjacent walls previously drawn.

   FYI: Doors are not labeled to be single flush. Also, dimensions are to centerline of interior walls and to the finished face of the exterior walls.

FIGURE 4-2.1 Level 1 - Added walls

2. Similar to step 1, add the walls and doors shown in Figure 4-2.2 to **Level 3**.

FIGURE 4-2.2 Level 3 - Added walls

3. Use the *Mirror* command to mirror the walls in Figure 4-2.2 to the other three corners of Level 3.

   TIP: Draw a "horizontal" reference plane.

4. Finally, modify the small office on the south, each side of building (Figure 4-2.3 and Figure 4-2.4).

   TIP: If you use the Trim tool (per the TIP in Figure 4-2.3), you will need to select "Delete Instance" to tell Revit to delete the door from the portion of wall that is being deleted.

   FYI: Your modifications to level 3 included adding a few executive offices to the top floor with the "good" views. You deleted the small office on the south side to make room for a reception desk at the main doors from the atrium. Ideally you would add windows to the interior walls of the executive offices to let borrowed light into the open office area. The center area will be open office area for executive assistants. You will add doors to the stair shaft in Exercise 4-4, when you add the stairs.

5. Save your project as **ex4-2.rvt**.

Remove small office here
(drawn in steps 2 and 3
above)

*TIP: Use the trim tool to
quickly modify this corner as
shown.*

FIGURE 4-2.3 Level 3 - Modify walls

FIGURE 4-2.4 Level 3 - Final layout

Exercise 4-3:
Setting the Floor-to-Floor Height

You will modify the building's floor-to-floor height in this lesson. The reasons for doing this vary. Some examples might be to make the building shorter or taller to accommodate ductwork in the ceilings or the depth of the floor structure (the longer the span the deeper the structure). The default floor-to-floor height in the template file you started from is 10'-0", which is not typically feasibly for commercial construction.

Don't forget to keep a backup of your files on a separate disk (i.e., Flash Drive, CD or DVD). Your project file should be about 3 MB when starting this exercise. Remember, your Revit project is one large file (not many small files). You do not want anything to happen to it!

Modify the Building's Floor-to-Floor Height:

1. Open ex4-2.rvt, Save As **ex4-3.rvt**.

2. Open the **South** exterior elevation from the *Project Browser*.

Next you will change the floor-to–floor height to be 12'-0" for each level.

3. Select the Level 2 level datum, and then select the text displaying the elevation. You should now be able to type in a new number. Type **12** and then press **Enter** to see the changes. Notice the windows move because the sill height has not been changed. (Figure 4-3.1)

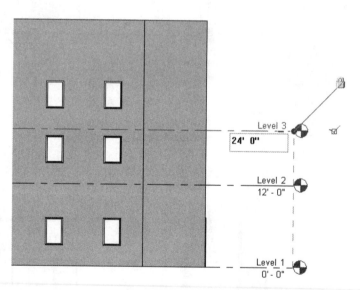

4. Change Level 3 to **24'-0"**.

5. **Save** your project.

FIGURE 4-3.1
Exterior elevation: modifying Level 3 elevation

Exercise 4-4:
Stairs

Next you will add stairs to your East and West stair shafts. Revit provides a powerful *Stair* tool that allows you to design stairs quickly with various constraints predefined (i.e., 7″ maximum riser).

Type Parameters:

Before you draw the stair it will be helpful to review the options available in the stair family.

1. Open ex4-3.rvt and Save As **ex4-4.rvt**.

2. From the *Project Browser*, expand the Families → Stairs → Stair (i.e., click the plus sign next to these labels).

3. Right-click on the stair type: **7″ max riser 11″ tread**, and select the **Type Properties** option from the pop-up menu.

You should now see the options shown in Figure 4-4.1.

Take a couple minutes to see what options are available. You will quickly review a few below.

- Tread: depth of tread in the plan view.

- Nosing Length (Depth): Treads are typically 12″ deep (usually code min.) and 1″ of that depth overlaps the next tread. This overlap is called the nosing.

- Riser: This provides Revit with the maximum dimension allowed (by code, or if you want it, less). The actual dimension will depend on the floor-to-floor height.

- Stringer dimensions: These dimensions usually vary per stair depending on the stair width, run and materials, to name a few. A structural engineer would provide this information after designing the stair.

- Cost: Estimating placeholder.

FIGURE 4-4.1 Stair type properties

Drawing the Stairs in Plan:

You will be drawing a standard switch-back stair. At first, when using Revit to draw stairs, it may be helpful to figure out the number of risers and landings. That information will be helpful when drawing the stair. As you become more familiar with the *Stair* tool you will not need to do those calculations to draw a stair. Dividing the floor-to-floor height of 12'-0" by 7" we get 20.57. Obviously you cannot have a fraction of a riser so you need to round up to 21 (rounding down would make the riser higher than 7"). Therefore, 12'-0" divided by 21 equals 6.86". Thus you have 21 risers that are 6.86" high. Additionally, most codes would require a landing in a stair rising 12'-0".

4. Make sure you are in the **Level 1** floor plan view.

5. **Zoom in** to the West stair shaft.

6. Click on the **Architecture** tab on the *Ribbon*.

7. Select the **Stairs** tool (circulation panel). Stairs

8. On the *Options Bar*, set the *Location Line* to **Exterior Support: Right**.

9. Also on the *Options Bar*, set the *Actual Run Width* to **3'-6"**.

10. Position the cursor approximately as shown in **Figure 4-4.3**; you are selecting the start point for the first step. Make sure you are snapping to the wall with *nearest*.

11. Pick the remaining points as shown in Figures 4-4.4, 4-4.5 and 4-4.6.

12. Hold the **Ctrl** key and then select the two runs of stairs (but not the landing or railings).

13. Click the **green check mark** to finish the stairs (Figure 4-4.2).

FIGURE 4-4.2 Stair Contextual Tab

14. Switch to **Level 2** and repeat the previous steps to add stairs from Level 2 up to Level 3.

Notice as you draw the stairs, Revit will display the number of risers drawn and the number of risers remaining to be drawn to reach the next level. If you click *Finish Stairs* before drawing all the required risers, Revit will display an error message. You can leave the problem to be resolved later.

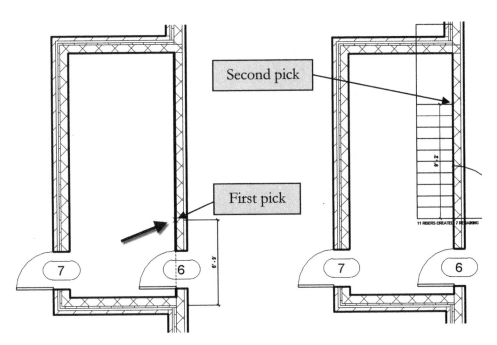

FIGURE 4-4.3 1st pick   **FIGURE 4-4.4** 2nd pick

FIGURE 4-4.5 3rd pick   **FIGURE 4-4.6** 4th pick

FYI: Revit has drawn the intermediate landings between levels. However, the landings at the main floor levels have not been created, but could be using the Landing option within the Stair tool. Some projects extend the primary floor structure into the stair shaft to act as the landing for that level and also support the stair. In a later lesson you will draw a floor system that extends into the stair shaft.

15. Repeat these steps for the East stair shaft.

16. **Add doors** to the <u>second</u> and <u>third floors</u> for both the East and West stair shafts (interior doors only!).

17. **Save** your project.

The final stairs still need some work, but with just a few steps you have a nice placeholder. Revit will add railings to both sides of the stair by default (this can be turned off on the *Ribbon* while in the Stair tool). The railings are separate elements which are hosted to the stair, much like a door is hosted to a wall. You can select a railing and delete it without deleting the stair. But if the stair gets deleted, the railings must go.

Stair Sample File from Revit's Web Site:

Make sure to examine the stair sample file available on Autodesk's online content library (seek.autodesk.com – search for "Revit samples" and select the stair option). You can download this file and see examples of several different stair types side-by-side (see image below). You can select one and view its properties to see how it is done. You can also Copy/Paste one into your project, select your stair, and then select the newly imported type(s) from the *Type Selector*. The partial view of the sample file, shown below, has open riser, single stringer, no stringer, spiral…

3D Ortho 1 View

Metal Pan Stair

Brick/Concrete Stair

Concrete Stair

Residential - Closed 2 Sides

Level 1 Plan View

Self-Exam:

The following questions can be used as a way to check your knowledge of this lesson. The answers can be found at the bottom of this page.

1. The default settings for the floor plan view shows the walls for the floor below. (T/F)

2. It is not possible to add a new floor level while in an elevation view. (T/F)

3. You should start drawing your floor plan generally centered on the default elevation tags in a new project. (T/F)

4. You can use the *Align* tool to align one wall with another across a hallway from the other line. (T/F)

5. Where do you change the maximum riser height? _____

Review Questions:

The following questions may be assigned by your instructor as a way to assess your knowledge of this section. Your instructor has the answers to the review questions.

1. It is not possible to copy/paste objects from one floor to another and have them line-up (with the original objects). (T/F)

2. If a shaft wall is to be built from the lowest level to the roof, and not interrupted at each floor level, the wall should be drawn with that height (not separate walls on each floor level). (T/F)

3. Each Revit view is saved as a separate file on your hard drive. (T/F)

4. You select the part of the wall to be deleted when using the *Trim* tool. (T/F)

5. You can change the floor-to-floor height by changing the level datum (e.g., 24'-0" to 22'-0") in elevation. (T/F)

6. What parameter should be set to none, in the view's properties, if you do not want to see the walls from the floor below? _____

7. You use the _____ tool to create a new floor plan level when in an elevation view.

8. You can use the _____ tool to quickly select a certain type of element from a large group of selected elements.

9. The number of _____ remaining is displayed while sketching a stair.

Lesson 5
Office Building: ROOF:

This lesson will look at some of the powerful options and tools for designing a roof for your building. You will also add skylights.

Exercise 5-1:
Hip Roof

The first step is to create a floor plan view at the roof level, at the top of your exterior masonry wall. This will create a working plane, called a level datum, for the *Roof* tool.

Add Level Datum:

1. Open ex4-4.rvt and **Save As ex5-1.rvt**.

2. Open the **South** elevation view.

Level

3. Select **Architecture → Datum → Level** tool from the *Ribbon*.

4. Draw a *Level* datum at the top of the exterior wall, at elevation 36′-0″; see the wall properties. Draw the datum "line" so both ends align with the other datum "lines" below it.

Next, you will rename the level datum. By default Revit will name the level based on the previous level created, plus 1. Thus, the new level should be named "Level 4". You will change this name so you (and others working on the same project) know it is the top of the masonry view and not another floor in the building.

5. Press **Esc** or select **Modify** from the *Ribbon*.

6. Now select the level datum you just drew (click on the line).

7. With the level datum selected, click on the [level name] text to rename the level label.

8. Change the label to **T.O. Masonry** (Figure 5-1.1).

    FYI: T.O. means "Top Of".

FIGURE 5-1.1 Renamed level datum

9. Click **Yes** when prompted to rename corresponding views (Figure 5-1.2).

FIGURE 5-1.2 Rename prompt

These steps are the same you used to add the third floor. Notice the "T.O. Masonry" label is now listed in the *Floor Plans* section of the *Project Browser*. You can delete the T.O. Masonry ceiling plan if you'd like as it will not be needed; simply right-click and select delete from the pop-up menu.

Add a Hip Roof:

10. Open the newly created **T. O. Masonry** Floor Plan view.

11. Select **Architecture → Build → Roof** (down-arrow).

12. Select **Roof by Footprint** from the drop-down list.

Before you start the roof you will change the slope (pitch) of the roof.

13. Click the **Properties Filter** drop down and select New <Sketch> as pointed out in Figure 5-1.3.

14. Make sure **Defines Slope** is checked and then change the **Slope** to **6″/12″**. Click **Apply**.

This will make the roof pitch 6/12, which means; for every 12″ horizontally the roof will *rise* 6″ vertically.

15. You are now prompted to select exterior walls to define the footprint. Select ONLY the wall segments that define the 120′-0″ x 60′-0″ portion of the building (Figure 5-1.4). Pick the exterior side of the walls.

You will notice in Figure 5-1.4 that there are three sections along the perimeter of the rectangle that are open because no wall is available to pick. You will need to draw three lines to close the "footprint."

FIGURE 5-1.3 Properties Palette

Pick these walls with dots (dots not in Revit) – Step 15

Draw lines (shown dashed here) – Step 17

FIGURE 5-1.4 Creating a roof

16. Select the **Line** tool from the *Ribbon* (Figure 5-1.5).

FIGURE 5-1.5 Ribbon: Roof tool active

17. Draw three lines to create a complete rectangle, making sure you use the snaps to accurately snap to the endpoint of the lines already present; one line across the atrium and the other two at the stair shafts (Figure 5-1.4).

18. Now click the **green check mark** from the *Ribbon*.

19. Click **NO** when prompted to attach the highlighted walls to the roof (Figure 5-1.6).

You will now see a portion of the roof in your plan view. The cutting plane is 4'-0" above the "floor" level, so you are seeing the roof thickness in section at 4'-0" above the T.O. Masonry level.

FIGURE 5-1.6 Prompt

- Switch to an elevation view to see the roof, South elevation, shown in Figure 5-1.7.

- You can also switch to the default 3D view to see the roof in isometric view; via the *Quick Access Toolbar.*

FIGURE 5-1.7 South elevation

After looking at the roof you have created, switch back to the plan view: **T.O. Masonry**. You will now add a roof over the East stair shaft.

20. **Zoom in** on the East stair shaft.

21. Select the **Roof** tool and click "*Roof by Footprint.*"

22. With **Defines slope** checked in the *Options Bar* (Figure 5-1.5), pick the three exterior walls at the stair shaft.

23. Uncheck **Defines Slope**, and then select the **Line** tool and draw a line as shown in Figure 5-1.8 to close the footprint. Be sure to use snaps to accurately draw the enclosed area.

24. Pick the **Modify** button and then select the line you just drew.

FIGURE 5-1.8 Roof footprint; East stair

FIGURE 5-1.9 Modified roof footprint; East stair

25. Use the **Move** command to move the line **6′-0″** to the West (Figure 5-1.9).

26. Select the **green check mark** from the *Ribbon* to finish the roof.

27. Click **NO** when prompted to attach the highlighted walls to the roof (Figure 5-1.6).

28. Switch to the **South** elevation view (Figure 5-1.10).

29. Switch back to the **T.O. Masonry** view.

30. Select the roof element over the East stair shaft.

31. Switch to the *Default* **3D View** and adjust your view to look similar to Figure 5-1.11.

Notice in the South elevation that the ridge of the stair roof does not extend into the main roof. You will adjust this next.

FIGURE 5-1.10 South elevation; East stair

T.O. Masonry
36' - 0"

Level 3
24' - 0"

TIP: Drag on the ViewCube.

32. Select **Modify → Geometry → Join/Unjoin Roof**.

You will now select the two edges of the roofs that you want to come together.

Select in this area for Step #34

Select in this area for Step #33

FIGURE 5-1.11 Default 3D View

33. Select the edge of the smaller roof; see Figure 5-1.11.

34. Select the edge of the larger roof; see Figure 5-1.11.

FIGURE 5-1.12 Joined roof

Your roof should now look similar to Figure 5-1.12. Take another look at the South elevation to see the revision.

35. Repeat the previous steps to create a roof over the West stair shaft.

TIP: You can also try mirroring about your Reference Plane.

Atrium Roof:

Next you will create a roof over the atrium area. We want a 4′-0″ high aluminum panel above the curtain wall, thus pushing the atrium roof up higher. You will need to create a new wall type for the aluminum panels.

36. Switch to the **T.O. Masonry** view listed under *Floor Plans*.

37. Select the **Wall** tool and then select the *Basic Wall*: **Generic – 5″** type.

38. Click *Type Edit* on the *Properties Palette*, and then **Duplicate**.

39. Enter **exterior wall – aluminum** for the name.

40. Click **Edit** next to the *Structure* parameter. Add a new *Layer* using the *Insert* button. Set the exterior finish with the material set to **Aluminum** and then edit the thickness to be **5/8″** (Figure 5-1.13).

41. Draw three walls, so their exterior faces align with the exterior face of the curtain wall below. Be sure to use *Snaps* and set the wall height to **4′-0″** (Figure 5-1.14).

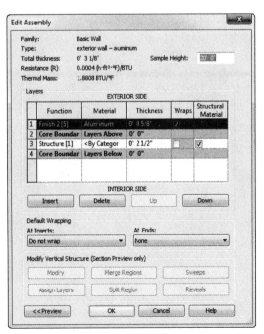

FIGURE 5-1.13 New wall structure

The walls running north-south need to extend far enough back into the main roof to avoid any holes.

Line drawn to close footprint – Step 43

4'-0" high wall (30'-0" long) – Step 41

FIGURE 5-1.14 4'-0" high wall above curtain wall in atrium

42. Use the **Roof** tool and select the three walls just drawn, using the footprint option; "Defines slope" checked.

43. Use the **Line** tool to draw a line to close the open side (Figure 5-1.14). This will create a closed rectangle to complete the roof; "Defines slope" unchecked.

44. Before finishing the roof, set the **Base offset from level** to **4'-0"** in the *Properties Palette*. This will place the roof on top of the 4'-0" high wall you just drew.

FIGURE 5-1.15 3D view

45. Select the **green check mark**.

Your 3D view should look similar to **Figure 5-1.15**. Like the stair roof, the atrium roof needs to be joined to the main roof.

46. Click **NO** when prompted to attach the highlighted walls to the roof (Figure 5-1.6).

47. Use the **Join/Unjoin Roof** tool to join the atrium roof to the main roof. (similar to steps 32-34 in this section)

Look at the side elevations. If the roof does not extend all the way to the main roof, select the roof and pick *Edit Footprint* (on the *Ribbon*) to move the line further into the building. When finished it should look like Figure 5-1.16.

FIGURE 5-1.16 Atrium roof

FIGURE 5-1.17 Setting model graphics style

Next you will take a quick look at the project, thus far, in an isometric view.

48. Click the *3D View* icon on the *Quick Access Toolbar*.

The 3D view can be improved by shading the surfaces.

49. Set the *Model Graphics Style* to **Shaded** via the *View Control Bar* (Figure 5-1.17).

TIP: *You can also turn on shadows from the View Control Bar (see image to right). This can make viewing and printing on larger, complex models much slower so use it sparingly.*

The 3D Model should now be shaded (Figure 5-1.18).

Revit automatically makes windows and curtain walls transparent.

FIGURE 5-1.18 Shaded model

Before moving on you will adjust the top constraint of the Level 3 interior walls to be tied to the new level.

50. Switch to the Level 3 Floor Plan view and select all the interior walls. Adjust their *Top Constraint* to the new level: *T.O. Masonry*.

51. **Save** your project.

Try adjusting the view; click and drag on the *ViewCube*.

Exercise 5-2:
Skylights

This short exercise covers inserting skylights in your roof. The process is much like inserting windows. In fact, Revit lists the skylight types with the window types, so you use the *Window* tool to insert skylights into your project. Technically, a skylight is a roof hosted window.

Inserting Skylights:

You will place the skylights in an elevation view.

1. Load project file **ex5-1.rvt**.

2. Switch to the **South** elevation view.

3. Select the **Window** tool and load the *skylight* family (skylight.rfa) into the project (via the *Load family* button on the *Ribbon*).

Load
Family

4. Select *Skylight*: **24″ x 27″** from the *Type Selector*.

You are now ready to place skylights in the roof. Revit will only look for roof elements when placing skylights, so you don't have to worry about a skylight ending up in a wall.

5. Roughly place four skylights as shown in Figure 5-2.1.

FIGURE 5-2.1 South elevation, skylights added

6. Press **Esc** or click the **Modify** tool to cancel the *Window* tool.

Next, you will want to align the skylights with each other.

7. Switch to the **West** elevation view.

8. Select one of the visible skylights.

You should now have the skylight selected and see the temporary dimensions that allow you to adjust the exact location of the element. Occasionally, the dimension does not go to the point on the model that you are interested in referencing from. Revit allows you to adjust where those temporary dimensions point to.

9. Click and drag the grip shown in Figure 5-2.2 (wait until it snaps) to the ridge of the main roof (Figure 5-2.3).

FIGURE 5-2.2 West elevation: default dimension shown when selecting skylight.

Click on the dimension text and change the text to **22'-8"**.

NOTE: This will adjust the position of the skylight relative to the roof.

10. Select the other skylight on the west elevation and adjust it to match the one you just revised.

11. Switch to the East elevation and repeat the above steps to adjust.

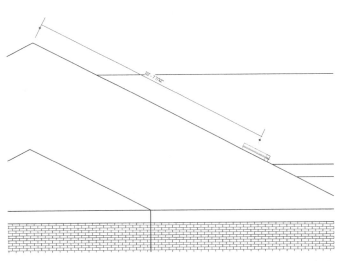

FIGURE 5-2.3 West elevation: default dimension shown when selecting skylight.

FIGURE 5-2.4 South elevation: with skylights added

Your drawing should look similar to the one above. Notice that the skylight tag is right on top of the skylight. You will adjust that next.

12. **Zoom in** on one of the skylights and **click** on the skylight tag (South view).

13. You should see a symbol appear near the bottom of the tag; drag on this symbol to move the tag down (Figure 5-2.5).

14. Position the skylight tag so the tag does not overlap the skylight (Figure 5-2.6).

15. Adjust the other skylight tags; as you reposition these tags you may see a reference line appear indicating the symbol will automatically align with an adjacent symbol.

Take a minute to look at your shaded 3D view and try changing the view so you can see through the skylight glass into the spaces below (Figure 5-2.7).

16. **Save** as **ex5-2.rvt**.

Figure 5-2.5 Enlarged skylight detail

FIGURE 5-2.7 Shaded skylight view

FIGURE 5-2.6 Enlarged skylight detail – revised

Exercise 5-3:
Roof Design Options (Style, Pitch and Overhang)

In this lesson you will look at the various ways to use the *Roof* tool to draw the more common roof forms used in architecture today.

Start a New Revit Project:

You will start a new project for this lesson so you can quickly compare the results of using the *Roof* tool.

1. Start a new project using the **default.rte** template.

2. Switch to the **North** elevation view and rename the level named *Level 2* to **T.O. Masonry**. This will be the reference point for your roof. Click **Yes** to rename corresponding views automatically.

    TIP: Just select the Level *datum and click on the level datum's text to rename.*

3. Switch to the *Level 1 Floor Plan* view.

T.O. Masonry
10' - 0"

Drawing the Buildings:

4. Set the Level 1 *"Detail Level"* to **medium**, so the material hatching is visible within the walls.

    TIP: Use the View Control Bar at the bottom.

5. Using the *Wall* tool with the wall *Type* set to **"Exterior - Brick on Mtl. Stud,"** draw a **40'-0" x 20'-0"** building (Figure 5-3.1).

    FYI: The default Wall height is OK; it should be 20'-0".

Be sure to draw the building
within the elevation tags.

*TIP: You can draw the building
in one step if you use the
Rectangle option on the Ribbon,
while using the Wall tool.*

Elevations tags – (4) are shown which
correspond to the (4) elevation views
listed in the *Project Browser.*

FIGURE 5-3.1 Bldg. and Elev. tags

You will copy the building so that you have a total four buildings. You will draw a different
type of roof on each one.

6. Drag a window around the walls to select them. Then use the **Array** command to set
    up four buildings **35'-0" O.C.** (Figure 5-3.2). See the *Array Tip* below.

*TIP: Zoom in and make
sure the brick is on the
exterior side of the wall. If
not, you can select each wall
and click its flip icon.*

*ARRAY TIP: Select the
first building, select Array,
and then, just like the
Copy command, define a
copy 35' to the right; then
enter the number of copies.*

FIGURE 5-3.2 Four buildings

7. Select all of the buildings and click **Ungroup**
    from the *Ribbon.*

Ungroup

Hip Roof:

The various roof forms are largely defined by the *"Defines slope"* setting. This is displayed in the *Options Bar* while the *Roof* tool is active. When a wall is selected and the *"Defines slope"* option is selected, the roof above that portion of wall slopes. You will see this more clearly in the examples below.

8. Switch to the **T.O. Masonry** *Floor Plan* view.

9. Select the **Architecture → Build → Roof** *(down-arrow)* → **Roof by Footprint** tool.

10. Set the overhang to **2′-0″** and make sure **Defines slope** is selected (checked) on the *Options Bar*.

11. Select the four walls of the West building, clicking each wall one at a time.

    TIP: Make sure you select towards the exterior side of the wall; notice the review line before clicking.

12. Click **Finish Edit Mode** (i.e., the green check mark) on the *Ribbon* to finish the *Roof* tool.

13. Click **Yes** to attach the roof to the walls.

14. Switch to the **South** elevation (Figure 5-3.3).

FIGURE 5-3.3 South elevation – Hip roof

You will notice that the default wall height is much higher than what we ultimately want. However, when the roof is drawn at the correct elevation and you attach the walls to the roof, the walls automatically adjust to stop under the roof object. Additionally, if the roof is raised or lowered later, the walls will follow; you can try this in the South elevation view by simply using the *Move* tool. **REMEMBER:** *You can make revisions in any view.*

15. Switch to the **3D** view using the icon on the *QAT* (Figure 5-3.4).

You can change the "model graphics style" to **Shading** if you would like. Select the *Visual Style* icon on the *View Control Bar* at the bottom.

FIGURE 5-3.4 3D view – hip roof

Gable Roof:

16. Switch back to the **T.O. Masonry** view (not the ceiling plan for this level).

17. Select the **Roof** tool, and then **Roof by Footprint**.

18. Set the overhang to **2'-0"** and make sure **Defines slope** is selected (checked) on the *Options Bar*.

19. Only select the two long (40'-0") walls.

20. **Uncheck** the **Defines slope** option.

21. Select the remaining two walls (Figure 5-3.5).

22. Pick the **green check mark** on the *Ribbon* to finish the roof.

23. Select **Yes** to attach the walls to the roof.

24. Switch to the **South** elevation view (Figure 5-3.6).

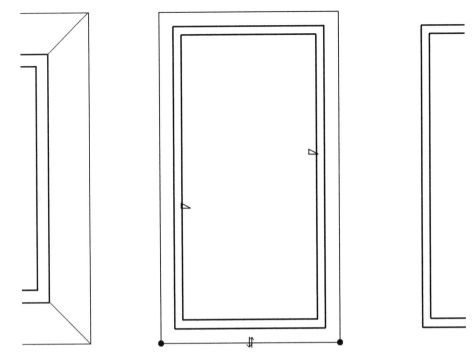

FIGURE 5-3.5 Gable – plan view

FIGURE 5-3.6 South elevation – gable roof

25. Switch to the **3D** view (Figure 5-3.7).

Notice the wall extends up to conform to the underside of the roof on the gable ends.

FYI: You may be wondering why the roofs look odd in the floor plan view. If you remember, each view has its own cut plane. *The cut plane happens to be lower than the highest part of the roof – thus, the roof is shown cut at the cut plane. If you go to Properties Palette → View Range (while nothing is selected) and then adjust the cut plane to be higher than the highest point of the roof, then you will see the ridge line.*

FIGURE 5-3.7 3D view – gable roof

Shed Roof:

26. Switch back to the **T.O. Masonry** view.

27. Select the **Roof** tool, and then **Roof by Footprint**.

28. Check **Defines slope** on the *Options Bar*.

29. Set the overhang to **2'-0"** on the *Options Bar*.

30. Select the East wall (40'-0" wall, right-hand side).

31. Uncheck **Defines slope** in the *Options Bar*.

32. Select the remaining three walls (Figure 5-3.8).

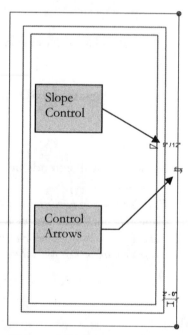

FIGURE 5-3.8 Selected walls

33. Set the **Slope**, or roof pitch, to 3/12 (Figure 5-3.9) on the *Properties Palette*.

34. Click **Apply** on the *Properties Palette*.

35. Pick the **green check mark** on the *Ribbon* to finish the roof.

36. Select **Yes** to attach the walls to the roof.

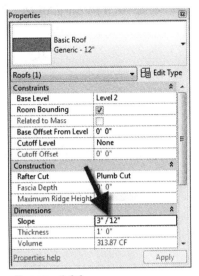

FIGURE 5-3.9
Properties for Roof tool

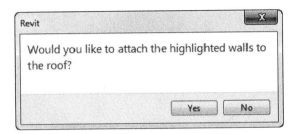

FYI: You can also change the slope of the roof by changing the Slope Control text (see Figure 5-3.8); just select the text and type a new number.

TIP: You can use the Control Arrows, while the roof line is still selected, to flip the orientation of the roof overhang if you accidentally selected the wrong side of the wall and the overhang is on the inside of the building.

37. Switch to the **South** elevation view (Figure 5-3.10).

FIGURE 5-3.10 South elevation – shed roof

38. Switch to the **Default 3D** view (Figure 5-3.11).

FIGURE **5-3.11** Default 3D view – shed roof

Once the roof is drawn, you can easily change the roof's overhang. You will try this on the shed roof. You will also make the roof slope in the opposite direction.

39. In **T.O. Masonry** view, Select **Modify** from the *Ribbon*, and then select the shed roof.

40. Click **Edit Footprint** from the *Ribbon*.

Edit
Footprint

41. Click on the East roof sketch-line to select it.

42. Uncheck **Defines slope** from the *Options Bar*.

43. Now select the West roofline and check **Defines slope**.

If you were to select the green check mark now, the shed roof would be sloping in the opposite direction. But, before you do that, you will adjust the roof overhang at the high side.

44. Click on the East roofline again, to select it.

45. Change the overhang to **6'-0"** in the *Options Bar*.

Changing the overhang only affects the selected roofline.

46. Select the **green check mark**.

47. Switch to the South view to see the change (Figure 5-3.12).

Thus you can see it is easier to edit an object than to delete it and start over. Just remember you have to be in sketch mode (i.e., *Edit Sketch*) to make changes to the roof. Also, when a sketch line is selected, its properties are displayed in the *Properties Palette*. That concludes the shed roof example.

FIGURE 5-3.12 South elevation – shed roof (revised)

Flat Roof:

48. Switch back to the **T.O. Masonry** *Floor Plan* view.

49. Select **Architecture → Roof → Roof by Footprint**.

50. Set the overhang to **2'-0"** and make sure **Defines slope** is not selected (i.e., unchecked) in the *Options Bar*.

51. Select all four walls.

52. Pick the **green check mark**.

53. Select **Yes** to attach the walls to the roof.

FIGURE 5-3.13 South elevation – flat roof

54. Switch to the South elevation view (Figure 5-3.13).

55. Also, take a look the **Default 3D view** (Figure 5-3.14).

FIGURE 5-3.14 Default 3D view – flat roof

56. Save your project as **ex5-3.rvt**.

Want More?

Revit has additional tools and techniques available for creating more complex roof forms. However, that is beyond the scope of this book. If you want to learn more about roofs, or anything else, take a look at one of the following resources:

- Revit **Web Site** (www.autodesk.com)
- Revit **Newsgroup** (potential answers to specific questions)
  www.augi.com; www.revitcity.com; www.autodesk.com; www.revitforum.org
- Revit **Blogs** information from individuals (some work for Autodesk and some don't)
  www.revitoped.com, revitclinic.typepad.com, do-u-revit.blogspot.com

Reference material: Roof position relative to wall

The remaining pages in this chapter are for reference only and do not need to be done to your model. You are encouraged to study this information so you become more familiar with how the *Roof* tool works.

The following examples use a brick and concrete wall example. The image below shows the *Structure* properties for said wall type. Notice the only item within the *Core Boundary* section is the *Masonry – Concrete Block* (i.e., CMU) which is 7⅝″ thick (nominally 8″). Keep this in mind as you read through the remaining material.

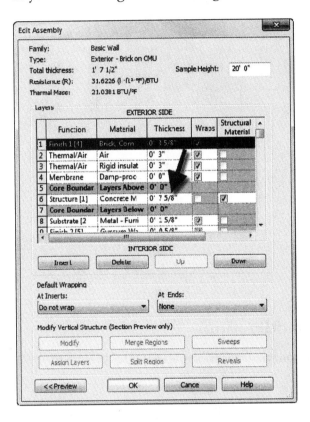

The following examples will show you how to control the position of the roof system relative to the wall below, both vertically and horizontally. The roof properties that dictate its position basically involve relationships between three things: the **Level Datum**, the exterior **Wall System** and the bottom edge of the **Roof System**. There are several other properties (e.g., pitch, construction, fascia, etc.) related to the roof that will not be mentioned at the moment so the reader may focus on a few basic principles.

The examples on this page show a sloped roof sketched with *Extend into wall (to core)* enabled and the *Overhang* set to 2′-0″. Because *Extend into wall (to core)* was selected, the bottom edge of the roof is positioned relative to the *Core Boundary* of the exterior wall rather than the finished face of the wall. See the discussion about the wall's *Core Boundary* on the previous page.

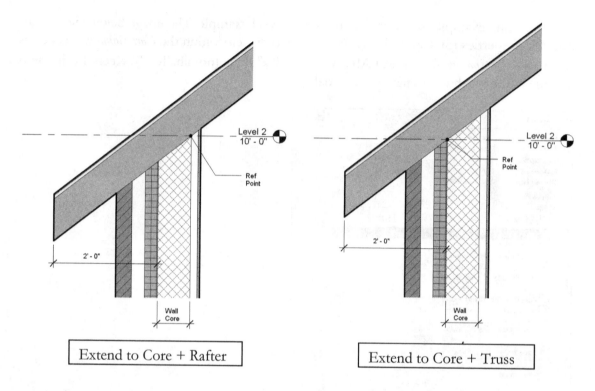

| Extend to Core + Rafter | Extend to Core + Truss |

Revit Roof Properties under Consideration:

Extend Into Wall: (To Core) This option was *checked* on the *Options Bar* while sketching the roof.

Rafter Or Truss: This option is an *Instance Parameter* of the roof object; the example on the above left is set to *Rafter* and the other is set to *Truss*.

NOTE: The Extend into Wall (to core) *option affects the relative relationship between the wall and the roof, as you will see by comparing this example with the one on the next page.*

Base Level: Set to *Level 2:* By associating various objects to a level, it is possible to adjust the floor elevation (i.e., *Level Datum*) and have doors, windows, floors, furniture, roofs, etc., all move vertically with that level.

Base Offset: From Level Set to *0′-0″:* This can be a positive or negative number which will be maintained even if the level moves.

The examples on this page show a sloped roof sketched with *Extend into wall (to core)* NOT enabled and the *Overhang* set to 2'-0". Notice that the roof overhang is derived from the exterior face of the wall (compared to the *Core Boundary* face on the previous example when *Extend into wall* was enabled).

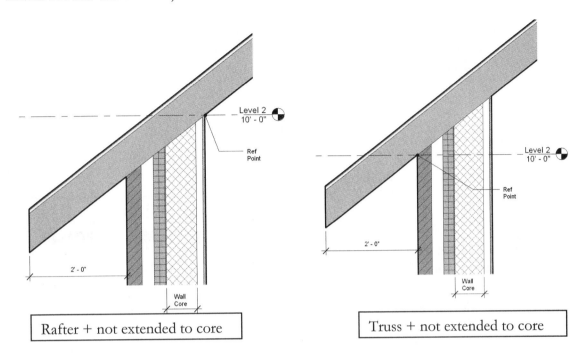

| Rafter + not extended to core | Truss + not extended to core |

Revit Roof Properties under Consideration:

Extend Into Wall: (To Core) — This option was *NOT checked* on the *Options Bar* while sketching the roof.

Rafter Or Truss: — This option is an *Instance Parameter* of the roof object; the example on the above left is set to *Rafter* and the other is set to *Truss*.

NOTE: The Extend into wall (to core) *option affects the relative relationship between the wall and the roof, as you will see by comparing this example with the one on the previous page.*

Base Level: — Set to *Level 2.* By associating various objects to a level, it is possible to adjust the floor elevation (i.e., *Level Datum*) and have doors, windows, floors, furniture, roofs, etc., all move vertically with that level.

Base Offset: From Level — Set to *0'-0".* This can be a positive or negative number which will be maintained even if the level moves.

As you can see from the previous examples, you would most often want to have *Extend to wall (to core)* selected while sketching a roof because it would not typically make sense to position the roof based on the outside face of brick or the inside face of gypsum board, for commercial construction.

Even though you may prefer to have *Extend to wall (to core)* selected, you might like to have a 2'-0" overhang relative to the face of the brick rather than the exterior face of concrete block. This can be accomplished in one of two ways:

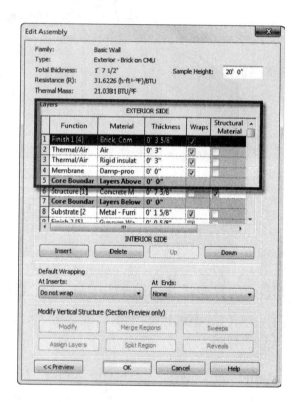

(A) You can modify the overhang, while sketching the roof, to include the wall thickness that occurs between the face of wall and face of core: 2'-0" + 9⅝" = 2'-9⅝". See the image to the right.

(B) The second option is to manually edit the sketch lines. You can add dimensions while in *Sketch* mode, select the sketch line to move, and then edit the dimension. The dimension can also be *Locked* to maintain the roof edge position relative to the wall. When you finish the sketch the dimensions are hidden.

Energy Truss:

In addition to controlling the roof overhang, you might also want to control the roof properties to accommodate an energy truss with what is called an *energy heal*, which allows for more insulation to occur directly above the exterior wall).

To do this you would use the *Extend into wall (to core) + Truss* option described above and then set the *Base Offset from Level* to 1'-0" (for a 1'-0" energy heal). See the image and the *Properties Palette* shown on the next page.

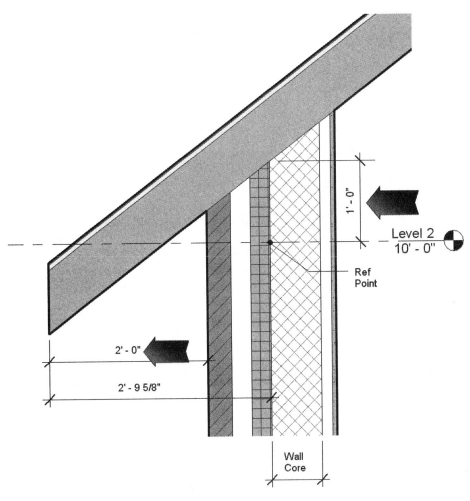

Level 2
10' - 0"

1' - 0"

2' - 0"

2' - 9 5/8"

Ref
Point

Wall
Core

Many other properties and techniques exist which one can use to develop the roof for a project, things like the *Rafter Cut* and *Fascia Depth* which control the fascia design. Also, you can apply a sweep to a roof edge to add a 1x fascia board around the building. These are intermediate to advanced concepts and will not be covered here.

This concludes the study of the *Roof* tool!

Self-Exam:

The following questions can be used as a way to check your knowledge of this lesson. The answers can be found at the bottom of this page.

1. You don't have to click *Finish Roof* when you are done defining a roof. (T/F)

2. The wall below the roof automatically conforms to the underside of the roof when you join the walls to the roof. (T/F)

3. The roof overhang setting is available from the *Options Bar*. (T/F)

4. To create a gable roof on a building with 4 walls, two of the walls should not have the _____ option checked.

5. Is it possible to change the reference point for a temporary dimension that is displayed while an object is selected? (Y/N)

Review Questions:

The following questions may be assigned by your instructor as a way to assess your knowledge of this section. Your instructor has the answers to the review questions.

1. When creating a roof using the "*roof by footprint*" option, you need to create a closed perimeter. (T/F)

2. Can the "*Defines Slope*" setting be changed after the roof is "finished?" (Y/N)

3. Skylights need to be rotated to align with the plane (pitch) of the roof. (T/F)

4. Skylights automatically make the glass transparent in shaded views. (T/F)

5. While using the **Roof** tool, you can use the _____ tool from the *Ribbon* to fill in the missing segments to close the perimeter.

6. You use the _____ parameter to adjust the vertical position of the roof relative to the current working plane (view).

7. While using the **Roof** tool, you need to select the _____ tool from the *QAT* before you can select a roofline for modification.

8. You need to use the _____ _____ to flip the roofline when you pick the wrong side of the wall and the overhang is shown on the inside.

Lesson 6
Office Building: FLOOR SYSTEMS and REFLECTED CEILING PLANS:

In this lesson you will learn to create floor structures and reflected ceiling plans.

Even though you currently have floor levels defined, you do not have an object that represents the mass of the floor systems. You will add floor systems with holes for stairs, elevators, and the atrium.

Ceiling systems allow you to specify the ceiling material by room and the height above the floor. Once the ceiling has been added it will show up in section views (sections are created later in this book).

Exercise 6-1:
Floor Systems

Similar to other Revit elements, you can select from a few pre-defined system families. You can also create new types.

Level 1, Slab on Grade:

Sketching floors is a lot like sketching roofs (Lesson 5); you can select walls to define the perimeter and draw lines to fill in the blanks and add holes (cut-outs) in the floor element.

1. Open ex5-2.rvt and **Save As ex6-1.rvt**.

2. Switch to the **Level 1** floor plan view.

3. Select **Architecture → Build → Floor** *(down-arrow)* **→ Floor**.

4. Click **Edit Type** on the *Properties Palette*.

5. Select type **Generic – 12″** from the *Type* drop-down list at the top.

6. Click **Duplicate** to start a new floor type.

7. Type **6″ Slab on Grade**, then **OK**.

8. Click the **Edit** button next to the *Structure* Parameter.

9. Change the material for the structure layer shown to **Concrete: cast-in-place concrete**, and change the thickness to **6″**.

10. Next you will add carpet on top of the slab. Click **Insert** and use the **Up/Down** buttons to position the *Layer* correctly (Figure 6-6.1).

11. Add another layer:

    a. *Function*: **Finish 1 [4]**
    b. *Material*: **Carpet (1)**
    c. *Thickness*: **1/4″**
        (Figure 6-1.1)

12. Click **OK** to close the open dialog boxes.

13. Select all the exterior walls on **Level 1**; this should include the curtain wall at the atrium and the stair shafts (Figure 6-1.3).

    TIP: Select the interior side of the wall; you can use the control arrows if needed.

14. Click the **green check mark**.

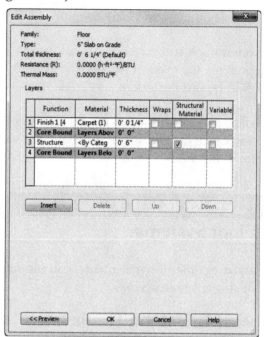

FIGURE 6-1.1 New Floor System

You will most likely get an error message. This is because the main exterior walls extend into the atrium (past the curtain wall). Because this is not a perfect corner (and it does not need to be), you can trim the "edge of slab" lines while in sketch mode to create a true corner, i.e., a closed line for the floor (Figure 6-1.2).

15. *(If you did not get an error, skip ahead to Step 18.)* Click **Continue**.

16. Use the **Trim** tool; select the two lines leading to the corner that needs to be trimmed. Do this for both sides of the atrium (Figure 6-1.3).

FIGURE 6-1.2 Floor error message

17. Click the **green check mark**.

Corners to trim before finishing floor; Step 16

FIGURE 6-1.3 Floor creation; highlighted walls

You now have a floor at the first level. You should see a stipple pattern representing the floor area. You would most likely want to turn that pattern off for a floor plan. You will do that next.

18. Click **Modify** on the *Ribbon* to unselect the new floor.

19. Select **Edit**, next to the *Visibility* parameter in the *Properties Palette* (Figure 6-1.4).

    TIP: Type VV to skip Steps 19 and 20!

20. In the *Visibility Graphic Overrides* dialog, click the "cell" at the intersection of *Floors* (row) and *Surface / Patterns* (column); select **Override** (Figure 6-1.5).

21. Uncheck **Visible**.

22. Click **OK** to close the dialogs.

The stipple pattern is no longer visible.

FIGURE 6-1.4 Level 1 view properties

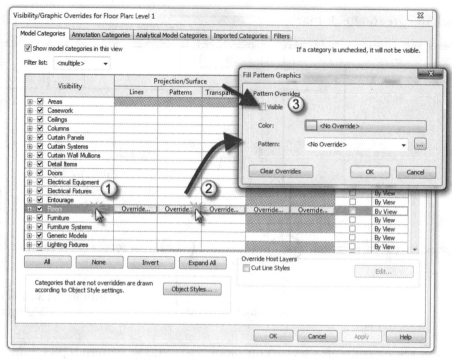

Figure 6-1.5 View Visibility

Levels 2 and 3, Conc. + Metal Deck + Bar Joists:

23. Switch to **Level 2** view.

Next you need to load a profile to properly define the upper floors.

24. Use the **Load Family** tool to load the following: Profiles\Metal Deck\ **Form Deck_Non-Composite**. If prompted, select overwrite.

25. Activate the **Floor** tool and create a new floor type named: **Steel Bar Joist 14″ – Carpet on Concrete**.

> *TIP: Use a similar floor type as a starting point (duplicate) when creating new floor types.*

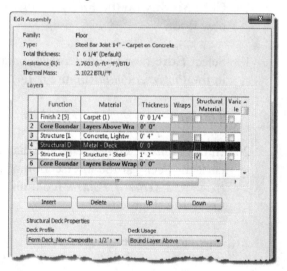

FIGURE 6-1.6 Floor system – edit structure

26. Adjust/add the layers shown in **Figure 6-1.6**.

   a. Be sure to set the *Structural Deck Properties* correctly near the bottom of the *Edit Assembly* dialog. Select the 1 1/2″ deck; this will appear in sections.

> *NOTE: In an actual project you might not want to include the finishes, sych as VCT and Carpet. These can be added seperately to better control their locations.*

Creating the second and third floors will be a little more involved than was the first floor. This is because the upper floors require several openings. For example, you need to define the openings for the elevator, the stair shafts and the atrium space. Revit makes the process very simple however.

You should still be in the *Floor* tool.

27. On the *Options Bar*, check "**Extend into wall (to core)**."

FYI: The "Extend into wall (to core)" option will extend the slab to your CMU (CMU is the core in our example), and go under the furring. Depending on the design, the floor may extend to the exterior face of the CMU, allowing the CMU to bear on the floor slab at each level. In this exercise you will select the interior side.

28. Select the exterior walls indicated in Figure 6-1.7.

REMEMBER: To select the interior side of the wall, use the control arrows if needed.

FIGURE 6-1.7 Level 2 –
exterior walls to select

Next you will define the portion of floor that extends into the stair shaft to be the landing at this level. You will need to use the *Line* tool and the *Trim* tools to define this area.

29. Click on the **Line** tool from the *Draw* panel on the *Ribbon*.

30. **Zoom In** to the West stair shaft.

31. Draw a <u>horizontal</u> line defining the edge of the landing; use Revit's snaps to accurately pick the top riser as shown in **Figure 6-1.8**.

Draw your line to the CMU face

Start line here with endpoint snap

DN UP

FIGURE 6-1.8 Level 2 – West stair

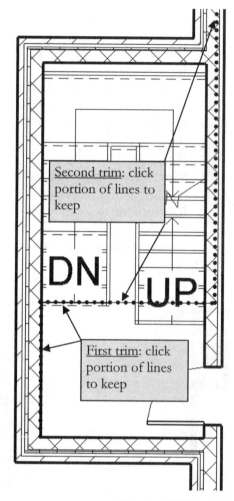

Second trim: click portion of lines to keep

DN UP

First trim: click portion of lines to keep

FIGURE 6-1.9 Level 2 – West stair trim lines

32. Select the **Trim** tool and trim the three lines referenced in **Figure 6-1.9**.

33. Repeat these steps for the East stair shaft.

34. Next you will pick the four walls at the elevator shaft, selecting the shaft side of the wall; be sure to use the **Pick Walls** feature from the *Draw* panel on the *Ribbon*.

Draw

You are now ready to define the edge of the slab at the atrium.

35. Use the **Line** tool (from the *Draw* panel) to draw the edge of slab in the atrium (5 lines) as shown in **Figure 6-1.10**.

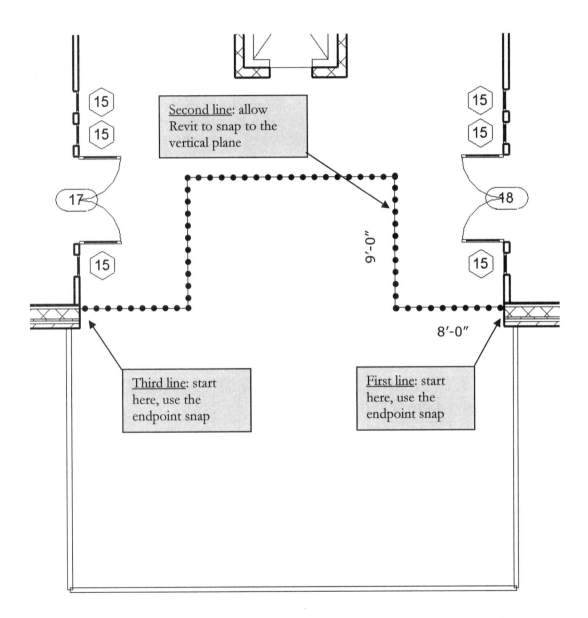

FIGURE 6-1.10 Atrium slab definition

36. Click the **green check mark** to finish the floor.

37. Click **Yes** to the prompt *"Would you like the walls that go up to this floor's level to attach to its bottom?"*

38. Click **Yes** for the prompt to join the walls that overlap the floor system (Figure 6-1.11).

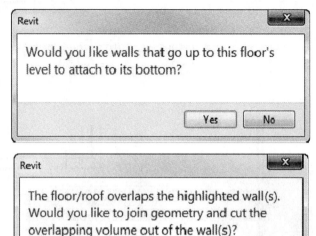

FIGURE 6-1.11 Finish floor prompts

39. Change Level 2's *Visibility* to turn off the floor pattern.

That completes the Level 2 floor system. Next you will copy the floor you just created to Level 3. You could switch to Level 3 and manually draw a floor following the same steps as for Level 2; however, because the two floors are identical, it would be faster to copy it.

40. Select the Level 2 floor element you just created and select **Modify Floors →** **Clipboard → Copy** from the *Ribbon*.

TIP: *Selecting elements that overlap, like the exterior walls and the edge of slab (floor system), may require the use of the TAB key. The only way to select a floor element is by picking its edge. Revit temporarily highlights elements when you move your cursor over them. But, because the floor edge may not have an "exposed" edge to select (e.g., like we have in the atrium area), you will have to toggle through your selection options for your current cursor location. With the cursor positioned over the edge of the floor (probably with an exterior wall highlighted), press the TAB key to toggle through the available options. A tooltip will display the elements; when you see floor:floor-name, click the mouse to select it.*

41. Switch to **Level 3**.

42. Select *Modify → Clipboard → Paste (down arrow) →* **Aligned to Current View**.

43. Change Level 3's *Visibility* to turn off the floor pattern.

Explore your work by looking at the model in 3D (Figure 6-1.12).

Notice again how Revit automatically applies colors and patterns to surfaces to help you (and your client) better visualize your design with minimal effort. These colors and materials relate to the materials applied to each element. You will learn more about this in the rendering chapter.

44. Save your project as **ex6-1.rvt**.

FIGURE 6-1.12 3D view with floors

Ceiling Systems (Susp. ACT and Gypsum Board)

This lesson will explore Revit's tools for drawing reflected ceiling plans. This will include drawing different types of ceiling systems.

Suspended Acoustical Ceiling Tile System:

1. Open ex6-1.rvt and Save As **ex6-2.rvt**.

2. Switch to the **Level 1** ceiling plan view, from the *Project Browser*.

Notice the doors and windows are automatically turned off in the ceiling plan views. The ceiling plan views have a cutting plane similar to floor plans. You can see this setting by selecting *Edit*, next to **View Range** in the *Properties Palette*.

The default value is 7'-6". You might increase this if, for example, you had 10'-0" ceilings and 8'-0" high doors. Otherwise, the doors would show because the 7'-6" cutting plane is below the door height (Figure 6-2.1).

FIGURE 6-2.1 Properties: View Range settings

3. Select **Architecture → Build → Ceiling**.

Ceiling

You have 4 ceiling types (by default) to select from (Figure 6-2.2).

4. Select _Compound Ceiling:_ **2'x4' ACT System** from the _Type Selector_.

Next you will change the ceiling height. The default setting is 8'-0" above the current level. You will change the ceiling height to 9'-0" to make the large open office areas feel more spacious. This setting can be changed on a room by room basis.

5. Set the _Height Offset From Level_ setting to **9'-0"** in the _Properties Palette_ (Figure 6-2.3).

You are now ready to place ceiling grids. This process can not get much easier, especially compared to traditional CAD programs.

6. Move your cursor anywhere within the large open office area in the West side of the building. You should see the perimeter of the room highlighted.

7. Pick within the large room; Revit places a grid in the room (Figure 6-2.4).

FIGURE 6-2.2 Type Selector

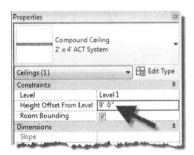

FIGURE 6-2.3 Properties Palette

You now have a 2x4 ceiling grid at 9'-0" above the floor (Level 1 in this case).

FIGURE 6-2.4 Level 1: Ceiling

When you place a ceiling grid, Revit centers the grid in the room. The general rule-of-thumb is you should try to avoid reducing the tile size by more than half at its perimeter. You can see in Figure 6-2.4 that the East and West sides look okay. However, the North and South sides are small slivers. You will adjust this next.

8. Select **Modify** from the *Ribbon*.

9. **Select** the ceiling grid (only one line in the ceiling grid will be highlighted).

10. Use the **Move** tool to move the grid 24″ to the North (Figure 6-2.5).

11. Place ceiling grids as shown in Figure 6-2.5.
    a. *Be sure to adjust the ceiling heights shown.*
    b. *Adjust the grids to avoid small tiles at the perimeter.*

FIGURE 6-2.5 Level 1: Ceiling Grids

Modifying the Suspended Acoustical Ceiling Tile System:

Making modifications to the grid is relatively easy. Next, you will adjust the ceiling height and rotate the grid.

12. Zoom in to the room in the upper right corner on *Level 1*.

13. Change the height to **8′-6″** in the *Properties Palette*, and then click **Apply**.

14. With the grid still selected, pick *Compound Ceiling:* **2′x2′ ACT System** from the *Type Selector* on the *Properties Palette*.

15. Again, with the grid still selected, use the *Rotate* tool to rotate the grid 45 degrees.

TIP: *When using the Rotate tool* ↻ *you need to pick two points. The first point is your reference line. The second point is the number of degrees off that reference line. In this example, try picking your first point to the right as a horizontal line. Then move the cursor counter-clockwise until 45 degrees is displayed. You can also type the angle instead of picking a second point.*

16. Your drawing should look similar to **Figure 6-2.6**.

FIGURE 6-2.6 Level 1: Modified Ceiling

The image below shows a camera view, looking South, of the large open office area, showing the ceiling. You will learn how to create camera views later in the text.

Next, you will look at drawing gypsum board (or drywall) ceiling systems. The process is identical to placing the grid system. Additionally, you will create a new ceiling type.

Gypsum Board Ceiling System:

You will create a new ceiling type for a gypsum board ceiling. To better identify the areas that have a gypsum board ceiling, you will set the ceiling type to have a stipple pattern. This will provide a nice graphical representation for the gypsum board ceiling areas.

17. From the *Manage* tab, select **Materials**.
    This is the list of materials you select from when assigning a material to each layer in a wall system, etc.

    TIP: *Change the* In Document Materials *view to a list via the icon pointed out.*

18. Select *Gypsum Wall Board*, right-click on it and select **Duplicate** and then enter the name: **Gypsum Ceiling Board**.

19. In the *Surface Pattern* area, pick the down-arrow and select **Gypsum-Plaster** from the list, and then click **OK** (Figure 6-2.7).

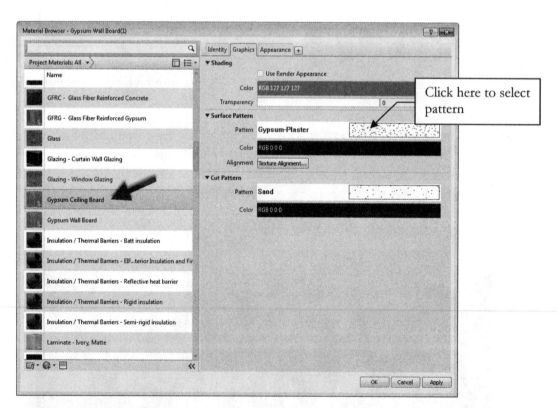

FIGURE 6-2.7 Materials dialog

The *Surface Pattern* setting is what will add the stipple pattern to the gypsum board ceiling areas. With this set to *none*, the ceiling has no pattern (like the basic ceiling type).

Thus, if you wanted Carpet 1 finish to never have the stipple hatch pattern, you could change the surface pattern to none via the *Materials* dialog and not have to change each view's visibility override.

20. Select **Architecture → Build → Ceiling**.

21. Click **Edit Type** on the *Properties Palette*.

22. Set the *Type* drop-down to **GWB on Mtl. Stud**.

> *FYI: You are selecting this because it is similar to the ceiling you will be creating.*

23. Click *Duplicate* and type **Gypsum Ceiling Board** for the name.

24. Select **Edit** next to the *Structure* parameter.

25. Set the values as follows (Figure 6-2.8):
    a. **1½″ Mtl. Stud**
    b. **¾″ Mtl. Stud**
    c. **Gypsum Ceiling Board**
       (This is the material you created in Step 18.)

26. Click **OK** two times.

FYI: The ceiling assembly you just created represents a typical suspended gypsum board ceiling system. The Metal Studs are perpendicular to each other and suspended by wires, similar to an ACT (acoustical ceiling tile) system. You are now ready to draw a gypsum board ceiling.

27. Make sure **Gypsum Ceiling Board** is selected in the *Type Selector* on the *Properties Palette*.

28. Set the ceiling height to **8′-0″**.

FIGURE 6-2.8 New ceiling – Edit assembly

29. Pick the two bathrooms on Level 1; which are the two rooms North of the elevator (Figure 6-2.9).

Figure 6-2.9 Gyp. Bd. Ceiling

You now have a gypsum board ceiling at 8'-0" above the finished floor in the toilet rooms.

Sketching a Ceiling:

Next, you will draw a ceiling in the atrium area. However, you cannot simply pick the room to place the ceiling because of the opening in the floor. You will need to sketch the ceiling just like you sketched the floor system in the previous exercise. First, you will need to draw a bulkhead at the edge of the second floor slab. A bulkhead is a portion of wall that hangs from the floor above and creates a closed perimeter for a ceiling system to tie into.

30. While still in the Level 1 Reflected Ceiling Plan view, select the **Wall** tool.

31. Set the wall properties to:
    Interior - 4 7/8″ Partition (1-hr) and
    the *Base Offset* to **9′-6″**. *(This will put the
    bottom of the wall to 9′-6″ above the current
    floor level, Level 1 in this case.)* (Figure 6-
    2.10)

32. Set the *Top Constraint* to:
    Up to level: Level 2 (Figure 6-2.10).

*TIP: The next time you draw a wall you will have to
change the Base Offset back to 0′-0″ or your wall will
be 9′-6″ off the floor.*

33. **Draw the bulkhead**; make sure you
    snap to the edge of the slab. Also, make
    sure the wall is under the floor system,
    not out in the opening. Do this by
    drawing the wall either from right to
    left or left to right depending on how
    you have the *Location Line* set (Figure
    6-2.11).

FIGURE 6-2.10 Bulkhead (wall) properties

Dashed line added to
indicate edge of slab
location.

FIGURE 6-2.11 Bulkhead drawn

34. Select the **Ceiling** tool and then click **Sketch Ceiling** from the *Ribbon*.

Sketch
Ceiling

35. Use the **Pick Walls, Line,** and **Trim** tools to sketch a line at the perimeter of the ceiling area as shown in **Figure 6-2.12**. You will also need to sketch a line around the toilet/elevator area to define the area within the larger area that will not receive the ceiling pattern: **2'x2' ACT ceiling, with the ceiling height set to 9'-6".**

36. Click the **green check mark** and save project as **ex6-2.rvt**.

FIGURE 6-2.12 Atrium Ceiling

Exercise 6-3:
Placing Fixtures (Lights and Diffusers)

In this exercise, you will learn to load and place light and mechanical fixtures in your reflected ceiling plans.

Loading Families:

Before placing fixtures, you need to load them into your project.

1. Select **Architecture → Build → Component** from the *Ribbon*.

2. Select **Load Family** on the *Ribbon* (Figure 6-3.1).

FIGURE 6-3.1 Component
tool active; Ribbon

3. Double-click the *Lighting\Architectural\Internal* folder, and then double-click **Troffer Light- 2x4 Parabolic.rfa** (Figure 6-3.2).

FIGURE 6-3.2 Load family

Before placing the light fixture you will load the other families first.

4. Select **Load Family** again, browse to the *Mechanical\Architectural\Air-Side Components\Air Terminals* folder.

5. Select **Square Supply Diffuser** and **Square Return Register** (you can select both while holding the Ctrl key) and then **Open**.

   TIP: *You can hold the Ctrl key to select and load multiple components at once.*

Placing Families:

You are now ready to place the elements in your ceiling plans.

6. With **Component** still selected from the *Ribbon*, pick *Troffer Light – 2′x 4′ Parabolic:* **2′x4′ (2 Lamp) – 277V** from the *Type Selector*.

7. On **Level 1 RCP**, place fixtures as shown in **Figure 6-3.3**.

FIGURE 6-3.3 RCP; lights added

TIP: You can use array to quickly place several lights.

You may have to use the *Move* command (or better, the *Align* tool) to move the fixture so it fits perfectly in the ACT grid.

8. Now place another **2x4 light fixture** as shown in **Figure 6-3.4**.

Notice the fixture does not automatically orientate itself with the ceiling grid. There may be an occasion when you want this.

Also, notice the light fixture hides a portion of the ceiling grid. This is nice because the grid does not extend through a light fixture.

TIP: You may press the Space bar while placing the light fixture to rotate it.

9. Use **Rotate** and **Move** to rotate the fixture to align with the grid (Figure 6-3.5).

FIGURE 6-3.4 RCP; lights added

10. Once you have one fixture rotated, it is easier to use the *Copy* tool and the snaps to add rotated light fixtures. **Copy** the light fixture to match the layout in **Figure 6-3.5**.

TIP: You can check "multiple" on the Options Bar to quickly copy several lights at once.

11. Select *Square Supply Diffuser:* **24"x24"** from the *Type Selector*.

12. Place the diffusers as shown in Figure 6-3.6.

13. Select *Square Return Register:* **24"x24"** from the *Type Selector*.

14. Place the registers as shown in Figure 6-3.6.

15. Save your project as **ex6-3.rvt**.

FIGURE 6-3.5 RCP; rotated lights

FIGURE 6-3.6 RCP; mechanical

Reflected Ceiling Plan Symbols:

Revit provides many of the industry standard symbols necessary in drawing reflected ceiling plans (RCP). As shown in Figure 6-3.5, supply air is represented with an X and return air has a diagonal line. It is typical to have a RCP symbol legend showing each symbol and material pattern and list what each one represents.

Component Properties

If you want to adjust the properties of a component, such as a light fixture, you can browse to it in the *Project Browser* and right click on it *(notice the right click menu also has the option to select all instances of the item in the drawing)* and select *Properties*. You will see the dialog below for the 2x4 (2 Lamps).

You can also click duplicate and add more sizes (e.g., 4'x4' light fixture).

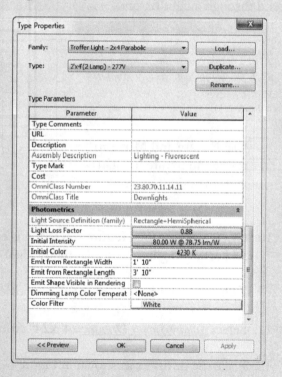

You can also select an inserted component and review the *Properties Palette* for additional properties for that particular instance.

Exercise 6-4:
Annotations

This short section will look at adding notes to your RCP.

Adding Annotations:

1. Select **Annotate → Text → Text** from the *Ribbon*.

2. Pick **3/32″ Arial** from the *Type Selector*.

3. Select the **Leader** option pointed out in **Figure 6-4.1**.

FIGURE 6-4.1 Text; Ribbon

Next, you will add a note indicating that the atrium area is open to the floor above (i.e., no floor or ceiling here). First you will draw a leader, and then Revit will allow you to type the text.

4. Add one of the leaders (i.e., arrows) shown in Figure 6-4.2.

5. Add the note "**OPEN TO ABOVE**" shown in **Figure 6-4.2**.

    a. Do the following to add the right-hand arrow:
       i. Click **Modify**;
      ii. Click the text to select it;
      iii. Click the right-hand arrow icon on the *Ribbon*.

Notice in the image of the *Ribbon* above, with the text selected, the ability to remove leaders is available (i.e., *Remove Last*). The arrows are removed in the order they were added.

OPEN TO ABOVE

FIGURE 6-4.2 Text with leaders

Adding Text Styles to Your Project:

You can add additional text styles to your project. Some firms prefer a font that has a hand lettering look and others prefer something like the Arial font. These preferences can be saved in the firm's template file so they are consistent and always available. You will add a new text style next.

6. Click on the **Text** tool.

7. Select **Edit Type** on the *Properties Palette*.

8. Select **Duplicate** and enter **1/4″ Outline Text** (Figure 6-4.3).

9. Next, make the following adjustments to the *Type Properties* (Figure 6-4.4):

    a. *Text Font:* **Swis721 BdOul BT**
    b. *Text Size:* **1/4″**

NOTE: You can use any Windows True-Type font. If you do not have this font, select another that best matches (see Figure 6-4.5 below).

FIGURE 6-4.3 New text name

The text size you entered in step 9 is the size of the text when printed. If you change the scale of the drawing, the text size will automatically change, so the text is always the correct size when printing. It is best to set the drawing to the correct scale first. As changing the drawing scale can create a lot of work; repositioning resized text that may be overlapping something or too big for a room.

10. Select **OK** to close the open dialog boxes.

You should now have the new text style available in the *Type Selector* on the *Properties Palette*.

11. Use the new text style to create the text shown below (Figure 6-4.5).

12. Erase the sample text (unless your instructor tells you otherwise).

13. Save as **ex6-4.rvt**.

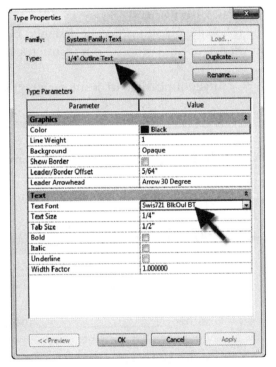

FIGURE 6-4.4 New text properties

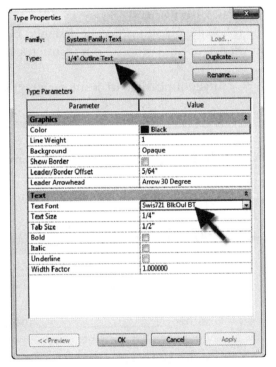

FIGURE 6-4.5 New text style sample

Self-Exam:

The following questions can be used as a way to check your knowledge of this lesson. The answers can be found at the bottom of this page.

1. You must pick Walls to define floor areas. (T/F)

2. Use the Ctrl key to cycle through the selection options. (T/F)

3. When you add a floor object in the plan view, the floor does not show up right away in the other views; i.e., 3D, Sections, etc. (T/F)

4. You use the _____ tool if you need to add a new product, like exterior plaster, so you can add it to wall types and other systems.

5. You have _____ different types of leader options with the *Text* tool.

Review Questions:

The following questions may be assigned by your instructor as a way to assess your knowledge of this section. Your instructor has the answers to the review questions.

1. It is not possible to create new text styles. (T/F)

2. You can add additional diffuser sizes to the Family as required. (T/F)

3. The light fixtures automatically turn to align with the ceiling grid. (T/F)

4. You can adjust the ceiling height room by room. (T/F)

5. Use the _____ button to add additional elements, for insertion, into the current project (e.g., ceiling: linear box family).

6. Leaders can only be removed in the order in which they were originally drawn (T/F).

7. Use the _____ tool if the ceiling grid needs to be at an angle.

8. Use the _____ tool to adjust the ceiling grid location if a ceiling tile is less than half its normal size.

9. Use the _____ tool to adjust whether an object's surface pattern is displayed (i.e., the stipple for the gypsum board ceiling).

10. What is the current size of your project (after completing Exercise 6-4)?

    _____ MB.

Lesson 7
Office Building: INTERIOR and EXTERIOR ELEVATIONS:

This lesson will cover interior and exterior elevations. The default template you started with already has the four main exterior elevations set up for you. You will investigate how Revit generates elevations and the role the elevation tag plays in that process. You will also be introduced to a feature called *Design Options*.

Exercise 7-1:
Creating and Viewing Parametric Exterior Elevations

Here you will look at setting up an exterior elevation and how to control some of the various options.

Setting Up an Exterior Elevation:

Even though you already have the main exterior elevations set, you will go through the steps necessary to set one up. Many projects have more than four exterior elevations, so all exterior surfaces are elevated.

1. Open your project, ex6-4.rvt, and **Save As ex7-1.rvt**.

2. Switch to your **Level 1** *Floor Plan* view.

3. Select **View → Create → Elevation**.

   TIP: Select the main part of the split-button, not the down arrow.

4. Place the temporary elevation tag in the plan view as shown in Figure 7-1.1.

   NOTE: As you move the cursor around the screen, the elevation tag automatically turns to point at the building.

You now have an elevation added to the *Project Browser* in the *Elevations* grouping.

Add this ⟶ elevation tag

FIGURE 7-1.1 Added elevation tag

After placing an elevation tag, you should rename the elevation label in the *Project Browser*.

5. In the *Project Browser*, under *Elevations*, select the elevation label that was just added; it should be "Elevation 1 – a".

6. Right-click on the view label and select **Rename**.

7. Type: **South Temp**

The name should be fairly descriptive so you can tell where the elevation is just by the label. This will be essential on a large project that has several exterior elevations and even more interior elevations.

8. Double-click on **South Temp** in the *Project Browser*.

The elevation may not look correct right away. You will adjust this in the next step. Notice, though, that an elevation was created simply by placing an elevation tag in the plan view.

9. Switch back to your **Level 1** floor plan view.

Next you will study the options associated with the elevation tag. This, in part, controls what is seen in the elevation.

10. The elevation tag has two parts: the pointing triangle (pointer) and the square center (body). Each part will highlight as you move the cursor over it. **Select the square center part**.

You should now see the symbol shown on the right (Figure 7-1.2).

View direction boxes:
The checked box indicates which way the elevation tag is looking. You can check (or uncheck) the other boxes. Each checked box relates to an elevation view in the *Project Browser*.

Rotation control:
Allows you to look perpendicular to an angled wall in plan, for example.

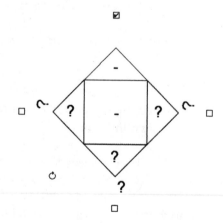

FIGURE 7-1.2 Selected elevation tag

Adjusting elevation tags:

While selected, you simply drag the tag to move it.

11. Press the **Esc** key to unselect the elevation tag.

12. Select the "pointing" portion of the elevation tag.

13. In the *Properties Palette*, set *Far Clipping* to "Clip without line" and then click **OK**.

Your elevation tag should look similar to Figure 7-1.3.

FIGURE 7-1.3 Selected elevation tag

The elevation tag, as selected in Figure 7-1.3, has several features for controlling how the elevation looks. Here is a quick explanation:

- **Cutting plane/extent of view line:** This controls how much of the 3D model is elevated from left to right (i.e., the width of the elevation).

- **Far clip plane:** This controls how far into the 3D model the elevation can see.

- **Adjustment grips:** You can drag this with the mouse to control the features mentioned above.

14. Select the view label **South Temp** in the *Project Browser*, now look at the *Properties Palette* settings for the view (see notes on the next page).

You have several options in the *Properties Palette* (Figure 7-1.4). Notice the options under the *Extents* heading, below is an examination of three of these settings:

- **Crop View**: This crops the width and height of the view in elevation. *Adjusting the width of the cropping window in elevation also adjusts the "extent of view" control in the plan view.*

- **Crop Region Visible**: This displays a rectangle in the elevation view indicating the extent of the cropping window (described above). *When selected in elevation view, the rectangle can be adjusted with the adjustment grips.*

- **Far Clipping**: If this is turned "off", Revit will draw everything visible in the 3D model *(within the "extent of view").*

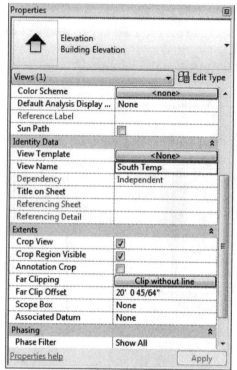

FIGURE 7-1.4 Elevation view: South Temp - Properties

You will manipulate some of these controls next.

15. With the elevation tag still selected (as in Figure 7-1.3), drag the "cutting plane/ extent of view" line up into the atrium as shown in Figure 7-1.5.

FIGURE 7-1.5 Revised cutting plane

16. Now switch to the *Elevation view:* **South Temp**.

Your elevation should look similar to Figure 7-1.6. If required, click on the cropping region and resize it to match Figure 7-1.6.

The atrium curtain wall and roof are now displayed in section because of the location of the "cutting plane" line in the plan.

Cropping window

FIGURE 7-1.6 Elevation with cutting plane thru atrium

Notice that the roof is not fully visible. This is not related to the cropping window shown in Figure 7-1.6. Rather, it is related to the "Far Clip Plane" set in the plan view.

17. Adjust the "Far Clip Plane" in the **Level 1** plan view so that the entire roof shows in the **South Temp** view.

Next you will adjust the elevation tag to set up a detail elevation for the atrium curtain wall.

18. In **Level 1** plan view, adjust the elevation tag to show only the atrium curtain wall (Figure 7-1.7).

19. Switch to **South Temp** view to see the "detail" elevation (Figure 7-1.8).

20. Adjust the South Temp view's **Properties** to turn off the crop region's visibility; this can also be done via the *View Control Bar*.

21. **Save** your project as **ex7-1.rvt**.

FIGURE 7-1.7 Atrium curtain wall detail elevation

Crop region: visibility should be turned off in Step 20.

T.O. Masonry
36' - 0"

Level 3
24' - 0"

Level 2
12' - 0"

Level 1
0' - 0"

DETAIL ELEVATION:
A detail elevation like this would be used to dimension the curtain wall member spacing (not drawn yet) and add notes about glass types and finish, etc. This might be placed on a sheet with the window types or on the sheet with the curtain wall details.

FIGURE 7-1.8 Atrium curtain wall detail elevation

Exercise 7-2:
Modifying the Project Model: Exterior Elevations

The purpose of this exercise is to demonstrate that changes can be made anywhere and all other drawings are automatically updated.

Modify an Exterior Elevation:

1. Open ex7-1.rvt and **Save As ex7-2**.

2. Open the **East** exterior elevation view.

3. Use the **Window** tool and select _Fixed:_ **32″ x 48″** in the _Type Selector_.

You will insert a window in elevation. This will demonstrate, first, that you can actually add a window in elevation not just plan view, and second, that the other views are automatically updated.

Notice, with the window selected for placement, you have the usual dimensions helping you accurately place the window. As you move the window around you should see a dashed horizontal cyan colored line indicating the default sill height.

4. Place a window as shown in **Figure 7-2.1**; make sure the bottom of the window "snaps" to the cyan sill line.

FIGURE 7-2.1 Placing a window

5. Switch to **Level 1** plan view; notice the window is added (Figure 7-2.2).

TIP: If the window is towards the inside, use the control arrows to flip the window within the wall. It should look like the window in Figure 7-2.2.

FIGURE 7-2.2 Level 1 – south-east corner

6. Switch back to the **East** elevation view.

7. Add windows as shown in Figure 7-2.3.

FIGURE 7-2.3 East elevation – windows added

If you laid out the interior walls as described in Lesson 3, you should get a warning message when inserting the windows on Level 1, towards the North side of the building. This is because the interior wall for the room in the north-east corner conflicts with the exterior window. Revit is smart enough to see that conflict and bring it to your attention. In this case you probably want the windows to be uniformly spaced, so you will ignore the conflict and move the wall in the plan view.

8. Click the red X (in the upper right) to ignore the wall/window conflict warning (Figure 7-2.4). *If you did not get this warning, skip this step.*

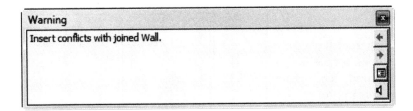

FIGURE 7-2.4 Conflict warning

9. Switch to **Level 1** plan view and revise the wall as shown in **Figure 7-2.5**.

    TIP: You will need to use the Split tool to break the wall where it offsets. You can then select the wall (just the wall; the doors will automatically move with the wall) and use the Move tool to move it north (check Disjoin on the Options Bar). Also notice that the windows on the east wall need to be flipped.

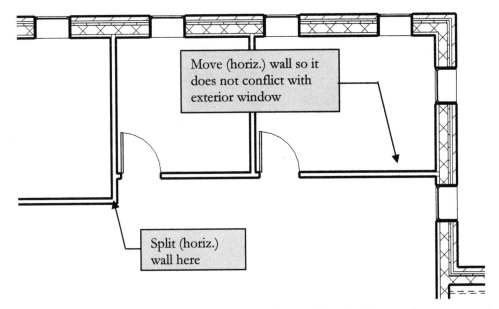

FIGURE 7-2.5 Level 1 – north-east corner

10. Switch to the **Level 1** RCP view. Fix the ceiling.

> *NOTE: The ceiling grids are likely not aligned with the revised walls. If this is the case, see the explanation below (Figure 7-2.6).*

Most of the time, when you move a wall, Revit will automatically update the ceiling gird to fit the new room. However, occasionally the definition of the room boundary is lost while making modifications. In this case, you will have to delete the grid and reinsert it - or select it and "edit sketch".

Deleting a Ceiling Grid:

When selecting a ceiling grid, Revit only selects one line. This does not allow you to delete the ceiling grid. To delete: hover cursor over a ceiling grid line and tap the TAB key until you see the ceiling perimeter highlight, then click the mouse. The entire ceiling will be selected. Press Delete.

FIGURE 7-2.6 Level 1 RCP – north-east corner

11. Add the same layout of windows (Figure 7-2.2) to the West elevation.

> *TIP: Mirror the windows in plan view, each floor.*

12. **Save** your Project as **ex7-2.rvt**.

TIP: ENTERING DIMENSIONS IN REVIT
*As your experience with Revit grows, you will want to learn some of the shortcuts to using the program. One of those shortcuts is how you enter dimensions when drawing. You probably already know, maybe by accident, that if you enter only one number (e.g., 48) and press enter, Revit interprets that number to be feet (e.g., 48'-0"). So, if you want to enter 48", you may be typing 0'-48" or 48". Both work, but having to press the **Shift** key to get the inch symbol takes a little longer.*

Here are some options for entering dimensions:

0 48	*Revit reads this as 48" (zero space forty-eight)*
48	*Revit reads this as 48'-0"*
5.5	*Revit reads this as 5'-6"*
0 5.5	*Revit reads this as 5 ½"*
2 0 1/4	*Revit reads this as 2'-0¼" (two space zero space fraction)*

Exercise 7-3:
Creating and Viewing Parametric Interior Elevations

Creating interior elevations is very much like exterior elevations. In fact, you use the same tool. The main difference is that you are placing the elevation tag inside the building, rather than on the exterior.

Adding Interior Elevation Tag:

1. Open project ex7-2.rvt and **Save As ex7-3.rvt**.

2. Switch to **Level 1** floor plan view, if necessary.

3. Select the **Elevation** tool.

4. Select *Elevation:* **Interior Elevation** from the *Type Selector* and then place an elevation tag, looking East, in the atrium area (Figure 7-3.1); place as shown in the center of the room.

REMEMBER: The first thing you should do after adding a new view is to give it an appropriate name in the Project Browser list.

5. Change the name of the elevation to **East Atrium**.

6. Switch to the East Atrium view. *Try double-clicking on the pointer part of the elevation tag to open the view.*

Initially, your elevation should look something like Figure 7-3.2. You will adjust this view next. *Notice how Revit automatically controls the line weights of things in section vs. things in elevations.*

FIGURE 7-3.1 Level 1 - Atrium

FYI: The elevation tags are used to reference the sheet and drawing number so the client or contractor can find the desired elevation quickly while looking at the floor plans. This will be covered in a later lesson. It is interesting to know, however, that Revit automatically does this (fills in the elevation tag) when the elevation is placed on a sheet, and will update it if the elevation is moved.

7. Switch back to the **Level 1** view.

8. Pick the "pointing" portion of the elevation tag, so you see the view options (Figure 7-3.3).

You should compare the two drawings on this page (Figures 7-3.2 and 7-3.3) to see how the control lines in the plan view dictate what is generated/visible in the elevation view, for both width and depth.

FIGURE 7-3.2 East Atrium – initial view

The goal is to set up an interior elevation of the entire east atrium wall, with the floor structure and roof shown in section.

FIGURE 7-3.3 Elevation tag selected

9. Adjust the control lines for the elevation tag as shown in Figure 7-3.4. Drag the "cutting plane/extent of view" line to the location shown. Make sure the "far clip plane" extends past the door alcove; otherwise it will not show up.

10. Switch back to the **East Atrium** view.

Other than adjusting the height of the view, you have the view ready.

11. Select the cropping region and drag the top middle grip upward, to increase the view size vertically (Figure 7-3.5).

Top middle grip

FIGURE 7-3.5 East Atrium
Elevation – crop region selected

FIGURE 7-3.4 Elevation tag
adjustments

If the ceiling were drawn for the third floor (your instructor may have assigned this), you would probably stretch the crop region down to it. Interior elevations don't normally show walls, roofs and floors in section. An atrium elevation like this could be an exception for the floors.

12. Now stretch the top of the crop region down to approximately 9'-6" above Level 3. (Go to the ceiling if you have drawn one for Level 3).

13. Stretch the bottom of the crop region up to align with the top of the Level 1 floor slab.

14. On the **View Control Bar**, set the scale to ¼"=1'-0".

Your elevation should look like Figure 7-3.6.

FIGURE 7-3.6 East Atrium Elevation

You can leave the crop region on to help define the perimeter of the elevation. You can also turn it off. However, some lines that are directly under the crop region might disappear. You could use the *Detail Line* tool to manually define the perimeter.

Also, notice the level datum automatically resized to match the new scale. When space permits, most interior elevations are ¼" = 1'-0".

15. Save your project as **ex7-3.rvt**.

Exercise 7-4:
Modifying the Project Model: Interior Elevations

This short exercise, similar to Exercise 7-2, will look at an example of Revit's ability to change anything anywhere. All drawings are generated from one 3D model.

Modify the Interior Elevations:

1. Open ex7-3.rvt and **Save As ex7-4.rvt**.

2. Open the **East Atrium** elevation view.

You will move two doors and add one.

3. Select both of the single doors on Levels 2 and 3; use the Ctrl key to select multiple objects at one time.

4. Use the **Move** tool to move the door 6'-0" to the right (South). (Figure 7-4.1)

5. In the East Atrium elevation view, use the **Door** tool to place a *Sgl Flush:* **36" x 84"** door on Level 2 to the far left (North). (See Figure 7-4.1.)

Relocated doors

Added door

FIGURE 7-4.1 East Atrium - modified

Now it's time to see the effects to the plan views.

6. Switch to **Level 2** floor plan view (Figure 7-4.2).
    You can also see a similar change on Level 3.

Added door

Relocated door

FIGURE 7-4.2 Level 2 plan with changes

When placing a door in elevation, you may have to switch to plan view to verify the door swing is the way you want it; you cannot control the door swing in elevation (well, actually, you can via a right-click on the door in elevation, but you would first need to know which way it is swinging).

In elevation, you can adjust many things this way. Some examples are: ceiling height, interior and exterior windows, wall locations (perpendicular to the current view), etc.

7. Save your project as **ex7-4**.

Exercise 7-5:
Adding Mullions to a Curtainwall

This exercise will cover the steps involved in designing a curtainwall system (only from an aesthetic viewpoint, not structurally). This is surprisingly simple to do.

Adding Curtain Grid:

First, you draw a grid on your curtainwall. This sets up the location for your mullions, which you will add later.

1. Open ex7-4.rvt and **Save As ex7-5.rvt**.

2. Switch to your **South Temp** view.

3. Select **Architecture → Build → Curtain Grid**.

Curtain Grid

4. Draw the grid as shown in **Figure 7-5.1**.
   Be sure to add horizontal grids at Levels 2 and 3.

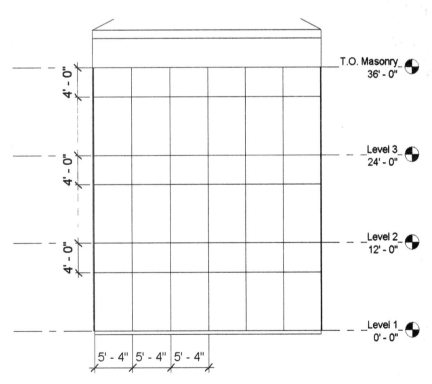

FIGURE 7-5.1 South Temp view – curtain grid added

If a curtain grid line did not land in the correct place, you can select it and adjust the dimensions that will appear on the screen. To select the grid you need to place your cursor over the grid line and press the *Tab* key until the curtain grid is highlighted, and then click to select.

5. Select the *Curtain Grid* tool and then click on the **One Segment** option on the *Ribbon* (Figure 7-5.2).

FIGURE 7-5.2 Ribbon options for Curtain Grid tool

6. Draw two vertical lines to set up the main entry door location (Figure 7-5.3). *You do not need to draw the dimensions shown.*

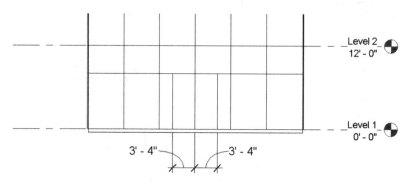

FIGURE 7-5.3 Curtain grid for door location

Notice that the *One Segment* option limits the grid to the "cell" you clicked in, rather than extending from top to bottom as the others did.

Next, you will setup the curtain grid lines around the corners. This can be done from the East or West views, similar to the previous steps. However, this can also be accomplished in a 3D view.

7. Click on the **3D** icon on the *Quick Access Toolbar*.

8. Using the **Curtain Grid** tool, add the grid lines shown in **Figure 7-5.4**. Starting at the outside corner, space the grids 5'-4" (the last space will be smaller).

FIGURE 7-5.4 Curtain grid – 3D view

As you move the cursor, while placing the horizontal grids, you should see the grid "snap" to the grid around the corner; that is when you click the mouse.

Drag your cursor on the ViewCube to see your project from different views. Clicking the "Home" icon (visible when your cursor is over the ViewCube) will reset the view.

Adding Doors:

9. Switch back to **South Temp** view and select one of the 3'-4″ wide cells; place your cursor over the cell [edge] and press the *Tab* key until that cell is highlighted and then click to select.

10. With the cell selected, pick **Curtain Wall Sgl Glass** from the *Type Selector* on the *Properties Palette* (Figure 7-5.5).

    FYI: If that type is not loaded, use Load Family to load the style from the Doors folder.

11. Repeat the previous two steps for the other 3'-4″ wide cell (Figure 7-5.6).

FIGURE 7-5.5 Type selector with curtain wall cell selected

FIGURE 7-5.6 Curtain grid with doors added

Adding Curtain Wall Mullions:

Thus far you have simply setup the spacing for the curtain wall mullions. Next you need to place the curtain wall mullions. This involves selecting a size for the mullion, as they typically come in many shapes and sizes. (The depth is usually related to the height of the curtain wall, as the mullion acts as the structure for the glass wall.)

12. Switch to the **3D** view.

13. Select **Architecture → Build → Mullion**.

14. Select _Rectangular Mullion:_ **2.5″ x 5″ rectangular** from the _Type Selector_ (Figure 7-5.7B).

15. Select all the grid lines you previously placed and the perimeter (excluding the outside corners and the bottom horizontal member on the south face).

FIGURE 7-5.7A
Ribbon for Mullion tool

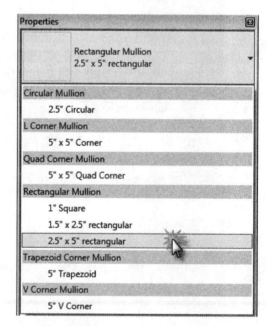

FIGURE 7-5.7B
Type selector for Mullion tool

Next, you will add the horizontal mullion at the bottom, on the south side. You need to place this mullion so it does not extend through the door openings.

16. With the Mullion tool selected, click **Grid Line Segment** from the *Ribbon* (Figure 7-5.7A).

17. Click on the bottom edge of the six cells (skipping the two door openings), to place the horizontal mullion (Figure 7-5.8).

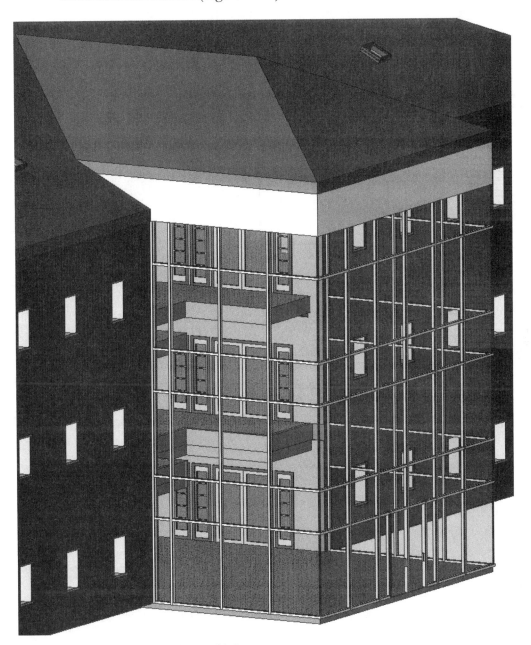

FIGURE 7-5.8 3D view with mullions added

18. Click on the two verticals next to each door to place a mullion (Figure 7-5.8).

In this example, you will not place a corner mullion. This will be a butt-joint condition where the two panes of glass are held together with silicon in the corner. However, figure 7-5.7B shows corner mullions that can be added.

All views will now be updated to show the curtain wall mullions.

19. Switch to the **Level 1** plan view to see the added curtain wall mullions and doors (Figure 7-5.9).

FIGURE 7-5.9 Level 1 plan view with curtainwall mullions

20. **Save** your project as **ex7-5.rvt**.

Exercise 7-6:
Design Options

This exercise will explore a feature called *Design Options*. This feature allows you to present two or more options for a portion of your design without having to save a copy of your project and end up having to maintain more than one project until the preferred design option is selected.

This feature can be used during the early design phase of a project or to manage bidding alternates all the way through construction documents. Design Options are different from phasing, which manages changes on the model over time, in that it manages changes to the model within the same time frame.

Design Options Overview:

A Revit project can have several design option studies at any given time. You might have an (A) entry canopy options study, (B) an executive board room options study, and a (C) toilet room layout options study in a project. Each of these studies can have several design options associated with them. For example, the entry canopy study might have three options: 1. flat roof, 2. gable roof, and 3. sloped glass roof.

A particular study of an area within your project is called a *Design Option Set*, and the different designs associated with a *Design Options Set* are called *Options*. Both the *Design Options Set* and the *Options* can be named.

One of the *Options* in a *Design Option Set* is specified as the *Primary* option (the others are called *Secondary* options); this is the option that is shown by default in all new and existing views. However, you can adjust the *Visibility* of a *View* to show a different option. Typically you would duplicate a *View*, adjust the *Visibility*, and *Rename* it to have each option at your finger-tips.

When the preferred design is selected, by you or the owner, you set that *Option* to *Primary*. Finally, you select a tool called *"Accept Primary"* which deletes the *Secondary Options* and the *Design Option Set*, leaving the *Primary Option* as part of the main building model.

Design Option Set

Option 1   Option 2

The following image (Figure 7-6.1) is an overview of the Design Options Dialog:

FIGURE 7-6.1 Design Options Dialog; Modern Layout Option selected

Notes about the *Design Options* dialog box:

Edit buttons:
You can edit a *Design Option* by selecting an *Option* (in the window area on the left) and then clicking the *"Edit Selected"* button. Next you add, move and delete elements in that Design Option.

When finished editing a *Design Option*, you reopen the *Design Options* dialog and click the *"Finish Editing"* button.

If you are currently in an Option Editing mode, the *Now Editing* area in the *Design Options* dialog displays the *Option* name being modified; otherwise it displays "Main Model".

Option Set buttons:
The *New* button is always available. You can quickly set up several *Option Sets*. Each time you create a new *Option Set*, Revit automatically creates a *Primary Option* named "Option 1".

The other buttons are only available when an Option Set label is highlighted (i.e., selected) in the window list on the left.

The *Accept Primary* button causes the Primary option of the selected Set to become a normal part of the building model and deletes the Set and Secondary Options. This is a way of "cleaning house", by getting rid of unnecessary information which helps to better manage the project and keeps the file size down.

Option buttons:
These buttons are only available when an *Option* (primary or secondary) is selected within an *Option Set*. You can quickly set up several *Options* without having to immediately add any content (i.e., walls, components, etc.) to them.

The *Make Primary* button allows you to change the status of a *Secondary Option* to *Primary*. As previously mentioned, the *Primary Option* is the *Option* that is shown by default in existing and new views.

The *Duplicate* button will copy all the elements in the selected Option into a new Option (this makes the file larger because you are technically adding additional content to the project). You can then use the copied elements (e.g., walls, furniture, etc.) as a starting point for the next design option. This is handy if the various options are similar.

Now you will put this knowledge to use!

Setting Up a Design Option Set:

In this exercise you will create two *Design Option Sets*; one for the curtain wall and another for the roof area above the curtain wall. You will create an alternate roof and curtain wall design for the office building project.

You could just create one *Design Option Set* and have two design options total. However, by placing the curtain wall options in one *Option Set* and the roof in another, you actually get a total of four design options. You can mix and match the curtain wall and roof options.

Setting Up Design Options in Your Project:

First you will setup the *Option Sets* and *Options*.

1.   Open ex7-5.rvt and **Save As ex7-6.rvt**.

2.   Select the **Design Options** icon on the *Status Bar* (see image below).

You are now in the *Design Options* dialog box (Figure 7-6.2). Unless you have modified your file to have *Option Sets*, your dialog will look like this one.

3.   In the *Option Set* area click **New**.

FIGURE 7-6.2 Design Options Dialog; initial view

Notice an *Option Set* named <u>Option Set 1</u> has been created. Revit also automatically created the *Primary Option* named <u>Option 1</u> (Figure 7-6.3). Next you will rename the *Option Set* to something that is easier to recognize.

FIGURE 7-6.3 Design Options Dialog; new option set created

4. (See warning below.) Select the *Option Set* currently named <u>Option Set 1</u> and then click the **Rename** button in the *Option Set* area.

    WARNING! *Be sure you are not renaming the Option but, rather, the Option Set.*

5. In the *Rename* dialog type: **Curtainwall** (Figure 7-6.4).

6. Click **OK** to rename.

Giving the *Option Set* a name that is easy to recognize helps in managing the various options later, especially if you have several.

FIGURE 7-6.4 Rename Option Set Dialog; enter Curtainwall

Next you will create a *Secondary Option* for the <u>Curtainwall</u> *Option Set*.

7. With the <u>Curtainwall</u> *Option Set* selected (or any option in that set), click **New** in the *Option* area.

Notice a secondary option was created and automatically named Option 2. If you have descriptive names for the options in a set, you should apply them. In this example you can leave them as they are.

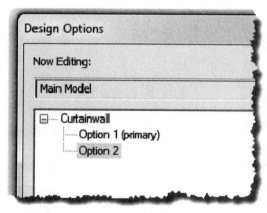

FIGURE 7-6.5 Design Options Dialog;
secondary option created

8. Create an *Option Set* for the roof (Figure 7-6.6):

   a. Name the set:
      Atrium Roof.
   b. Create one secondary option.

FIGURE 7-6.6 Design Options Dialog

The basic thinking with the *Design Options* feature is that you set up the *Option Set* and *Options* and then start drawing the elements related to the current *Option*. So, you select the option you wish to edit via the *Design Options* drop-down list on the *Status Bar*, make the additions and modifications relative to that *Design Option*, and finally set the drop-down list back to "Main Model".

However, in your case, you want to move content already drawn to *Option 1*. Revit has a feature that allows you to move content to a *Design Option Set*, which means the content gets copied to each *Option* in the *Set* you select. This option will work for the curtainwall because the second option will be similar to the first one.

Curtain Wall Design Option:

You are now ready to setup the different design options.

9. Switch to the **Default 3D view**.

10. Select the three curtain wall sections (three major areas around the atrium) and the three short walls above the curtain walls.

    TIP: Make sure you click when the entire curtain wall area is selected, not just an individual mullion or cell. You may need to use the Tab key to cycle through the available options below your cursor.

11. Select the **Add to Set** icon on the *Status Bar*.

12. Select *Curtainwall* from the dialog and then click **OK** (Figure 7-6.7).

The selected items are now in both *Option 1* and *Option 2* under the *Option Set: Curtainwall*.

From this point forward you can only modify the curtainwall when in *Option 1* or *Option 2* "edit mode" (in which case the tables are turned and you cannot edit the main building model; this is because "exclude options" is selected on the *Status Bar*).

FIGURE 7-6.7 Add to Set Dialog

13. Select **Curtainwall: Option 2** (i.e., <u>Option Set</u>: *Curtainwall*; <u>Option</u>: *Option 2*) from the *Design Options* list on the *Status Bar*. See image to right.

Now you should notice that the main building model is slightly grey and not editable. (It is not editable because "active option only" is selected on the *Status Bar*).

14. Zoom in on the curtain wall area in your 3D view.

15. Using the **Curtain Grid** tool on the *Modeling Tab*, add horizontal lines equally spaced between the larger vertical spaces as shown in Figure 7-6.8 (You should be able to place all the grid lines from this one view angle).

> *TIP: Use the "All except picked" setting on the Ribbon when placing the grid on either side of the doors on Level 1.*

FIGURE 7-6.8
3D View: horizontal
curtain grid lines added

16. Select the **Mullion** tool from the *Architecture* tab.

17. Select *Rectangular Mullion:* **2.5″ x 5″ rectangular** from the *Type Selector* (Figure 7-6.8).

18. Select each one of the gird lines to place the horizontal mullions (Figure 7-6.9).

FIGURE 7-6.9 3D View: horizontal mullions added

19. To finish editing the design option select **Main Model** from the *Design Options* list on the *Status Bar*.

It now appears like all your changes disappeared, right? Well, if you recall from the introduction to this exercise, the *Primary Option* is displayed by default for all new and existing views. So when you finished editing *Curtainwall:Option 2* the *Default 3D View* switched back to the primary option (which is currently set to Option 1).

Next you will create a new view and adjust its *Visibility* to display *Option 2* of the *Curtainwall Options Set.*

First you will create a duplicate copy of the 3D view.

20. In the *Project Browser*, under *3D Views*, right-click on the **{3D}** label.

21. Select **Duplicate View → Duplicate** from the pop-up menu.

You now have a copy of the 3D view named *Copy of {3D}*.

22. **Rename** the new view to **Curtainwall Option 2**.

23. Switch to your new view (if required).

24. Type **VV** on the keyboard to open the *Visibility/Graphics Overrides* for the current view.

25. Click on the **Design Options** tab at the top of the dialog. Note that this tab did not exist until you created *Design Options* in the project.

26. Change the *Design Option* parameter for *Curtainwall* to *Option 2* (Figure 7-6.10).

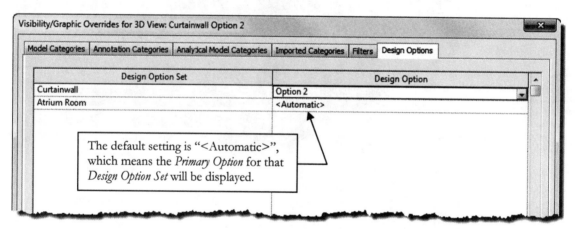

FIGURE 7-6.10 Visibility/Graphic Overrides dialog: modified Curtainwall design option visibility

27. Click **OK** to close the dialog.

Now, with the {3D} view and the *Curtainwall:Option 2* view, you can quickly switch between design options. Both views could be placed on the same sheet and printed out for a design critique. *FYI: When a design option is "hard wired" in this way you cannot ever edit any other curtainwall options in this view as they are not visible in this view (this only works when the view is set to automatic).*

Atrium Roof Design Option:

Similar to getting things ready to create the second option for the curtainwall, you will do the same for the atrium roof. However, the second roof option is totally different from the first option, so it does not make sense to move the current roof to each option in the *Atrium Roof Option Set*; you would end up completely deleting the roof from *Atrium Roof:Option 2* (deleting the roof would be no problem in this case, but another scenario might have hundreds of entities that need to be moved to Option 1, which would be more difficult to delete from Option 2). Next you will explore the how to move content to just one *Option* in an *Option Set*.

28. Switch to the *Default* **3D view**.

29. Select the roof over the atrium and curtain wall area.

30. Again, select **Add to Set** from the *Status Bar*.

You are now able to specify the *Option Set* and the specific *Options* to copy the selected elements to (Figure 7-6.11).

31. Select **Atrium Roof** from the drop-down list. (Figure 7-6.11)

32. Uncheck "Option 2" from the list.

33. Click **OK** to close the *Add to Set* dialog.

FIGURE 7-6.11 Add to Set dialog

You have now copied the roof into Option 1 for the *Option Set* named Atrium Roof, and Option 2 is still empty.

You are now ready to create the roof for Option 2.

34. Select **Atrium Roof: Option 2** from the *Design Options* list on the *Status Bar*. See image to the right.

Your view should now look similar to the image on the left. The roof is gone because *Atrium Roof:Option 2* does not currently have a roof in it.

35. Switch to the **South** elevation view.

36. Zoom in to the area above the curtain wall.

Next, you will create an *In-place Family* to represent a curved roof option over the atrium area. Basically, you will create a solid by specifying a depth and then drawing a profile of the curved roof with lines.

37. Click **Architecture →**
     Build → Component →
     Model In-Place.

Immediately, you are prompted to select a *Family Category*. This allows Revit to understand how other elements should interact with the object(s) you are about to create, and helps control visibility.

38. Select **Roofs** from the *Family Category* list (Figure 7-6.12).

39. Click **OK**.

Now you are prompted to provide a name for the new *Family*.

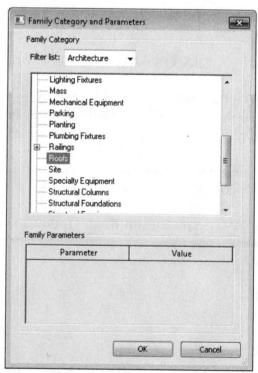

FIGURE 7-6.12
Family Category and Parameters dialog

For the *Family* name, type **Atrium Roof** (Figure 7-6.13).

FIGURE 7-6.13 Family name prompt

You are now in a mode where you draw the Atrium Roof. Notice that the *Architecture* tab on the *Ribbon* has changed (Figure 7-6.14) which has all the tools available to create a *Family*. You are continuously in the *Family* edit mode until you select *Green Check Mark* (to finish the roof) or the *Red X* (to cancel) from the *Ribbon*.

FIGURE 7-6.14
Model In-Place active; *Create* tab on the Ribbon

40. Select **Extrusion** from the *Ribbon*. (Figure 7-6.14)

Finally, you are prompted to select a plane in which to start drawing the profile of the solid to be extruded. Even though the view is a 2D representation of a 3D model, Revit needs to know where you want the 3D Solid created. You will select the wall above the curtain wall as a reference surface to establish a working plane.

41. Select **Pick a Plane** and click **OK** (Figure 7-6.15).

FIGURE 7-6.15 Work Plane dialog; select Pick a Plane

42. Move the cursor over the upper edge of the wall above the curtainwall and press the Tab key until a dashed line appears around the perimeter of the wall, and then click the mouse to select (Figure 7-6.16).

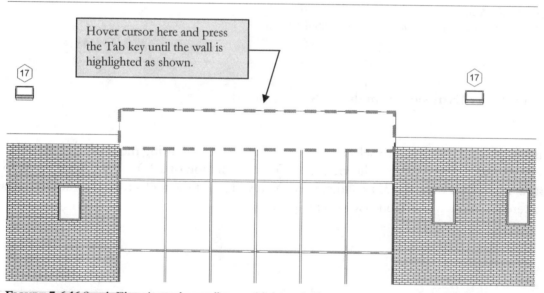

Hover cursor here and press the Tab key until the wall is highlighted as shown.

FIGURE 7-6.16 South Elevation; select wall to establish work plane

Next you will draw an arc to specify the bottom edge of the curved roof design option.

Notice the *Ribbon* changed again to show tools related to drawing an extruded solid (Figure 7-6.17).

FIGURE 7-6.17 Create Extrusion contextual tab

43. On the *Options Bar*, enter **-40'-0"** for the **Depth** (Figure 7-6.18).

    FYI: A positive number for the depth would cause the solid to project out from the curtain wall rather than back over the atrium.

44. Click **Arc** (Start End Radius) from the *Draw* panel on the Ribbon (Figure 7-6.17).

45. Pick the three points shown in Figure 7-6.18 to draw the arc. The angle 71.847° is not critical; get as close as possible.

    TIP: Zoom in on each arc endpoint to accurately select the corners.

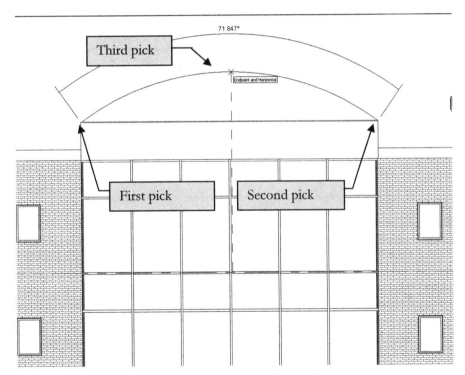

FIGURE 7-6.18 South Elevation; drawing arc to define roof

Now you will draw another arc 1'-0" above the previous one.

46. Select **Modify** on the *Ribbon.*

47. With the draw arc tool still selected, on the *Options Bar*, enter **1'-0"** for the *Offset.*

48. Pick the same three points shown in Figure 7-6.18.

Notice that an arc is drawn offset 1'-0" from the points you picked. If you pick the first two points in the other direction, the arc would be offset in the other direction (downward in this case).

Next, you will draw two short lines to connect the endpoints of the two arcs. This will create a closed area which is required before finishing the sketch. Think of it this way: you need to completely specify at least two dimensions before Revit can create the third.

49. Click the "straight" line icon on the *Draw* panel. This will switch you from drawing arcs back to drawing straight line segments.

50. Zoom in and draw a short line on each end of the arc as shown in Figure 7-6.19, try typing SE before picking to make it easier to snap to the arc's endpoints. (Make sure *Offset* is set back to zero.)

FIGURE 7-6.19 South Elevation; two arcs and two short lines define roof profile

51. Click the **green check mark** from the *Ribbon* to finish the solid extrusion.

> **TIP:** *If you get any warnings, it may be because one or more of the profile's corners do not create a perfect intersection. Zoom in to see and use the Trim tool to close the corners.*

You are still in the *Create Family* mode. Before you finish you will apply a material to the roof element.

52. Click the new roof to select it.

53. On the *Properties Palette*, click in the *Material* value field and then click the "**...**" icon that appears.

The Material dialog opens.

54. In the **AEC Material** library, under the **Metal** heading, double-click **Roofing, Metal** from the list of predefined *Materials* and then click **OK**.

> *FYI: Notice the rendering material is set to an Aluminum Anodized Bronze for **Roofing, Metal** on the Render Appearance tab.*

55. Click **Apply** to close the *Properties Palette*.

You are now ready to finish the Family.

56. From the *Ribbon* click **Finish Model** (Green Check Mark).

You are now also ready to finish editing the current design option for the time being.

57. Select **Main Model** from the *Design Options* list on the *Status Bar*.

As before, the option you were just working on was not the *Primary Option* in the *Atrium Roof Design Set*, so the current view reverted back to *Atrium Roof: Option 1* (which is the Primary view).

You will create a 3D view that has *Option 2* set to be visible for both the *Curtainwall* Option Set and the *Atrium Roof* Option Set.

58. Duplicate the *Default* **3D view**.

59. Rename the duplicated view to **Atrium – Option 2**.

60. Switch to the new view (Atrium – Option 2).

61. Type **VV** to access the *Visibility/Graphics Overrides*.

62. On the *Design Options* tab, set both *Option Sets* to **Option 2** in the *Design Option* column.

63. Click **OK** to close the dialog.

You can now see a 3D view of your new roof option. However, you realize that the walls above the curtainwall need to be modified based on the roof option; so it would make more sense to have the walls in the Atrium Roof Option Set rather than the Curtainwall Option Set.

Next, you will make this change and then modify the wall to conform to the curved roof option.

64. In the Default 3D View: open each of the two *Options* (i.e., enter edit mode) in the *Curtainwall* Option Set, select the three walls above the curtain wall and **Cut to Clipbaord**.

65. Now open each of the two *Options* for the *Atrium Roof* Option Set and **Paste** the three walls using *Paste Aligned\Same Place*.

FIGURE 7-6.20 Atrium – Option 2 view

The three walls should now exist in the *Atrium Roof:Option 1* set and the *Atrium Roof:Option 2* set. Next you will modify the *Option 2* walls.

66. Enter edit mode for *Atrium Roof:Option 2*.

67. In your newly created 3D view "Atrium Option 2", zoom in to the South wall above the curtain wall that needs to be extended up to the curved roof.

68. Click on the wall to select it.

69. Click the **Attach Top/Base**, from the *Ribbon* (Figure 7-6.21).

FIGURE 7-6.21 Ribbon with wall selected

This feature allows you to *Attach* a wall to another object. In this example you will pick the curved roof which will cause the wall to extend up and conform to the underside of the curved roof.

The *Edit Profile* button (also visible on the *Ribbon* when the wall is selected) would allow you to achieve the same results. Using that tool you sketch a new perimeter for the wall in an elevation or 3D view. This is particularly handy if you do not have another object to conform to; you simply want the top of the wall to do something unusual.

70. Hover the cursor over the curved roof until it highlights, and then click to select it.

Immediately the wall is modified; it should look similar to Figure 7-6.22.

71. Finish editing the current Design Option – switch to **Main Model**.

72. **Save** you project as **ex7-6.rvt**.

TIP: The Design Options feature can also be used to manage alternates, where both the base bid and the alternate(s) need to be drawn.

FIGURE 7-6.22 Atrium – Option 2 view; Wall attached to curved roof

Self-Exam:

The following questions can be used as a way to check your knowledge of this lesson. The answers can be found at the bottom of this page.

1. The plan is updated automatically when an elevation is modified, but not the other way around. (T/F)

2. You can use the Elevation tool to place both interior and exterior elevations. (T/F)

3. You can rename elevation views to better manage them. (T/F)

4. You have to resize the Level datum symbols and annotations after changing a view's scale. (T/F)

5. How do you enter 5 ½″ without entering the foot or inch symbol?

_____

Review Questions:

The following questions may be assigned by your instructor as a way to assess your knowledge of this section. Your instructor has the answers to the review questions.

1. The visibility of the crop region can be controlled. (T/F)

2. You have to manually adjust the line weights in the elevations. (T/F)

3. As you move the cursor around the building, during placement, the elevation tag turns to point at the building. (T/F)

4. There is only one part of the elevation tag that can be selected. (T/F)

5. You cannot adjust the "extent of view" using the crop region. (T/F)

6. What is the first thing you should do after placing an elevation tag? _____

7. In addition to the Window tool, if one window is already placed, you can use

   the _____ tool to place additional instances of that window.

8. With the elevation tag selected, you can use the _____ to adjust the tag orientation to look at an angled wall.

9. You need to adjust the _____ to see elements, in elevation that are a distance back from the main elevation.

10. What feature allows you to develop different ideas? _____

Lesson 8
Office Building: SECTIONS and DETAILS:

Sections are one of the main communication tools in a set of architectural drawings. They help the builder understand vertical relationships. With traditional CAD software, architectural sections can occasionally contradict other drawings, such as mechanical or structural drawings. One example is a beam shown on the section is smaller than what the structural drawings call for; this creates a problem in the field when the duct does not fit in the ceiling space. The ceiling gets lowered or the duct gets smaller, ultimately compromising the design to a certain degree.

Revit takes great steps toward eliminating these types of conflicts. Sections, like plans and elevations, are generated from the 3D model. So it is virtually impossible to have a conflict between the architectural drawings. As structural and mechanical engineers begin to use Revit the coordination get betters as the various discipline's models are linked together.

Exercise 8-1:
Specify Section Cutting Plane in Plan View

Similar to elevation tags, placing the reference tags in a plan view actually generates the section view. You will learn how to do this next.

Placing Section Tags:

1. Open ex7-6.rvt and **Save As ex8-1.rvt**.

2. Switch to **Level 1** view.

Section

3. Select **View → Create → Section** button from the *Ribbon*.

4. Draw a Section tag as shown in Figure 8-1.1. Start on the left side in this case. Use the *Move* tool if needed to accurately adjust the section tag after insertion. The section should go through the doors in the stair shaft (Figure 8-1.1).

FIGURE 8-1.1 Section tag (selected)

Figure 8-1.1 shows the section tag selected. The section tag features are very similar to the elevation tags covered in the previous lesson. You can adjust the depth of view (*Far Clip Plane*) and the width of the section with the *Adjustment Grips*.

Section views are listed under that heading in the *Project Browser*. Similar to newly created elevation views, you should name section views as you create them.

5. Rename the new section view to: **Longitudinal Section**.

6. Switch to the **Longitudinal Section** view (Figure 8-1.2).

FIGURE 8-1.2 Longitudinal section view

You can see that the stairs are cut off on the back side because of the *Far Clip Plane* location in the plan view (Figure 8-1.1). Also, you can see the roof is shown in section exactly where the section line is shown in plan. Figure 8-1.2 also shows the *Crop Region*.

7. Adjust the *Far Clip Plane* in plan view so the entire stair shows and the *Crop Region* is not visible (Figure 8-1.3).

FIGURE 8-1.3 Longitudinal view - updated

8. On the *View Control Bar*, change the view *Properties* so the **Detail Level** is set to **Medium**. *(Notice how the walls change to show more detail.)*

9. Zoom in to the elevator shaft area as shown in **Figure 8-1.4**.

FIGURE 8-1.4 Section view – zoomed in

You should notice an added level of detail in the section view. For example, the concrete hatch in the floor and the CMU joint lines in the elevator shaft. This added detail helps the drawing read better.

Next you will add a cross sectional view.

10. Create a **Section** as shown in **Figure 8-1.5**.

>   *TIP: You can use the control arrows to make the section look the other direction.*

FIGURE 8-1.5 Level 1 view; Section tag (selected)

11. Rename the new section view to **Cross Section 1** in the *Project Browser*.

12. Adjust the **Far Clip Plane** (if required) so the entire atrium roof will be visible in the **Cross Section 1** view.

13. Switch to the **Cross Section 1** view.

14. Set the *Detail Level* to **Medium** and turn off the **Crop Region** visibility via the *View Control Bar* (Figure 8-1.6).

>   *TIP: Both of these settings can be controlled via the Properties Palette as well.*

Revit automatically displays lines heavier for objects that are in section than for objects beyond the cutting plane (i.e. in projection) and shown in elevation.

Also, with the *Detail Level* set to medium, the walls and floors are hatched to represent the material in section.

Figure 8-1.6 Cross Section 1 view

Notice that the Longitudinal Section tag is automatically displayed in the Cross Section 1 view. If you switch to the Longitudinal Section view you will see the Cross Section 1 section tag. Keeping with Revit's philosophy of change anything anywhere, you can select the section tag in the other section view and adjust its various properties, like the Far Clip Plane.

15. **Save** your project as **ex8-1.rvt**.

FYI: In any view that has a Section Tag in it, you can double-click on the round reference bubble to quickly switch to that section view.

Exercise 8-2:
Modifying the Project Model in Section View

Again, similar to elevation views, you can modify the project model in section view. This includes adjusting door locations and ceiling heights.

Modifying Doors in Section View:

In this section you will move a door and delete a door in section view.

1. Open ex8-1.rvt and **Save As ex8-2.rvt**.

2. Open **Cross Section 1** view.

3. On **Level 2**, move the *Single Glass* door **5′-0″** to the north and **delete** the door added in a previous lesson, see modified section view Figure 8-2.1. (See Figure 8-1.6 for an unmodified view.)

4. Adjust the **ceiling height** in the lower right room to be **9′-0″** above Level 1 (Figure 8-2.1).

    TIP: Select the ceiling and simply change the temporary dimension that appears (or use the Properties Palette).

FIGURE 8-2.1 Cross Section 1 view (modified)

5. Switch to the **Level 2** view (Figure 8-2.2).

FIGURE 8-2.2 Level 2 view

You should see the door in its new location and the other door has been deleted.

6. Switch to the **East Atrium** view (Figure 8-2.3).

FIGURE 8-2.3 East Atrium view

You can see the changes here as well. Compare this elevation with Figure 7-4.1 from lesson 7. Also, notice that the section mark was automatically added to the elevation. Remember, you can double-click on the section bubble to switch to that view.

7. Save your project as **ex8-2.rvt**.

Exercise 8-3:
Wall Sections

So far in this lesson you have drawn building sections. Building sections are typically 1/16″ or 1/8″ scale and light on the details and notes. Wall sections are drawn at a larger scale and have much more detail. You will look at setting up wall sections next.

Setting Up the Wall Section View:

1. Open ex8-2.rvt and **Save As ex8-3.rvt**.

2. Switch to the **Cross Section 1** view.

Callout

3. Select **View → Create → Callout**.

4. Place a **Callout** tag as shown in Figure 8-3.1.

   TIP: Pick in the upper left and then in the lower right (don't drag) to place the Callout tag.

   a. Select *Section:* **Wall Section** from the *Type Selector*.

5. Use the *Control Grips* for the *Callout* tag to move the reference bubble as shown in Figure 8-3.1.

FIGURE 8-3.1 Cross Section 1 view
with Callout added

Notice that a view was added in the *Sections* category of the *Project Browser*. Because *Callouts* are detail references off of a section view, it is a good idea to keep the section view name similar to the name of the callout.

Additionally, *Callouts* differ from section views in that the callout is not referenced in every related view. This example is typical, in that the building sections are referenced from the plans and wall sections are referenced from the building sections. The floor plans can get pretty messy if you try to add too much information to them.

6. Double-click on the reference bubble portion of the *Callout* tag to open the **Callout of Cross Section 1** view (Figure 8-3.2).

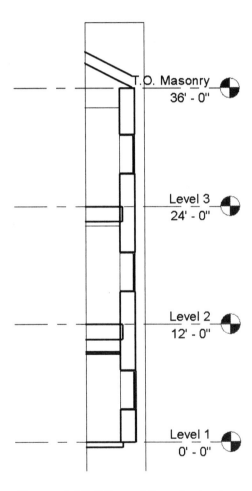

FIGURE 8-3.2 Callout of Cross Section 1

7. In the View properties, set the *View Scale* to ¾″ **= 1′-0″** and the *Detail Level* to **Fine** (Figure 8-3.3).

    TIP: This can all be done from the View Control Bar as well.

    Notice the Level datum symbol size changed as well as the Detail Level (Figure 8-3.4).

FIGURE 8-3.3 View properties

FIGURE 8-3.4 Revised Detail Level and view scale

If you zoom in on a portion of the *Callout* view, you can see the detail added to the view. The wall's interior lines (i.e., veneer lines) are added and the materials in section are hatched (Figure 8-3.5).

FIGURE 8-3.5 Callout view (zoomed in)

Join ▾

You can use the **Join** tool to clean up the floor to wall condition shown above. Simply click the icon and the two elements you want to join (this works on many types of elements). See Figure 8-3.6 for a "joined" condition; every view is updated!

You can use the **Detail Lines** tool to add more detailed information to the drawing. For example, you could show the masonry coursing, window trim, brick vents/weeps and flashing.

As before, you can turn off and adjust the crop region.

8. **Save** your project as **ex8-3.rvt**.

FIGURE 8-3.6 Joined wall/floor

Exercise 8-4:
Annotation

This exercise will explore adding notes and dimensions to your wall section.

Add Notes and Dimensions to Callout of Cross Section 1:

1. Open ex8-3.rvt and **Save As ex8-4.rvt**.

2. Switch to **Callout of Cross Section 1** view.

3. Adjust the View Properties so the crop region is not visible (via the *Properties Palette* when nothing is selected in the model).

4. Add two dimensions and adjust the Level datum symbol location as shown in **Figure 8-4.1**.

   TIP: Dimension to the masonry opening.

These dimensions are primarily for the masons laying up the CMU and Brick. Typically, when an opening is dimensioned in masonry, the dimension has the suffix M.O. This stands for Masonry Opening, clearly representing that the dimension identifies an opening in the wall. You will add the suffix next.

5. Select the dimension at the window opening and pick the **Blue text** (i.e., 4'-0").

6. Type **M.O.** in the Suffix field (Figure 8-4.2).

7. Click **OK**.

FIGURE 8-4.1 Added dimensions

FIGURE 8-4.2 Editing dimension text

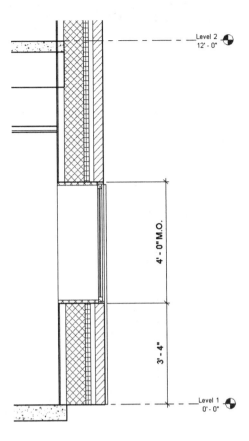

FIGURE 8-4.3 Dimension with suffix

Figure 8-4.3 shows the dimension with the added suffix.

8. Add the additional dimensions shown in Figure 8-4.4; be sure to add the suffixes.

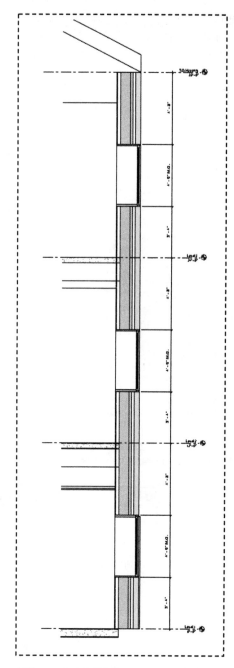

9. Add the notes with leaders shown in Figure 8-4.5. *(See step 10.)*

   a. Aluminum window system, typical
   b. Brick cavity wall
   c. Concrete and metal deck and stl. bar joists
   d. Concrete slab on grade over vapor barrier

FIGURE 8-4.5 Notes added

Figure 8-4.4 All dimensions added

10. The text style should be set to **3/32″ Arial**; it may still be set to the last text style you used (¼″ Outline Text, in this book).

11. Select the text and use the grips and the justification buttons to make the text look like **Figure 8-4.5**.

FYI: Architectural text is typically all uppercase.

12. **Save** your project.

Exercise 8-5:
Details

This exercise shows you how to develop 2D details which are not tied to the 3D model in any way. Why would you want to do this, you might ask? Many design firms have developed detail libraries over the years for typical conditions. These details contain a significant amount of embodied knowledge of the firm as a whole. Many notes and dimensions have been added which cover certain situations that have come up and created problems or cost the firm money. For example, a window head detail might show flashing, which directs any moisture in the wall out – rather than into – the window or inside the building. Well, a note might have been added to instruct the contractor to turn the flashing up at each side of the window to ensure the moisture does not just run off the end of the flashing and stay in the wall.

If every detail were a live cut through the model, the designer would have to spend the time adding all these notes and dimensions, and more importantly try not to forget any, even if typing them from a printed reference page – similar to what you are doing with this book. (Have you missed anything yet, and had to go back and make a correction?) Furthermore, if the part of the model changes, the detail could be messed up. Or, an item being detailed from the live model might change and not be the typical condition anymore.

So, as you can see, there are a number of reasons a design firm maintains and utilizes static 2D details. *NOTE: Sometimes these details are used as starting points for similar details. This saves time not having to start from scratch.*

It should also be pointed out that standard details should always be reviewed before "dumping" them into a project. If a note says "Apply fireproofing to underside of metal roof deck" and your building has precast concrete plank, you need to change the note and the drawing. All other parts of the detail may perfectly match the project design you are working on.

Linking an AutoCAD Drawing

This first exercise will explore linking AutoCAD drawings into Revit when the need to use legacy details arises.

It is better to recreate these details in native Revit format rather than linking an AutoCAD drawing. Any external files linked in have the potential to slow your BIM experience and introduce corruption. This is especially true with site plans created in AutoCAD or AutoCAD Civil 3D. Site plans are often a great distance from the origin (i.e., 0,0,0 coordinate in an AutoCAD drawing) and this creates several issues.

In general, it is best to avoid AutoCAD DWG files within Revit. However, when it is required, they should always be *Linked* in and not *Imported*, and never *Exploded*. Importing DWG files makes them difficult to manage and exploding them creates lots of extra text styles, fill patterns and other items that clutter the BIM database.

- Open ex8-4.rvt and **Save As ex8-5.rvt**.

AutoCAD DWG files can be linked directly into a plan view and be used as an underlay to sketch walls and place doors and windows, when modeling an existing building in Revit that has been drawn in a traditional CAD program.

In our example, we have a DWG file which contains a detail we want to reference and place on a sheet for our office building project. To do this, you create a *Drafting View* and link the CAD file into the drafting view. A *Drafting View* is a 2D drawing within the BIM project that has no direct relationship to the 3D model.

- Click **View → Create → Drafting View** from the *Ribbon*.

Drafting
View

Now you are prompted for a name and scale for the new drafting view; this can be changed later if needed.

- Enter the following (Figure 8-5.1):

    a. *Name:* **Typical Roof Drain Detail**

    b. *Scale:* **1½″ = 1′-0″**

- Click **OK** to create the new *Drafting View*.

FIGURE 8-5.1 Creating a drafting view

You now have a new section, under *Views* in the *Project Browser*, called *Drafting Views* (Detail). Within this section is your new *Drafting View* – Typical Roof Drain Detail.

Within this new drafting view you could begin sketching a detail from scratch using the various tools on the *Annotate* and *Modify* tabs. Or, in this example, you may link in a DWG file.

This roof drain detail is a good example of why 2D details are still useful in Revit, either DWG or native Revit. As previously mentioned, many firms spend years developing standard details. These details have notes that have been added to and edited as building materials change and problems occur. It would take a lot of time to cut a section at a 3D roof drain in the model and then add all the notes, if one can even remember what all the notes are. Now, repeat this for 20 to 50 other items throughout the building project.

Now you will link in the DWG file from the CD that came with this textbook.

- While in the newly created drafting view, select **Insert → Link → Link CAD** from the *Ribbon*.

Link
CAD

- Browse to the **DWG Files** folder on the CD.

- Select the file **Typical Roof Drain Detail.DWG**.

- Set the *Colors* options to **Black and White** (Figure 8-5.2).

FIGURE 8-5.2 Linking an AutoCAD detail file

- Click **Open** to place the linked AutoCAD DWG file.

- Type **ZF** (for *Zoom Fit*) on the keyboard; do **not** press **Enter**.

You should now see the roof drain detail, with line weights.

FIGURE 8-5.3 DWG file linked into drafting view

The drawing can be selected and moved around within the drafting view, but it cannot be edited. If you need to make changes to this drawing, you would have to do it in AutoCAD. Revit will automatically update any linked files when the project file is opened. It can also be done manually using the *Manage Links* tool.

When DWG files are linked into Revit, a specific set of line weights are used. These settings can be seen by clicking the small arrow (i.e., the dialog launcher) in the lower right corner of the *Import* panel on the *Insert* tab.

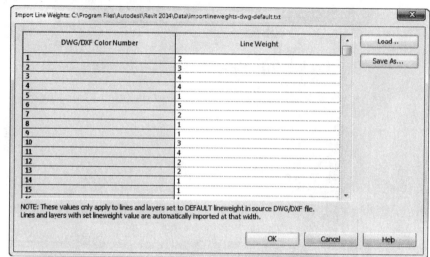

FIGURE 8-5.4 DWG color to Revit line weight conversion

Applying line weights is a onetime conversion process when the DWG file is linked in. Changing the line weight setting after a DWG has been linked in has no effect on it (only on new DWG files to be linked in).

> **TIP:** *Go to* **Manage → Settings → Additional Settings → Line Weights** *to see what each line weight number is equal to.*

If you type **VV** in the drafting view and then select the *Imported Categories* tab, you can see the AutoCAD *Layers* that exist in the imported DWG file (Figure 8-5.5). Unchecking a *Layer* will hide that information within the drafting view. You can also control the color and line weight of the lines on each *Layer*.

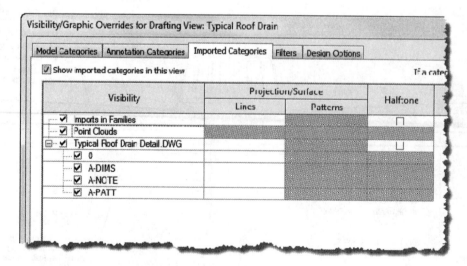

FIGURE 8-5.5 Controlling DWG layer visibility in Revit

Creating 2D Details:

Autodesk Revit Architecture has a large array of 2D detail components that can be used to create 2D details. These components allow for efficient detail drafting and design. Not every detail in Revit is generated from the 3D model; the amount of modeling required to make this happen is restricted by time, file size and computing power. The following is an outline of the overall process; this will be followed by a few exercises for practice:

- To create a 2D detail one would create a **drafting view** via *View > Create > Drafting View*, providing a name and selecting a scale.

- Once the *drafting view* has been created, **Detail Lines** and **Filled Regions** (via the *Annotate* tab) can be added.

- In addition to *Detail Lines* and *Filled Regions*, one can insert pre-drawn items from the Detail Library.

  i.   Select *Component > Detail Components* from the *Annotate* tab.

  ii. Select **Load Family** from the *Ribbon*.

  iii. Click **Imperial Detail Library** from the shortcut bar on the left of the *Open* dialog.

  iv. **Browse** to the specific "CSI organized" folder; for example, *Div 5-Metals → 052100- Steel Joists Framing → K-Series Bar Joist-Side.rfa.*

  v.   Click **Open** to place the component.

- Add notes and dimensions to complete the 2D detail.

FIGURE 8-5.6
Loading detail components

Flooring Details

The first two details you will draw are simple details consisting of *Detail Lines*, *Filled Regions*, *Text* and *Dimensions*.

You will draw a high-end floor and wall base detail known as terrazzo. This finish is poured in a liquid state, allowed to dry and then polished to a smooth finish. The colors and aggregate options are virtually unlimited (for example, you could use a clear epoxy resin and place leaves within the flooring).

1. Per the steps previously covered in this section, create a new drafting view.

   a. *Name*: **Terrazzo Base Detail**
   b. *Scale*: **3"=1'-0"**

You will now draw the detail shown below. See the next page for specific steps.

Terrazzo floor example with brass inlay

FIGURE 8-5.7 Terrazzo floor and wall base detail

2. Using the **Detail Lines** tool from the *Annotate* tab, draw the floor line **8″** long using **Wide Lines**.

> **FYI:** *The eight inch dimension is random, and does not represent anything other than a portion of the floor surface.*

3. Draw a vertical line, also **8″** long, using the **Medium Lines** style. This line should be about 2″ from the right edge of the floor line (just so your detail is generally proportional to the one presented in the book).

Next, you will offset the two lines just drawn to quickly create the terrazzo floor and base.

4. Select **Modify → Offset** on the *Ribbon*.

5. On the *Options Bar*, enter an offset value of **3/8″**.

6. Pick the floor line when the preview line appears above the horizontal line.

7. Now **Offset** the vertical line **3/8″** to the left.

Your drawing should now look like the image to the right (less the arrows). Next you will change the top horizontal line to a lighter line weight, offset it up 6″ to create the top of the wall base and then use the *Fillet Arc* feature to round off the corners.

8. Select the top horizontal line and change the *Line Style* from *Wide Lines* to **Medium Lines** via the *Ribbon*.

9. **Offset** the top horizontal line upward **6″** inches.

10. Select the new horizontal line and then drag its right end grip over to the vertical line.

Next you will trim and round the corners in one step.

11. Select the **Detail Line** tool from the *Annotate* tab.

    a.   Select **Fillet Arc** from the *Draw* panel.
    b.   Set the *Line Style* to **Medium Lines**.
    c.   Check and set the *Radius* to ¼″.

12. Click on the portion of the two lines you want to remain (see the two numbered clicks in the image to the right).

The line is now trimmed and an arc has been added.

13. Repeat these steps to round off the top edge of the wall base.

Next you will add a *Filled Region* to represent the terrazzo material with a pattern when viewed in a section. When creating the perimeter of a *Filled Region* you also specify a *Line Style* (similar to the *Detail Line* tool). In this case you will use *Thin Lines* for all but the left edge of the floor thickness. There you will change the *Line Style* to be an invisible line so as not to suggest a joint or the end of the flooring; but rather, that the flooring material continues.

14. Select **Annotate** → **Detail** → **Region** → **Filled Region** from the *Ribbon*.

    a.   Select the **Pick Lines** option from the *Draw* panel.

    b.   Select **Thin Lines** from the *Lines Style* panel.

Selecting *Pick Lines* will allow you to quickly create the boundary of your *Filled Region* based on lines already drawn. So you simply click on a line rather than pick two points to define the start and endpoints of each edge. However, with the *Line* and *Arc* options you could also snap to the endpoints of the previously drawn linework. The one drawback to using the *Pick Lines* option is you will have to trim a few corners, because the *Filled Region* tool requires that a clean perimeter be defined (similar to the floor and roof tools).

15. Pick the five lines and two arcs which define the edges of the floor and wall base.

16. Switch to the **Line** option in the *Draw* panel and then set the *Line Style* to **<Invisible Lines>**.

While in *Sketch Mode* (i.e., the green check mark and red X are visible) for the *Filled Region* tool, the invisible lines are not actually invisible. This allows you to select and modify them as needed.

17. Draw a line to close off the open edge of the flooring on the left hand side.

18. Use the **Trim** tool to clean up the two corners where the lines run past.

19. Click the **green check mark** to finish the *Filled Region*.

Your drawing should look like the one shown to the right. The default pattern is a cross hatch. You will change this next.

20. Select the *Filled Region*; you must click on one of the edges (and you may need to use *Tab*).

21. Expand the **Type Selector** to see the options currently available.

Looking at the list, we notice an option for concrete is not listed (which is what we decided we want). Next you will learn how to add this.

22. Press **Esc** to close the *Type Selector*.

23. Click **Edit Type**.

24. Click **Duplicate**.

25. Enter **Concrete** for the name.

26. Click in the *Fill Pattern* field and then **click the icon** that appears to the right.

27. Select **Concrete** from the list and click **OK**.

Notice the option to hatch the fill background opaque or transparent and the line weight setting.

28. Click **OK** to close the *Type Properties*.

Your terrazzo now has a concrete pattern. You can import additional fill patterns (using any AutoCAD hatch pattern file) or create custom ones with specific line spacing. This *Filled Region* tool can be used in floor plans as well; maybe you want to highlight the corridors or private office areas. When a *Filled Region* is selected the square foot area is listed in the *Properties Pallet*. Thus, you could quickly create a *Filled Region* just to list the area and then delete the *Filled Region*.

The last thing you will do is add the notes and dimensions. These will be the correct scale based on the *View Scale* setting (which should be 3″ = 1′-0″). Once you place the dimension you will learn how to adjust the dimension style so the 0′ does not show up.

29. Add the dimension and two notes as shown.

30. Select the dimension.

31. Select **Edit Type**.

32. Click the button to the right of **Units Format**.

33. Uncheck **Use Project Settings**.

34. Check **Suppress 0 feet**.

35. Click **OK** twice, to close both open dialog boxes.

Your dimension should now only say 6″ rather than 0′-6″. Because you changed this in the *Type Properties*, all dimensions will have this change applied (both previously saved and new). If you want to have both options, you would first need to *Duplicate* the dimension type, which is similar to creating new wall, door and window types!

The last thing you will look at is adjusting the arrow style for the notes.

36. Select one of the notes.

37. Click **Edit Type**.

38. Change the *Leader Arrowhead* to **Arrow Filled 30 Degree**.

39. Click **OK**.

Your detail should now look similar to the one presented at the beginning of this exercise. This detail can now be placed on a sheet (covered in chapter 12). You can also export this detail and save it in a detail library that you and others in your firm can utilize. To export the detail, simply right-click on the view name in the *Project Browser* and select *Save to new File*. Place the file on a server so everyone can get at it. To load this file into another project: Select **Insert → Insert from File → Insert Views from File**.

Now you will draw another detail using the same tools and techniques. Keep in mind, every detail needs to go in its own *drafting view*. This is required for Revit to manage the reference bubbles on the sheets.

40. Create a new **drafting view**;
    a. *Name:* **Floor Transition Detail**
    b. *Scale:* **3″ = 1′-0″**

41. Draw the detail per the following guidelines:
    a. The detail will be plotted at 3″=1′-0″ (this determines the text and leader size).
    b. Tile pattern is **Diagonal Up–Small**; this requires a new *Fill Region* style (see the previous exercise for more information).
    c. The grout (i.e., area under tile) is to be hatched with **Sand – Dense**; this also requires a new *Fill Region* style.
    d. Draw the tile ¼″ thick and 4″ wide.
    e. The grout is ¼″ thick.
    f. The resilient flooring is shown ⅛″ thick.
    g. The solid surface (e.g., Corian) threshold is 1⅞″ wide; draw an arc between the two floor thicknesses.
    h. Hatch the threshold with the solid hatch:
        i. **Duplicate** the **Solid Black** *Filled Region* style.
        ii. Name the new style: **Solid Gray**.
        iii. Set the hatch's color to a light gray (RGB color 192).
    i. The bottom concrete floor line is to be the heaviest line.

RESILIENT FLOORING

SOLID SURFACE THRESHOLD

THIN SET CERAMIC TILE

CONCRETE FLOOR

FIGURE 8-5.8 Floor transition detail: ceramic tile to resilient flooring

The previous drawing would typically occur in a door opening and the location of the door would also be shown in the detail. This lets the contractor know that the threshold is to occur directly below the door slab.

Base Cabinet with Drawers:

This section will dive right into drawing cabinet details. These are often based on industry standard dimensions so many of the dimensions and material thicknesses can be omitted (assuming the project manual/specification covers this).

42. Create a **drafting view**:

   a. *Name:* **Base Cabinet Detail – Drawers**
   b. *Scale:* **1″ = 1′-0″**

Revit provides many *Detail Components* which aid in creating 2D details. Things such as side views of bar joists, section views of steel beams and angles, and more are available in the *Detail Component* library. The detail below takes advantage of three *Detail Components* which ship with Revit: particle board, lumber and the counter top. The only things drawn with the *Detail Line* tool are the tops of the drawers, the drawer pulls (i.e., handles) and the heavy wall/floor lines.

FIGURE 8-5.9 Cabinet section (with drawers)

43. Using the *Detail Line* tool, draw the floor and wall line, shown in the image to the right, using the **Wide Lines** style. (Do not add the dimensions.)

Next, you will load the countertop *Family* from the *Detail Component* library.

44. Select **Annotate → Detail → Component → Detail Component** from the *Ribbon*.

45. Click **Load Family** from the *Ribbon*.

46. Click the **Imperial Detail Library** shortcut on the left (or just open the *Detail Items* folder).

47. Now, browse to: *Div 12-Furnishings → 123000-Casework →123600-Countertops*.

48. Select **Countertop-Section.rfa** and then click **Open**.

Countertop-Section with type *24″ Depth* is current, in the *Type Selector*, and ready to be placed.

49. Place the countertop as shown:
    a. Aligned with wall
    b. 3′-0″ above the floor (dimension to the line second from the top; the open heavy line is an exaggeration to highlight the added plastic laminate surface.
    c. With the countertop selected, adjust the values in the *Properties Palette*:
        i.   *Backsplash Depth:* **0′ 1″**
        ii. *Counter Depth:*   **2′-1″**
        iii. *Thickness:*   **0′ 1⅝″**
    d. Do not add dimensions yet.

Be careful not to click on the grips when the countertop is selected as this will adjust its dimensions; this is because the values are associated with an *instance parameter* rather than a *type parameter*.

Next, you will load and place the 2x lumber. The two on the floor are 4″ high, which are cut down from a 2x6. So you will load a 2x4 *Family* and then create a duplicate and adjust the height from 3½″ to 4″.

50. Per the step just covered, load **Nominal Cut Lumber-Section.RFA** from the following location: *Detail Item → Div 06-Wood and Plastic → 061100-Wood Framing*.

To minimize the number of *Types* for the lumber *Family*, you are presented with the *Specify Types* dialog. This lets you pick just the sizes you want – more can be added later.

51. Hold the **Ctrl** key and select **1x4** and **2x4** and then pick **OK**.

52. Select **2x4** in the *Type Selector*.

53. Click **Edit Type**.

54. Click **Duplicate**.

55. Enter **2x4 Base Cabinets** for the name.

56. Change the *Height* from 3½″ to **4″**.

57. Click **OK** to close the *Type Properties*.

58. Place the two **2x4 Base Cabinet** detail components on the floor as shown in the image to the right. (Do not add the dimension.)

59. Place the two **1x4** components as shown.

Next, you will load the detail component used to draw particle board. This *Family* is somewhat like the *Wall* tool. You pick two points and two lines and a fill pattern is generated. The *Type Selector* also has a number of standard thicknesses ready to use.

60. Per the step just covered, load **Particle board-Section.rfa** from the following location: *Detail Items → Div 06-Wood and Plastic → 061600-Sheathing*.

61. Select the **3/4"** type from the *Type Selector*.

62. Draw the two pieces of particle board shown in the image to the right; these are the top and bottom of the base cabinet. *TIP: Use the space bar to flip the thickness while drawing, if needed.*

63. Draw the cabinet back; use the **3/8"** thickness option and extend it **1/4"** into the top and bottom boards. See image below. *TIP: Draw temporary detail lines so you have a place to pick if needed. Delete them when done.*

The newest drawn particle board automatically shows up on top of any previously drawn particle board. This is how the notice is created. There was no trimming or erasing required. If you need to change the order of the overlap, simply select the component and use the *Arrange* options on the *Ribbon*.

64. Draw the rest of the base cabinet using the techniques previously covered and the following information:

   a. The "EQ" dimensions are 6".

   b. The drawer bottoms and backs are all ½" particle board; everything else is ¾".

   c. Use **Thin Lines** for the pulls and the top edge of the side drawer panel (seen in elevation in **Figure 8-5.9**). Use **Medium Lines** for the rubber base.

   d. Add dimensions not provided which can be approximated; make it look like the image in the book as much as possible.

   e. Add all the notes and dimensions shown on the first image only.

Some things you should know about detailing:

In the previous steps you drew a typical detail showing a standard base cabinet with drawers. Interior designers occasionally draw these details, but more often, they simply review them for finishes.

The countertop material needs to match that which is specified in the **Project Manual** and intended for the project. For example, a PLAM (i.e., plastic laminate) countertop would not be appropriate in a laboratory where chemicals would be used.

The base of the cabinet typically has the same wall base as the adjacent walls. For example, if the walls have a rubber base (also referred to as a resilient base), the toe-kick area of the base cabinet would also receive a rubber base; this is the type of base shown in the previous detail. If the project only had ceramic tile wall base, you would show that.

The **notes for details** (or any drawing) should be simple, generic and to the point. Notice in previously drawn detail that the note for the base does not indicate whether the base is rubber, tile or wood. This helps avoid contradictions with the room finish schedule. The note simply says the cabinet and floor are to receive a finish and instructs the contractor to go to the *Room Finish Schedule* to see what the finish is. This is particularly important in buildings that have several variations of floor and base finishes.

Notes should not have any **proprietary or manufactures names** in them either. For example, you should not say "Sheetrock" in a note because this is the brand name; rather, you should use the generic term "gypsum board". Similarly, you would use the term "solid plastic" rather than "Corian" when referring to countertops or toilet partitions. In any event, whatever term you use on the drawings should be the same term used in the Project Manual!

One last comment: the *Construction Documents* set should never have **abbreviations** within the drawings that are not covered in the *Abbreviations* list, usually located on the title sheet. *Construction Documents* are legal, binding documents, which the contractor must follow to a "T." They should not have to guess as to what the designers meant in various notes all over the set of drawings. It is better to spell out every word, if possible, only abbreviating when space does not permit. You would not want a bunch of abbreviations in your bank loan or mortgage papers you were about to sign! Plus, non-documented abbreviations would probably not have much merit before a judge or arbitrator in the case of a legal dispute!

65. Using the same steps just covered, draw the base cabinet shown below. Name the drafting view **Base Cabinet Detail**. The *Scale* is also **1" = 1'-0"**.

> *TIP: Duplicate the Base Cabinet Detail – Drawer view and modify it to be this detail; much of this detail is exactly the same.*

FIGURE 8-5.10 Cabinet section (door + drawer)

Cabinet details do not need to have every nook-and-cranny dimensioned because they are very much a standard item in the construction industry. Furthermore, the Project Manual usually references an industry standard that the contractor can refer to for typical dimensions, thicknesses and grades of wood.

The vertical dimension shown in the cabinet detail above says "VARIES - SEE ELEV". This notation, rather than an actual number, allows the detail to represent more than one condition. The interior elevations are required to have these dimensions, which may be the standard 36" or the lower handicap-accessible height.

Ceiling Detail:

Next, you will draw a typical recessed light trough detail at the ceiling. This is used often in commercial/public toilet rooms.

66. Create a new drafting view:

    a. *Name*: Toilet Room Ceiling Detail

    b. *Scale:* 1½" = 1'-0"

    c. *See the next page for additional notes.*

67. Load the following *Detail Components* into your project:

    a. Div 09-Finishes → 092000-Plaster and Gypsum Board → 092200-Supports → 092216-Non-Structural Metal Framing
        i. **Interior Metal Runner Channels-Section.rfa**
        ii. **Interior Metal Studs-Side.rfa**

    b. Div 09-Finishes → 092000-Plaster and Gypsum Board → 092900-Gypsum Board → **Gypsum Wallboard-Section.rfa**

    c. Div 09-Finishes → 095000-Ceilings → 095100-Acoustical Ceilings
        i. **Suspension Wall Angle-Section.rfa**
        ii. **Suspended Acoustic Ceiling-Square Edge-Section.rfa**

FIGURE 8-5.11 Ceiling detail

TIP: The notes in details should align on one edge as shown. Additionally, the leaders should not cross dimensions or other leaders unless it is totally unavoidable.

When using the *Detail Components* you will occasionally run into a few challenges getting things to look exactly the way you want them. For example, many firms have traditionally shown gypsum board as if it were continuous – not indicating the joints. Most contractors understand this and the designer usually does not want to imply the gypsum board be installed in a specific way or order. However, the *Detail Component* feature forces these edge lines to appear. Unfortunately we **cannot** use the *Linework* tool to set some of the lines in a *Detail Component* to be invisible.

Another problem you will run into, when using *Detail Components*, is the fact that everything is drawn true to life size. You may think, "Isn't that a good thing?" Usually it is, but some things often need to be exaggerated so they are legible on the printed page. Take the metal stud runner for example; when placed next to the *Gypsum Board* detail component it is totally hidden because the gypsum line weight is heavier than the runner stud. The best thing to do is to edit the *Family* so the runner stud has a heavier line weight and its thickness is exaggerated inward (you don't want to change the overall width. However, this type of change is outside the scope of this exercise, so you will do the following:

68. Erase the runner stud *Detail Components* and draw **Detail Lines** using **Medium Lines** – in bound from the gypsum board.

69. Make the light fixture **4½″ x 1¾″** with a 1″ circle for the light. Use the **Solid Gray** *Fill Region* previously created.

70. Sketch the egg-crate lens using **Detail Lines**. Create a new *Fill Region* using the **Vertical-Small** fill pattern.

71. Add the notes and dimensions shown.

Fixed Student Desk at Raised Seating Classroom:

This detail would work nicely for the fixed desks in the Lecture Classroom. However, assuming this detail came from a standard detail library, you would have to coordinate with what you have previously drawn in the floor plan. For example, the overall depth shown in the detail below is about 1'-5", and the depth drawn in plan is 2'-0" (see page 6-21). They would need to match. (You do not have to make any plan changes at this time.)

72. Create a new **Drafting View**:
    a. *Name:* **Fixed Student Desk**
    b. *Scale:* **1½" = 1'-0"**
    c. *See the next page for additional comments*

FIGURE 8-5.12 Fixed desk detail

73. Load the following detail component:
    a. Div 06-Wood and Plastic\062200-Millwork\Standard Millwork-Section.rfa
       i. Load the **1x2** and **1x4** sizes.

74. Develop the fixed student desk following these guidelines:
    a. All particle board and trim to be Detail Components.
    b. Tapered wood blocking to have **Wood 2** *Fill Pattern*.
    c. The curvy line pointing to the 1'-0″ dimension should be drawn like this:
       i. First add the "PLAM" note using a regular leader;
       ii. Use the **Detail Line** tool;
       iii. Select the **Spline** *Draw* option;
       iv. Set the *Line Style* to **Thin**;
       v. Sketch the curvy line starting at the corner of the leader.
    d. Add a horizontal Detail Line at the top of the sloped work surface so you have something to pick when adding the angle dimension.

As you can see, some of the *Detail Components* have odd line weights when placed side-by-side. Both the wood trim and particle board are in section so they should be the same line weight. You would have to edit the family to make this change, which will not be covered at this time.

Using the Keynotes Feature:

The content that ships with Revit, both 2D and 3D, has a default keynote value assigned to it. Keynotes are used to save room and make details look neater; it is a reference number rather than a full note, and then an adjacent legend lists what each number means. This legend is for all the details on a sheet. You will learn how this works next. You will make a copy of the *Fixed Student Desk*, add keynotes and then create a keynote legend.

75. Right-click on the **Fixed Student Desk** item in the *Project Browser*.

76. Select **Duplicate → Duplicated with Detailing**.

77. Rename the new view:
    Fixed Student Desk – Keynotes

78. **Erase all the notes**, but leave the dimensions.

79. Select **Annotate → Tag → Keynote** from the *Ribbon*.

FIGURE 8-5.13 Keynote added

80. With the *Keynote* tool active, click the ½″ particle board shown in Figure 8-5.13; you will see it highlight just before selecting it.

81. Click two additional points to define a leader and text location, just like placing text with a leader.

You now have a keyed note placed in your drawing. This only works on *Detail Components* (in drafting views) and not *Detail Lines* as they are too generic. Next, you will see where this keynote notation is coming from.

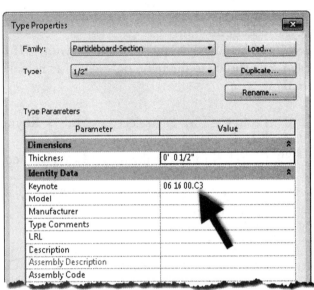

82. Select the ½″ particle board; go to its *Type Properties*.

Notice the *Keynote* value listed. This was defined in the *Family* you loaded.

Now you will view the *keynote text file* so you can see how a family could be changed to "mean" something else. You might change a family directly or create a duplicate *Type* first.

83. Click in the cell listing the *Keynote*.

84. Click the **small icon** that appears to the right.

You now see a rather extensive listing of keyed notes. Take a minute to explore the various sections and descriptions for the keynote references.

Notice the path listed at the top. This is the location of the text file being used for the keynotes. The path to this file is set via the *Keynoting Settings* icon located in the *Tag* panel expanded area on the *Annotate* tab.

85. After reviewing the keynote text file click **Cancel**.

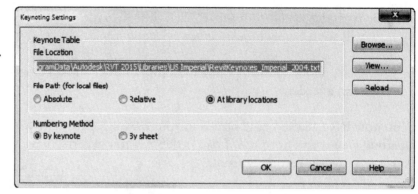

86. Click **OK** to close the *Type Properties* dialog.

The last thing to learn is how to create the **Keynote Legend**. This legend can be added to any sheet with keynotes. If the "By sheet" option is selected in the dialog box shown to the right, only keynotes actually found on that specific sheet will be listed.

87. From the *View* tab, select **Legend → Keynote Legend**.

88. Click **OK** to accept the name: **Keynote Legend**.

89. Click **OK** to accept the default properties and to create the legend.

You should now see the *Keynote Legend* shown to the below.

FYI: Make sure the numbering method is still set to By keynote in order to see all the keynotes at this time.

Later, in Chapter 12, you will learn how to place views on sheets.

Keynote Legend	
Key Value	Keynote Text
06 16 00.	1/2" Particleboard
06 16 00.	1" Particleboard
06 22 00.	1x2 Wood Trim
06 22 00.	1x4 Wood Trim
09 22 16.	3 5/8" Metal Stud Framing
09 22 16.	3 5/8" Metal Runner
09 29 00.	5/8" Gypsum Wallboard

90. Add the remaining keynotes and then **Save**.

Finally, you can create elevations and sections that reference a drafting view rather than a true view of the model. This is another one of those places where you are breaking the intelligence of Revit's drawing sheet and number coordination.

To do this, you select the *Elevation* or *Section* tool, and rather than picking points in the drawing right away, you select a view that already exists in the project from the *Options Bar*. Even though you have not placed any roof drains, you could switch to the **Roof** plan view and add a section mark that references the roof drain detail.

The following steps do not need to be performed at this time:

- Switch to the **Roof** floor plan view.

- Select the **Section** tool on the *View* tab.

- On the *Ribbon/Options Bar* settings (Figure 8-5.14):

   a. *Type Selector:*   **Detail View: Detail**

   b. *Reference other view:*   **check**

   c. *Reference other view drop-down list:* **Typical Roof Drain Detail**

FIGURE 8-5.14 Placing a section that references the roof drain detail

- Pick two points, roughly as shown in the image to the right.

Try double-clicking on the blue bubble head; it should bring you to the roof drain detail. Once the detail is placed on a sheet, the bubble head will be automatically filled out!

   13. Save as **8-5.rvt**.

Self-Exam:

The following questions can be used as a way to check your knowledge of this lesson. The answers can be found at the bottom of this page.

1. The controls for the section tag (when selected) are similar to the controls for the elevation tag. (T/F)

2. In large-scale <u>elevations</u> (and areas elevated within a section), Revit displays the masonry coursing. (T/F)

3. In large-scale <u>sections</u> (i.e., wall sections), Revit displays the masonry coursing in addition to the material hatching. (T/F)

4. The "Crop Region" is represented by a black rectangle in the section view. (T/F)

5. Use the _____ tool to reference a larger section off a building section.

Review Questions:

The following questions may be assigned by your instructor as a way to assess your knowledge of this section. Your instructor has the answers to the review questions.

1. The visibility of the crop region can be controlled. (T/F)

2. It's not possible to draw a leader (line with arrow) without placing text. (T/F)

3. When a section tag is added to a view, all the other related views automatically get a section tag added to it. (T/F)

4. It is possible to modify objects (like doors, windows and ceilings) in section views. (T/F)

5. You cannot adjust the "depth of view" using the crop region. (T/F)

6. What is the first thing you should do after placing a section tag?

    _____

7. If the text appears to be excessively large in a section view, the view's

    _____ _____ is probably set incorrectly.

8. The abbreviation M.O. stands for _____ _____.

9. Describe what happens when you double-click on the section bubble:

    _____ .

10. Revit provides _____ different leader options within the text command.

Lesson 9
Office Building: INTERIOR DESIGN:

This lesson explores the various "features," if you will, of a floor plan, such as toilet room layouts (i.e., fixtures and partitions), cabinets and casework (e.g., reception counters and custom cabinets). Additionally, you will look at placing furniture into your project.

Exercise 9-1:
Toilet Room Layouts

Toilet room layouts involve placing water closets (toilets), toilet partitions and sinks. These rooms have many code issues related primarily to handicapped accessibility. These codes vary from state to state (and even city to city).

You will start this exercise by loading several components to be placed into your project.

1. Open ex8-5.rvt and **Save As ex9-1.rvt**.

2. Select **Load Family** from the *Insert* tab and load the following items into the current project:

> **Local Files** *(i.e., on your hard drive)*
> a. Plumbing\Architectural\Fixtures\Water Closet\
> **Toilet-Comercial-Wall-3D.rfa**
> b. Plumbing Fixtures\Architectural\Fixtures\Urinals**Urinal-Wall-3D**

> **Online Files** *(i.e., Seek.autodesk.com via the Insert tab)*
> c. **Sink-Wall-Rectangular**
> d. **Grab Bar-3D**
> e. **Toilet Stall-Accessible-Front-Braced-3D**
> f. **Toilet Stall-Braced-3D**
> g. **Urinal Screen-3D**

These files represent various families that will be used to design the toilet room. It is possible to create custom families for non-typical conditions.

Figure 9-1.1 shows an example of the various families available for Toilet Stalls on Autodesk Revit's web site.

FIGURE 9-1.1 Toilet stalls online

3. Switch to **Level 1** view.

The next step will be to place the toilet stalls.

4. Using the **Component** tool, pick **Toilet Stall-Accessible-Front-Braced-3D: 60″ x 60″ Clear** from the *Type Selector*.

5. Zoom in to the toilet rooms (North of the elevator).

6. **Place** the toilet stall as shown and then move into place using the **Move** tool and your snaps or the *Align* tool (Figure 9-1.2).

Once you move the toilet stall North, you will have your first stall in place.

Next, you will place two standard size toilet stalls.

7. Place two toilet stalls; **Toilet Stall-Braced-3D: 36″ x 60″ Clear** as shown in Figure 9-1.3.

FIGURE 9-1.2 Accessible Toilet stall

As with most projects, you will need to modify the model as you develop the design. In this case we notice that toilets that are back-to-back and stacked on each floor will require a thicker wall to accommodate the fixture brackets (W.C.'s are not hung on the wall by light gauge metal studs) and larger piping. You will make this adjustment next.

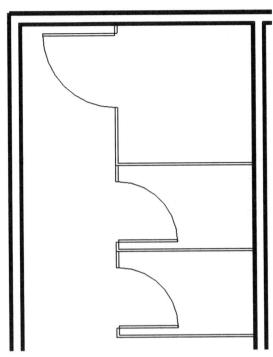

FIGURE 9-1.3 Toilet stalls placed

8. Select the middle wall and the West wall and **Move** them **6″** to the West.

9. **Move** the far East wall (of the two toilet rooms) **6″** to the east.

10. Add an additional **4⅞″** gyp. bd. wall as shown in **Figure 9-1.4**.

TIP: Make sure wall height and base offset are correct.

11. Modify the North wall of the elevator shaft to have furring and gyp. bd. on the toilet room side.

TIP: Use the wall type you created for the stair shafts.

12. Add the additional components as shown in **Figure 9-1.4**.

FIGURE 9-1.4 Toilet room layout

As mentioned previously, building codes vary by location. The toilets in the accessible stall area are usually mounted higher than the typical fixtures. When a room has more than one urinal, one is usually required to be mounted lower for accessibility. Another example is that Minnesota requires a separate vertical grab bar above the horizontal grab bar on the wall next to the toilet.

You will now copy the revised walls and toilet room layout to the other levels. The elevator shaft extends through each floor, so you will not have to copy that wall. Looking at the upper levels you can see the revised elevator shaft wall and the old wall layout (Figure 9-1.5). It will be easier to delete the stud walls rather than modify the existing walls.

13. Delete the walls, per **Figure 9-1.6**, for Levels 2 and 3.

14. **Copy** the walls and toilet room layout (for Level 1) to the clipboard and **Paste Aligned** to Levels 2 and 3.

FIGURE 9-1.5 Walls on upper levels   FIGURE 9-1.6 Walls deleted

Interior Elevation View:

Next, you will set up an interior elevation view for the Men's Toilet Room. You will also add a mirror above the sinks in elevation view.

15. Switch to **Level 1** and place an interior **Elevation** tag looking towards the west wall (wall with fixtures on it); see Figure 9-1.7.

16. Rename the new view to: **Men's Toilet – Typical** in the *Project Browser*.

17. Switch to the new view. Adjust the *Crop Region* so the concrete slab is not visible. Your view should look like Figure 9-1.8.

You may see the building section reference as shown in Figure 9-1.8. This would not typically be shown in an interior elevation view, especially because it does not intersect the elevation view. You will remove the reference in the next step. You cannot simply delete it, because that will remove it from all views and delete the section.

FIGURE 9-1.7 Elevation tag added

18. If you see the building section tag, click on the section reference to select it and then right-click and pick **Hide in View → Elements** from the pop-up menu (Figure 9-1.9).

FIGURE 9-1.8 Men's Toilet – Typical view

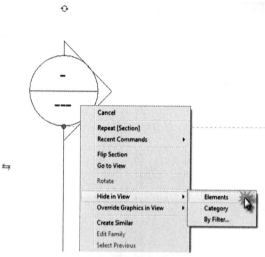

FIGURE 9-1.9 Hide annotation

19. Load component *Specialty Equipment\ Toilet Room Specialties* **Mirror.rfa** from the Online Revit library.

20. While in the interior elevation view, place a **72″ x 48″ Mirror** on the wall above the sinks. Use the *Align* tool to align the mirror with the middle sink (Figure 9-1.10).

21. Add the notes and dimensions shown in Figure 9-1.10. Adjust the heights and locations of the fixtures/components as required.

FIGURE 9-1.10 Updated interior elevation

FYI: *Keep in mind that many of the symbols that come with Revit (or any program for that matter) are not necessarily drawn or reviewed by an architect. The point is that the default values, such as mounting heights, may not meet ADA, national, state or local codes. Items such as the mirror have a maximum height off the floor to the reflective surface that Revit's standard components may not comply with. However, as you apply local codes to these families, you can reuse them in the future.*

Adjusting the Reflected Ceiling Plan:

Because you added a wall in the East toilet room, the definition of the room that the reflected ceiling plan uses is incorrect. You will adjust that next. You will have similar problems on Levels 2 and 3 if you added ceilings there, because you deleted walls and then pasted new walls.

22. Switch to **Level 1 RCP** (Figure 9-1.11).

23. Hide the Interior Elevation tag from this view (via right-click and Hide in View).

24. Delete the ceiling in the Men's Toilet room.

25. Place a new ceiling to fit within the room.

26. Select the ceiling grid in the atrium, and then pick **Edit Boundary** to adjust the reference lines for the perimeter of the ceiling grid in the atrium area (Figure 9-1.12).

FYI: You could have used this method for Steps 24/25 as well.

27. Correct the ceilings on Levels 2 and 3.

28. **Save** your project as **ex9-1.rvt**.

FIGURE 9-1.11 Level 1 RCP   **FIGURE 9-1.12** Revised Level 1 RCP

Exercise 9-2:
Cabinets

In this exercise you will look at adding cabinets and casework to your project. As usual, Revit provides several families to be placed into the project.

Placing Cabinets:

You will add base and wall cabinets in a break room on Level 1.

1. Open ex9-1.rvt and **Save As ex9-2.rvt**.

2. Switch to **Level 1** view and zoom into the area shown in **Figure 9-2.1**.

FIGURE 9-2.1 Level 1 – north-east corner

3. *Load* the following components into the project
   (*all local files – folder listed after filename*):

   a. **Counter Top w Sink Hole** (Casework\Counter Tops)

   b. **Base Cabinet-Double Door Sink Unit** (Casework\Base Cabinets)

   c. **Base Cabinet-Single Door** (Casework\Base Cabinets)

   d. **Base Cabinet-4 Drawers** (Casework\Base Cabinets)

   e. **Upper Cabinet-Double Door-Wall** (Casework\Wall Cabinets)

   f. **Sink Kitchen-Single** (*Plumbing\Architectural\Fixtures folder*)

   g. **Refrigerator** (*Specialty Equipment\Domestic folder*)

You are now ready to place the cabinets into your floor plan.

FYI: *As with other components (i.e., doors and windows), Revit loads several types to represent the most valuable/ useful sizes available. Cabinets typically come in 3″ increments with different types (i.e., single or double door unit) having maximum and minimum sizes.*

4. With the *Component* tool selected, pick *Base Cabinet-4 Drawers:* **24″** from the *Element Type Selector.*

5. Place the cabinet as shown in **Figure 9-2.2**.

TIP: *The control arrows are on the front side of the cabinet; the cursor is on the back. Press the spacebar to rotate while placing (i.e., before picking).*

6. Place the other two base cabinets as shown in **Figure 9-2.3**, with a 24″ single door base cabinet in the middle and a 48″ sink base to the north end.

FIGURE 9-2.2 First cabinet placed

FIGURE 9-2.3 Three base cabinets placed

Add the remaining items as shown in Figure 9-2.4; be sure to use snaps.
(E.g., place sink to one side, use move and snap to a mid-point of the sink bowl, and then to the mid-point of the same line representing the hole in the countertop).

Elevation Ref. – *Step #8*

Refrigerator: 35"x32" RH

Sink Kitchen-Single : 30" x 21"

Countertop : 24" Depth

Two upper cabinets : 48"

FIGURE 9-2.4 Completed plan view

7. Add an interior elevation tag to setup the interior elevation view. (Figure 9-2.4)

8. Rename the new elevation view to **Break Room (east)**.

9. Switch to the new view, **Break Room (east)**.

10. Adjust the **Crop Region** so the slab on grade is not visible.

11. Your view should look like **Figure 9-2.5**.

FIGURE 9-2.5 Interior elevation

You will add notes and dimensions to the elevation. You can also add 2D line work to the elevation.

12. Set the *View Scale* to **½″ = 1′-0″**.

13. Add the notes and dimensions per **Figure 9-2.6**.

FIGURE 9-2.6 Interior elevation with annotations

14. Use the **Model Line** tool, on the *Architecture* tab, to draw the line on the wall behind the refrigerator, indicating the vinyl base.

When you select the **Model Line** tool, Revit will ask you what plane you want to draw on (Figure 9-2.7). This will allow Revit to restrict all your line work to a particular plane. Otherwise you would not know exactly at what depth the lines would be drawn on.

15. Select **Pick a Plane** (Figure 9-2.7) and then pick the wall in the elevation view (use the TAB key and make sure the tool tip lists the wall before picking the plane).

> *TIP: If you are prompted to switch to a different view, you selected the wrong plane. Click cancel and try again.*

FIGURE 9-2.7 Work Plane prompt

16. Draw the line, snap to the endpoint of the base cabinet toe kick.

> *FYI: The main difference between the Model Line tool on the Architecture tab and the Detail Line tool on the Annotate tab is this: any line work drawn with the Model Line tool will show up on other views which see that surface. On the other hand, any line work drawn with the Detail Line tool will only show up in the view in which they were created. So in this example, you may want to draw the lines using the Detail Line tool so the base does not show up in building and wall sections. Do not change this at this time however.*

17. Select the line and in the *Type Selector*, change the *Line Style* to **Thin Lines**.

18. **Save** your project as **ex9-2.rvt**.

Exercise 9-3:
Furniture

This lesson will cover the steps required to lay out office furniture. The processes are identical to those previously covered for toilets and cabinets. Various manufacturers are beginning to provide Revit content; for example take a look at www.hayworth.com.

Loading the Necessary Families:

1. Open ex9-2.rvt and **Save As ex9-3.rvt**.

2. Select the **Component** tool and load the following items into the current project:

> <u>**Local Files**</u> *(i.e., on your hard drive)*
> a. **Work Station Cubicle.rfa** (Furniture System)
> b. **Work Station Desktops** (Furniture System)
> c. **Sofa-Pensi** (Furniture\Seating)
> d. **Chair-Breuer** (Furniture\Seating)
> e. **Chair-Executive** (Furniture\Seating)
> f. **Chair-Task Arms** (Furniture\Seating)
> g. **Table-Round** (Furniture\Table)
>
> <u>**Online Files**</u> *(i.e., Seek.autodesk.com)*
> h. **Copier-Floor**

These files represent various families that will be used to design the offices.

TIP:
You can set the View mode for the Open dialog box (which is displayed when you click Load Family). One option is Thumbnail mode; this displays a small thumbnail image for each file in the current folder. This makes it easier to see the many symbols and drawings that are available for insertion. You can make the preview images larger by holding down the Ctrl key and then spinning the wheel on your mouse.

View set to List mode

View set to Thumbnail mode

Designing the Office Furniture Layout:

3. Switch to the **Level 3** view.

4. Place the furniture as shown in Figure 9-3.1.

FIGURE 9-3.1 Level 3 – furniture layout

TIP: Use snaps to assure accuracy; use rotate and mirror as required.

The cubicles in the open office area should be centered in the North-South direction. The cubicle partitions should overlap so only one partition is visible. The items not labeled in Figure 9-3.1 should be compared to the families listed in step 2; it will be obvious as to what the items are.

3D View of Office Layout:

Next you will look at a 3D view of your office area. This involves adjusting the visibility of the roof and skylights.

5. Switch to the *Default* **3D** view.

6. Make sure nothing is selected and the *Properties Palette* is open.

7. Click **Edit** next to the *Visibility/Graphic Override* parameter.

8. Uncheck the *Roof* category and click **OK**.

The roof should not be visible now. However, you should still see the skylights floating in space. You will make those disappear next.

9. Select one of the skylights floating above the office area.

10. Click the **Temporary Hide/Isolate** from the *View Control Bar*.

You should see the menu shown in **Figure 9-3.2** show up next to the *Temporary Hide/Isolate* icon. This allows you to isolate an object (so it's the only thing on the screen) or hide it (so the object is temporarily not visible).

FIGURE 9-3.2 Hide/Isolate popup menu

11. Click **Hide Category** in the menu. (Figure 9-3.2)

    FYI: This makes all the skylights hide; you could leave it at "Hide Element" and select each skylight.

12. Adjust your 3D view to look similar to **Figure 9-3.3** by clicking and dragging your mouse on the *ViewCube*.

You will now restore the original visibility settings for the 3D view.

13. Click the *Hide/Isolate* icon and then select **Reset Temporary Hide/Isolate** from the popup up menu.

   NOTE: *The Temporary Hide/Isolate feature is just meant to be a temporary control of element visibility while you are working on the model. If you want permanent results, you can click the "Apply Hide/Isolate to View" option. Also, to the right of the Hide/Isolate icon is the Reveal Hidden Elements icon (the light bulb icon), which will clearly show any elements that have been previously hidden.*

14. Reset the 3D view's visibility settings so the roof is visible.

15. **Save** your project as **ex9-3.rvt**.

   Notice the furniture and toilet rooms are represented in 3D.

FIGURE 9-3.3 3D view with roof not visible

Online Content:

A few locations on the internet provide additional content for use in Revit. Some are free and some are not. Hopefully more product manufacturers will start providing content based on the products they make; making it easier for people to include that manufacturer's product in their project (both the virtual and real projects).

You have already spent a little time looking at Revit's online content library (Seek.autodesk.com). You should spend some more time there so you know what is generally available. This will help you to reduce duplicated effort.

The following sites also contain content that can be downloaded:
- www.revitcity.com
- Seek.autodesk.com
- revit.autodesk.com/library/html (old Revit content library)
- www.turbosquid.com/revit-market

You should occasionally search the internet to see if additional content becomes available. You can do an internet search for "revit content", make sure to include the quotation marks. The rendering content, such as that offered by www.archvision.com, will be covered in Chapter 11.

Exercise 9-4:
Adding Guardrails

This lesson will cover the steps required to lay out guardrails. The steps are similar to drawing walls; you select your style and draw its path.

Adding a Guardrail to the Atrium:

1. Open ex9-3.rvt and **Save As ex9-4.rvt**.

2. Switch to **Level 2** view.

3. Select **Architecture → Circulation → Railing → Sketch Path**.

4. **Zoom** into the Atrium area (South of the elevator).

At this point you will draw a line representing the path of the guardrail. The railing is offset to one side of the line, similar to walls. However, you do not have the *Location Line* option as you do with the *Wall* tool, so you have to draw the railing in a certain direction to get the railing to be on the floor and not hovering in space just beyond the floor edge.

5. Draw a line along the edge of the floor as shown in **Figure 9-4.1**.

   TIP: Select Chain from the Options Bar to draw the railing with fewer picks.

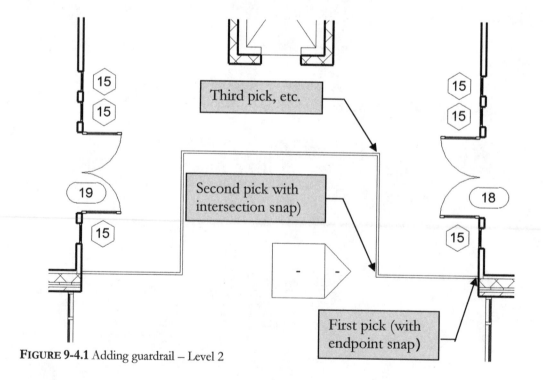

FIGURE 9-4.1 Adding guardrail – Level 2

6. Click the **green check mark** on the *Ribbon* to finish the Railing tool.

The railing has now been drawn. In the next step you will switch to a 3D view and see how to quickly change the railing style. This will also involve changing the height of the railing. Most building codes require the railing height be 42″ when the drop to the adjacent surface is more than 30″; this is called a guardrail.

7. Switch to the *Default* **3D** view.

8. Zoom into the railing shown on Level 2, looking at it through the curtain wall. (Notice the railing style – Figure 9-4.2.)

FIGURE 9-4.2 Added railing – 3D view

9. Select the railing. You may have to use the *Tab* key to cycle through the various selection options.

10. With the railing selected, select the various railing types available in the *Type Selector* on the *Ribbon*. When finished make sure **Railing: Guardrail – Pipe** is selected. (Figure 9-4.3)

FIGURE 9-4.3 Options for selected railing

Your railing should now look like Figure 9-4.4. Notice that a handrail was added to the railing. You should also notice that the handrail is on the wrong side of the guardrail. You will adjust that next.

FIGURE 9-4.4 Railing with new style

11. Switch to the **Level 2** plan view and select the railing.

12. Click on the **Control Arrows** to flip the railing orientation. (See the *FYI* below for additional information.)

13. You can switch back to the **3D view** to see the change.

14. Finally, from the Level 2 plan view, **Copy** the railing to the clipboard and **Paste** it into the Level 3 view.

15. **Save** your project as **ex9-4.rvt**.

FYI: The last modification, using the control arrows, flipped the railing about the sketch lines, so the railing is now hanging out in space. You can fix this by selecting the railing, clicking "edit path" on the Ribbon, and then moving the sketch lines in to compensate.

Make sure to examine the railing sample file available on Autodesk Seek; search for **Railing Samples**. You can download this file (railing samples.rvt), open it, select a railing and view its properties to see how it works.

FIGURE 9-4.5
Railing sample file downloaded
from Revit's website

You can Copy/Paste a railing style from this drawing into one of your project files. Then you select your railing and pick the newly imported one from the *Type Selector*. This process was done to achieve the image below (Figure 9-4.6). Notice the glass railing with brackets.

FIGURE 9-4.6 Optional railing configuration

Self-Exam:

The following questions can be used as a way to check your knowledge of this lesson. The answers can be found at the bottom of this page.

1. The toilet room fixtures are preloaded in the template file. (T/F)

2. You do not need to be connected to the internet when loading content from the online web library. (T/F)

3. Revit content is not always in compliance with codes. (T/F)

4. You can draw 2D lines on the wall in an interior elevation view. (T/F)

5. Use the _____ tool to copy fixtures to other floors.

Review Questions:

The following questions may be assigned by your instructor as a way to assess your knowledge of this section. Your instructor has the answers to the review questions.

1. Revit provides several different styles of toilet stalls for placement. (T/F)

2. Most of the time Revit automatically updates the ceiling when walls are moved, but occasionally you have to manually make revisions. (T/F)

3. It is not possible to draw dimensions on an interior elevation view. (T/F)

4. Cabinets typically come in 6″ increments. (T/F)

5. Base cabinets automatically have a countertop on them. (T/F)

6. What can you adjust so the concrete slab does not show in section?

   _____

7. How does Revit determine where to place 2D lines in an elevation view (based on the example in this lesson)?

   _____

8. What is the current size of your Revit Project? _____

9. What should you use to assure accuracy when placing furniture?

   _____

10. You use the _____ tool to make various components temporarily invisible.

Lesson 10
Office Building: SCHEDULES:

You will continue to learn the powerful features available in Revit. This includes the ability to create parametric schedules; you can delete a door number on a schedule and Revit will delete the corresponding door from the plan.

Exercise 10-1:
Room and Door Tags

This exercise will look at adding room tags and door tags to your plans. As you insert doors, Revit adds tags to them automatically. However, if you copy or mirror a door you can lose the tag and have to add it.

Adding Room Tags:

Room

You will add a Room Tag to each room on your Level 1 floor plan.

1. Select **Architecture → Room & Area → Room**.

FIGURE 10-1.1 Room tag – Level 1

TIP: Change the height of the Room element in the stairs to go up to Level 3 + 10'-0" via the Properties Palette – and then just "tag" the room at Levels 2 and 3 rather than adding new room objects.

Placing a *Room/Room Tag* is similar to placing a ceiling in the reflected ceiling plan; as you move your cursor over a room, the room (perimeter) highlights. When the room you want to place a *Room* element in is highlighted, you click to place it.

2. Click your cursor within the atrium area to place a **Room**, which will also automatically place a room tag (Figure 10-1.1).

By default, Revit will simply label the space "Room" and number it "1". You will change these to something different.

3. Press **Esc** or select **Modify** to cancel the *Room* command.

4. Click on the *Room Tag* you just placed to select it.

5. Now click on the room name text to change it; enter **Atrium**.

6. Now click on the room number to change it; enter **100**.

7. Add *Room Tags* (using the **Room** tool) for each room on Level 1, incrementing each room number by 1 (Figure 10-1.1).

The stair shafts typically are numbered Stair #1, Stair #2, etc. The same number is then placed on each level. This is because stair shafts are really one tall room and the finishes would apply to the entire shaft, not each floor. When you try to place a tag with the same name and number, Revit will warn you; see the tip on the previous page to avoid this problem.

8. Add Room/Tags to Levels 2 and 3. The numbering for Level 2 should start with 200 and Level 3 should start with 300. (For Level 2, see Figure 10-1.2; Level 3, see Figure 10-1.3.)

FIGURE 10-1.2 Level 2 – Room tags

FIGURE 10-1.3 Level 3 – Room tags

Adding Door Tags:

Next you will add Door Tags to any doors that are missing them. Additionally, you will adjust the door numbers to correspond to the room numbers.

Revit numbers the doors in the order they are placed into the drawing. This would make it difficult to locate a door by its door number if door number 1 was on Level 1 and door number 2 was on Level 3, etc. Typically, a door number is the same as the room that the door swings into. For example, if a door swung into an office numbered 304, the door number would also be 304. If the office had two doors into it, the doors would be numbered 304A and 304B.

9. Switch to **Level 1** view.

10. Select **Annotate → Tag → Tag by Category** button on the *Ribbon* (Figure 10-1.4).

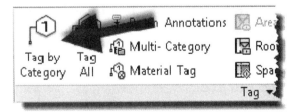

Figure 10-1.4 Annotate tab, Tag panel

Notice as you move your cursor around the screen Revit displays a tag, for any elements that can have tags, when the cursor is over it. Revit actually places a tag when you click the mouse.

11. **Uncheck** the **Leader** option on the *Options Bar.*

12. Place a door tag for each door that does not have a tag, do this for each level.

13. Renumber all the door tags to correspond to the room they open into; do this for each level. (Figure 10-1.5)

> *REMEMBER: Click Modify, select the Tag and then click on the number to edit it.*

FIGURE 10-1.5 Level 1 – door tags (scale changed to make tags larger on this page)

TIP: TAG ALL...
This tool allows you to quickly tag all the elements of a selected type (e.g., doors) at one time. After selecting the tool, you select the type of element from a list and specify whether or not you want a leader. When you click OK, Revit tags all the untagged doors in that view.

14. **Save** your project as **ex10-1.rvt**.

Exercise 10-2:
Generate a Door Schedule

This exercise will look at creating a door schedule based on the information currently available in the building model (i.e., the tags).

Create a Door Schedule View:

A door schedule is simply another view of the building model. However, this view displays numerical data rather than graphical data. Just like a graphical view, if you change the view it changes all the other related views. For example, if you delete a door number from the schedule, the door is deleted from the plans and elevations.

1. Open ex10-1.rvt and **Save As ex10-2.rvt**.

2. Select **View → Create → Schedule/Quantities** button from the *Ribbon*.

3. Select **Doors** under *Category*, Make sure *Phase* is set to **New Construction** and then click **OK** (Figure 10-2.1).

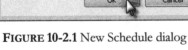

FIGURE 10-2.1 New Schedule dialog

You should now be in the *Schedule Properties* dialog where you specify what information is displayed in the schedule, how it is sorted and the text format.

4. On the **Fields** tab, add the information you want displayed in the schedule. Select the following (Figure 10-2.2):

    a. Mark

    *TIP: Click the **Add** → button each time.*

    b. Width
    c. Height
    d. Frame Material
    e. Frame Type
    f. Fire Rating

As noted in the dialog, the fields added to the list on the right are in the order they will be in the schedule view. Use the *Move Up* and *Move Down* buttons to adjust the order.

5. On the **Sorting/Grouping** tab, set the schedule to be sorted by the Mark (i.e., door number) in ascending order (Figure 10-2.3).

Figure 10-2.2 Schedule Properties – Fields

*TIP: **The Formatting and Appearance tabs** allow you to adjust how the schedule looks. The formatting is not displayed until the schedule is placed on a plot sheet. Also, you cannot print a schedule unless it is on a sheet. Only views and sheets can be printed – not schedules or legends.*

FIGURE 10-2.3 Schedule Properties – Sorting

6. Click the **OK** button to generate the schedule view.

You should now have a schedule similar to Figure 10-2.4.

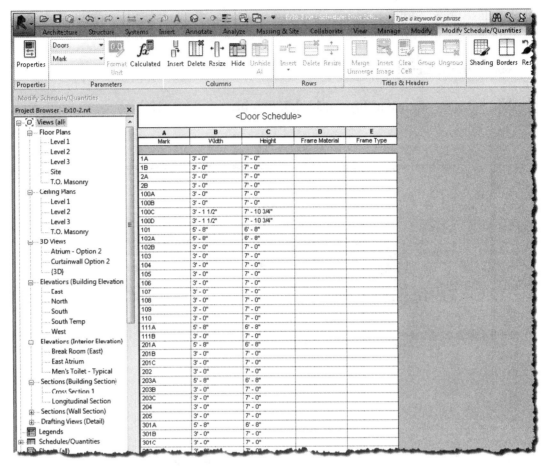

FIGURE 10-2.4 Door schedule view

*TIP: You can select **Application Menu → Export → Reports → Schedule** to create a text file (*.txt) that can be used in other programs such as MS Excel.*

The example below is from a real world Revit project, notice the detailed header information.

DOOR AND FRAME SCHEDULE												
DOOR NUMBER	DOOR				FRAME		DETAIL				FIRE RATING	HDWR GROUP	
	WIDTH	HEIGHT	MATL	TYPE	MATL	TYPE	HEAD	JAMB	SILL	GLAZING			
1000A	3' - 8"	7' - 2"	WD		HM		11/A8.01	11/A8.01					
1046	3' - 0"	7' - 2"	WD	D10	HM	F10	11/A8.01	11/A8.01 SIM				34	
1047A	6' - 0"	7' - 10"	ALUM	D15	ALUM	SF4	6/A8.01	6/A8.01	1/A8.01 SIM	1" INSUL		2	CARD READER N. LEAF
1047B	6' - 0"	7' - 2"	WD	D10	HM	F13	12/A8.01	11/A8.01 SIM			60 MIN	85	MAG HOLD OPENS
1050	3' - 0"	7' - 2"	WD	D10	HM	F21	8/A8.01	11/A8.01		1/4" TEMP		33	
1051	3' - 0"	7' - 2"	WD	D10	HM	F21	8/A8.01	11/A8.01		1/4" TEMP		33	
1052	3' - 0"	7' - 2"	WD	D10	HM	F21	8/A8.01	11/A8.01		1/4" TEMP		33	
1053	3' - 0"	7' - 2"	WD	D10	HM	F21	8/A8.01	11/A8.01		1/4" TEMP		33	
1054A	3' - 0"	7' - 2"	WD	D10	HM	F10	8/A8.01	11/A8.01		1/4" TEMP	-	34	
1054B	3' - 0"	7' - 2"	WD	D10	HM	F21	8/A8.01	11/A8.01		1/4" TEMP	-	33	
1055	3' - 0"	7' - 2"	WD	D10	HM	F21	8/A8.01	11/A8.01		1/4" TEMP	-	33	
1056A	3' - 0"	7' - 2"	WD	D10	HM	F10	9/A8.01	9/A8.01			20 MIN	33	
1056B	3' - 0"	7' - 2"	WD	D10	HM	F10	11/A8.01	11/A8.01			20 MIN	34	
1056C	3' - 0"	7' - 2"	WD	D10	HM	F10	20/A8.01	20/A8.01			20 MIN	33	
1057A	3' - 0"	7' - 2"	WD	D10	HM	F10	8/A8.01	11/A8.01			20 MIN	34	
1057B	3' - 0"	7' - 2"	WD	D10	HM	F30	9/A8.01	9/A8.01		1/4" TEMP	20 MIN	33	
1058A	3' - 0"	7' - 2"	WD	D10	HM	F10	9/A8.01	9/A8.01			-	33	

Image courtesy LHB (www.LHBcorp.com)

Next you will see how adding a door to the plan automatically updates the door schedule. Likewise, deleting a door number from the schedule deletes the door from the plan.

7. Switch to the **Level 1** view.

8. Add a door as shown in **Figure 10-2.5**; number the door **111C**.

FIGURE 10-2.5 Level 1 – door added

9. Switch to the **Door Schedule** view, under Schedules/Quantities in the *Project Browser*. Notice door 111C was added (Figure 10-2.6).

109	3' - 0"	7' - 0"
110	3' - 0"	7' - 0"
111A	6' - 0"	7' - 0"
111B	3' - 0"	7' - 0"
111C	3' - 0"	7' - 0"
201A	6' - 0"	7' - 0"
201B	3' - 0"	7' - 0"

FIGURE 10-2.6 Updated door schedule

Next you will delete door 111C from the door schedule view.

10. Click in the cell with the number **111C**.

11. Now click the **Delete** button from the *Ribbon* (Figure 10-2.7).

FIGURE 10-2.7
Ribbon for the door schedule view

You will get an alert. Revit is telling you that the actual door will be deleted from the project model (Figure 10-2.8).

12. Click **OK** to delete the door (Figure 10-2.8).

> **Revit**
>
> This will delete 1 instance(s).
>
> Please note that you are not just removing rows from the schedule, but also deleting the associated elements and geometry from the project.
>
> [OK] [Cancel]

FIGURE 10-2.8 Revit alert message

13. Switch back to the **Level 1** view and notice that door 111C and its tag have been deleted from the project model.

14. **Save** your project as **ex10-3.rvt**.

TIP: You can also change the door number in the schedule and even the size; however, changing the size actually changes the door family which affects all the doors of that type.

The image below shows a real world Revit project with several doors; notice the door numbers match the room numbers. Also, the shaded walls are existing (Revit can manage phases very well).

Image courtesy LHB (www.LHBcorp.com)

Exercise 10-3:
Generate a Room Finish Schedule

In this exercise you will create a room finish schedule. The process is similar to the previous exercise. You will also create a color-coded plan based on information associated with the *Room* element.

Create a Room Finish Schedule:

1. Open ex10-2.rvt and **Save As ex10-3.rvt**.

2. Select **View → Create → Schedule/Quantities** button from the *Ribbon*.

3. Select **Room** under *Category* and then click **OK** (Figure 10-3.1).

4. In the **Fields** tab of the *Schedule Properties* dialog, add the following fields to be scheduled (Figure 10-3.2):

    a. Number
    b. Name
    c. Base Finish
    d. Floor Finish
    e. Wall Finish
    f. Ceiling Finish
    g. Area

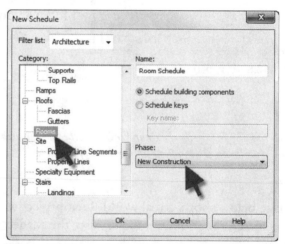

FIGURE 10-3.1 New Schedule dialog

Area is not typically listed on a room finish schedule. However, you will add it to your schedule to see the various options Revit allows.

5. On the **Sorting/Grouping** tab set the schedule to be sorted by the **Number** field.

6. On the **Appearance** tab, select ¼" **Arial** for the *Title Text* (Figure 10-3.3).

7. Select **OK** to generate the **Room Schedule**.

FIGURE 10-3.2
Schedule Properties – Fields

FIGURE 10-3.3
Schedule Properties – Appearance

Place cursor here to resize the column

<Room Schedule>

A	B	C	D	E	F	G
Number	Name	Base Finish	Floor Finish	Wall Finish	Ceiling Finish	Area
#1	Stair					168 SF
#2	Stair					168 SF
100	Atrium					1805 SF
101	RECEPTION &					313 SF
102	OPEN OFFICE					1977 SF
103	CONFERENCE					204 SF
104	WORK ROOM					437 SF
105	WOMENS					161 SF
106	MENS					161 SF
107	MECH / ELEC R					131 SF
108	BREAK ROOM					389 SF
109	OFFICE					104 SF
110	OFFICE					143 SF
111	OPEN OFFICE					2309 SF
200	Atrium					1759 SF
201	Open Office					3000 SF
202	TELECOMM					131 SF
203	Open Office					3000 SF
204	Womens					161 SF
205	Mens					161 SF
300	Atrium					1759 SF
301	Open Office					1870 SF
302	Room					240 SF
303	Room					243 SF
304	Office					232 SF
305	Office					229 SF
306	Office					125 SF
307	Room					131 SF
308	Misc / Storage					125 SF
309	Office					229 SF
310	Office					232 SF
311	Open Office					1870 SF
312	Office					243 SF
313	Office					240 SF
314	Room					161 SF
315	Room					161 SF

FIGURE 10-3.4 Room Schedule view

Your schedule should look similar to the one to the left. (Figure 10-3.4)

8. Resize the *Name* column so all the room names are visible. Place the cursor between the *Name* and *Base Finish* and drag to the right until all the names are visible. (Figure 10-3.4)

The formatting (i.e., Bold header text) will not show up until the schedule is placed on a plot sheet.

Modifying and Populating a Room Schedule:

Like the door schedule, the room schedule is a tabular view of the building model. So you can change the room name or number on the schedule or in the plans.

9. In the **Room Schedule** view, change the name for room **307** (this should be the room directly north of the toilet rooms) to **MECH/ELEC RM**.

    TIP: Click on the current room name and then click on the down-arrow that appears. This gives you a list of all the existing names in the current schedule; otherwise you can type a new name.

10. Switch to the **Level 3** view to see the updated room tag.

You can quickly enter finish information to several rooms at one time. You will do this next.

11. In the Level 3 plan view, select the *Rooms* (not the room tags) for all private offices – 9 total (Figure 10-3.5).

    REMEMBER: Hold the Ctrl key down to select multiple elements.

    TIP: Move the cursor near the room tag but not over it to select the room – the large "X" will appear when the Room is selectable (see image below).

FIGURE 10-3.5 Level 3 – selected room

12. Next you will make changes in the *Properties Palette*, type *PP* to open it if needed.

The *Parameters* listed here are the same as the *Fields* available for display in the room schedule. When more than one tag is displayed and a parameter is not the same (e.g., different names), that value field is left blank. Otherwise, the values are displayed for the selected *Room* element. Next you will enter values for the finishes.

13. If the *Name* field is blank enter **OFFICE**, so the nine rooms are labeled office.

14. Enter the following for the finishes (Figure 10-3.6):

    a. *Base Finish:*   **Wood**
    b. *Ceiling Finish:*   **ACT 1** *(ACT = acoustic ceiling tile)*
    c. *Wall Finish:*   **VWC 1** *(VWC = vinyl wall covering)*
    d. *Floor Finish:*   **Carpet 1**

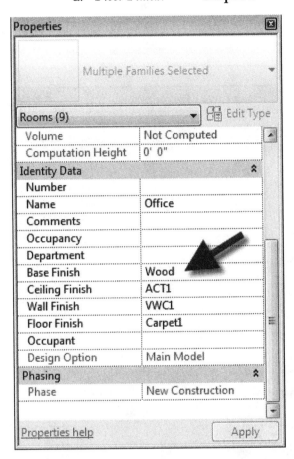

15. Click **Apply**.

16. Switch back to the **Room Schedule** view to see the automatic updates (Figure 10-3.7).

You can also enter data directly into the Room Schedule view.

17. Enter the following data for the Men's and Women's toilet rooms:

    a. *Base:*   **COVED CT**
    b. *Ceiling:*   **Gyp. Bd.**
    c. *Wall:*   **CT**
    d. *Floor:*   **CT**

Hopefully, in the near future, Revit will be able to enter the finishes based on the wall, floor and ceiling types previously created!

FIGURE 10-3.6 Element Properties – Room

TIP:
You can add fields and adjust formatting anytime by selecting one of the edit buttons in the Properties Palette. This gives you the same options that were available when you created the schedule.

204	WOMENS					161 SF
205	MENS					161 SF
300	Room					1786 SF
302	OFFICE	Wood	Carpet 1	VWC 1	ACT 1	229 SF
303	OFFICE	Wood	Carpet 1	VWC 1	ACT 1	232 SF
304	OPEN OFFICE					1896 SF
305	OFFICE	Wood	Carpet 1	VWC 1	ACT 1	232 SF
306	OFFICE	Wood	Carpet 1	VWC 1	ACT 1	229 SF
307	OFFICE	Wood	Carpet 1	VWC 1	ACT 1	125 SF
308	MECH / ELEC RM					98 SF
309	WOMENS					161 SF
310	MEN					161 SF
311	MISC. / STORAGE					125 SF
312	OFFICE	Wood	Carpet 1	VWC 1	ACT 1	229 SF
313	OFFICE	Wood	Carpet 1	VWC 1	ACT 1	232 SF
314	OPEN OFFICE					1896 SF
315	OFFICE	Wood	Carpet 1	VWC 1	ACT 1	232 SF
316	OFFICE	Wood	Carpet 1	VWC 1	ACT 1	229 SF
# 1	STAIR					168 SF

FIGURE 10-3.7 Partial Room Schedule with new data

Setting Up a Color-Coded Floor Plan:

With the *Rooms* in place you can quickly set up color-coded floor plans. These are plans that indicate (with color) which rooms are Offices, Circulation, Public, etc., based on the room name in our example.

18. Switch to **Level 3** view.

19. Select **Annotate** → **Color Fill** → **Color Fill Legend**.

20. Click just below the floor plan on the right side.

21. Select **Name** and then **OK** to the following prompt (Figure 10-3.8).

You now have a color-coded plan where the colors are assigned by room <u>name</u>; e.g., all the rooms named "Office" have the same color (Figure 10-3.9).

FIGURE 10-3.8 Color fill prompt

*TIP: You can use a **Room Separation Line**, drawn along the railing, to stop the Atrium "Room" from extending out over the multi-story atrium area (i.e. no floor area). This will also make the "area" correct.*

FIGURE 10-3.9 Color filled floor plan

22. Select the *Room Legend* shown in **Figure 10-3.9**.

23. Click **Edit Scheme** on the *Ribbon* (Figure 10-3.10).

FIGURE 10-3.10 Ribbon;
Color Legend key selected

Each unique room name will get a different color. Before you finish you will change one *Color* and one *Fill Pattern*.

24. Click on the *Color* for the **Atrium**.

FIGURE 10-3.11
Edit Color Scheme dialog

FIGURE 10-3.12 Color selector

25. Click the **PANTONE…** button to select a standard *Pantone* color (Figure 10-3.12).

26. Pick any color you like (Figure 10-3.13).

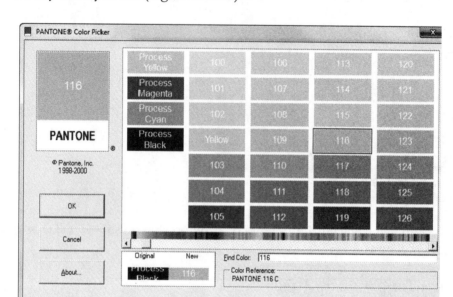

FIGURE 10-3.13 PANTONE Color Picker

27. Click **OK** to accept.

28. Now click on the *Fill Pattern* for the **MECH /ELEC RM**.

29. Click the down-arrow and select **Vertical-small** from the list.

30. Click **OK.**

Your plan should now have the new color you selected for the Atrium and a hatch pattern in the mechanical room. The color legend can also sort by *Department* (see Figure 10-3.11) in addition to many other variables common to the *Room* element. (Interior Designers can create a color filled plan based on the floor finishes for example.)

31. **Save** your project as **ex10-4.rvt**.

TIP: In the Properties Palette you can set the Color Scheme Location to "foreground" if you do not want 3D objects likes chairs and toilets to obscure the color beneath them.

Self-Exam:

The following questions can be used as a way to check your knowledge of this lesson. The answers can be found at the bottom of this page.

1. Revit is referred to as a Building Information Modeler (BIM). (T/F)

2. The area for a room is calculated when a *Room* element is placed. (T/F)

3. Revit can tag all the doors not currently tagged on a given level with the "*Tag All*" tool. *(T/F)*

4. You can add or remove various fields in a door or room schedule. (T/F)

5. Use the _____ tool to add color to the rooms in a plan view.

Review Questions:

The following questions may be assigned by your instructor as a way to assess your knowledge of this section. Your instructor has the answers to the review questions.

1. You can add a door tag with a leader. (T/F)

2. You can export your schedule to a file that can be used in MS Excel. (T/F)

3. A door can be deleted from the door schedule. (T/F)

4. The schedule formatting only shows up when you place the schedule on a sheet. (T/F)

5. It is not possible to add the finish information (i.e., base finish, wall finish) to multiple rooms at one time. (T/F)

6. When setting up a color scheme, you can adjust the color and the _____ pattern in the *Edit Scheme* dialog.

7. Use the _____ palette to adjust the various fields associated with each room in a plan view.

8. Most door schedules are sorted by the _____ field.

9. Revit provides access to the industry standard _____ color library.

Notes:

Lesson 11
Office Building: SITE and RENDERING:

In this chapter you will take a look at Revit's photo-realistic rendering abilities as well as the basic site development tools. Rather than reinventing the wheel, Revit chose to use an established architectural rendering technology called Mental Ray. Autodesk makes several high-end rendering programs like *Autodesk 3DS Max*, *Autodesk Maya* and *Mental Ray*, which work with Revit models in various ways, the integration options improve with each new release. You will need Revit Structure or Revit Architecture for the rendering exercises as Revit MEP does not support the rendering feature set.

Exercise 11-1:
Site tools

This lesson will give the reader a quick overview of the site tools available in Revit. The site tools are not intended to be an advanced site development package. Autodesk has other programs much more capable of developing complex sites such as Autodesk Land Desktop 2009 and AutoCAD Civil 3D 2015. These programs are used by professional Civil Engineers and Surveyors. The contours generated from these advanced civil CAD programs can be used to generate a topography object in Revit.

In this lesson you will create a topography object from scratch – you will also add a sidewalk.

Once the topography object (the topography object, or element, is a 3D mass that represents part *or* all of the site) is created the grade line will automatically show up in building and wall sections, exterior elevations and site plans. The sections even have the earth pattern filled in below the grade line.

As with other Revit elements you can select the object after it is created and set various properties for it; such as surface material, Phase, Etc. One can also return to Sketch mode to refine or correct the surface – this is done in the same way most other Sketched objects are edited – by selecting the item and clicking *Edit* on the *Options Bar*.

Overview of Site tools located on the Ribbon:

Below is a brief description of what the site tools are used for. After this short review you will try a few of these tools on your office project.

Toposurface: Creates a 3D surface by picking points (specifying the elevation of each point picked) or by using linework, within a linked AutoCAD drawing, that were created at the proper levels.

Subregion: Allows an area to be defined within a previously drawn *Toposurface* – the result is an area within the *Toposurface* that can have a different material than the *Toposurface* itself. The *Subregion* is still part of the *Toposurface* and will move with it when relocated. If a *Subregion* is selected and deleted the original surface/properties for that area are revealed.

Split Surface: This tool is similar to the *Subregion* tool in every way except that the result is separate surfaces that can intentionally, or accidentally, be moved apart from each other. If a split surface is selected and deleted it results in a subtraction or a void relative to the original *Toposurface*.

Merge Surfaces: After a surface has been split into one or more separate surfaces you can merge them back together. Only two surfaces can be merged together at a time. The two surfaces to be merged must share a common edge or overlap.

Graded Region: This tool is used to edit the grade of a *Toposurface* that represents the existing site conditions and the designer wants to use Revit to design the new site conditions. This tool is generally only meant to be used once; when used it will copy the existing site conditions to a new phase and set the existing site to be demolished in the new construction phase. The newly copied site object can then be modified for the new site conditions.

Property Line: Creates property lines (in plan views only).

Building Pad: Used to define a portion of site to be subtracted when created below grade (and added when created above grade). An example of how this might be used is to create a *Pad* that coincides with a basement floor slab – which would remove the ground in section above the basement floor slab (otherwise the basement would be filled with the earth fill pattern). Several pads can be imposed on the same *Toposurface* element.

Parking Component: These are parking stall layouts that can be copied around to quickly layout parking lots. Several types can be loaded – which specify both size and angle.

Site Component: Items like benches, dumpsters, etc. that are placed directly on the *Toposurface*, at the correct elevation at the point picked.

Label Contours: Adds an elevation label to the selected contours.
FYI: Contours are automatically created based on the Toposurface.

Site Settings:

The *Site Settings* dialog controls a few key project wide settings related to the site – below is a brief description of these settings.

The **Site Settings** dialog is accessed from the *arrow* link in the lower-right corner of the *Model Site* panel. You should note that various tools under the Settings menu affect the entire project, not just the current view.

Contour Line Display: This controls if the contours are displayed when the *Toposurface* is visible (via the check box) and at what interval. If the *Interval* is set to 1'-0" you will see contour lines that follow the ground's surface and each line represents a vertical change of 1'-0" from the adjacent contour line (the contour lines alone do not tell you what direction the surface slopes in a plan view – this is where contour labels are important). The *Passing Through Elevation* setting allows control over where the contour intervals start from. This is useful because architects usually base the first floor of the building on elevation 0'-0" (or 100'-0") and the surveyors and Civil Engineers will use the distance above sea level (e.g. 1009.2'). So this feature allows the contours to be reconciled between the two systems. The Additional Contours section allows for more "contour" detail to be added within a particular area (vertically) – on a very large site you might want 1'-0" contours only at the building and 10'-0" contours everywhere else. However, this only works if the building is in a distinctive set of vertical elevations. If the is site relatively level or an adjacent area shares the same set of contours you will have undesirable results.

Section Graphics: This area controls how the earth appears when it is shown in section (e.g. exterior elevations, building sections, wall sections, etc.). Here is where the pattern is selected that appears in section (the pattern is selected from the project "materials" similar to the process for selecting the pattern to be displayed within a wall when viewed in section. The

Elevation of poche base controls the depth of the pattern in section views relative to the grade line.

Property Data: This section controls how angles and lengths are displayed for information describing property lines.

Creating topography in Revit

1. Open file 10-3.rvt and *Save-As* **11-1.rvt**.

2. Switch to the **Site** plan view.

   a. Adjust the category visibility so your view matches Figure 11-1.1. Also, set the *Detail Level* to *Fine*. Hide elevation and section tags.

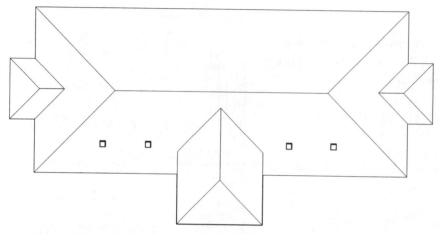

Figure 11-1.1 Site plan view

Here you will basically see what appears to be a roof plan view of your project (Figure 11-1.1). This view has the visibility set such that you see the project from above and the various "site" categories turned on so they are automatically visible once they are created. Next you will take a quick look at the *View Range* for this view so you understand how things are setup.

3. Make sure nothing is selected and a command is not active by clicking the **Modify** tool. This will insure you have access to the *View Properties* via the *Properties Palette*.

4. In the *Properties Palette*, scroll down and select **Edit** next to *View Range*.

Here you can see the site is being viewed from 200′ above the first floor level – so your building/roof would have to be taller than that before it would be "cut" like a floor plan. The *View Depth* could be a problem here: on a steep site, the entire site will be seen if part of it passes through the specified *View Range*. However, items completely below the *View Range* will not be visible.

Figure 11-1.2 Site Plan view range settings

5. In the *View Depth* section, set the *Level* to **Unlimited**.

This change will ensure everything shows up on a steeper site.

6. Click **OK**.

You are now ready to create the site object. The element in Revit which represents the site is called *Toposurface*.

TIP: Structural engineers can use the toposurface tool to model ledge rock, which would aid in determining how deep foundations need to be.

7. Select **Massing & Site → Model Site → Toposurface** from the *Ribbon*.

Toposurface

By default the *Place Point* tool is selected on the *Ribbon*, you are now in sketch mode. This tool allows you to specify points within the view at various elevations – Revit will generate a 3D surface based on those points, so the more points you provide the more accurate the surface. Notice, on the *Options Bar* (Figure 11-1.3) that you can enter an elevation for each point as you click to place them on the screen.

Figure 11-1.3 Options bar for Toposurface tool

What elevation should I enter on the Options Bar?

The elevation you enter for each point should relate to the level datums setup in your project – for example, look at your South exterior elevation (Figure 11-1.4). Recall that the first floor is set to 0'-0".

As you can see in the South elevation, the only place you would want to add points at an elevation of 0'-0" would be at the doors. Everywhere else should be at about -4" so the grade does not rise higher than the top of the foundation wall and come into contact with the brick, and possibly block the weeps and brick vents.

8. With the *Elevation* set to **0'-0"** pick the six points shown in Figure 11-1.5; these points are at the exterior door locations.

T.O. Masonry
36' - 0"

Level 3
24' - 0"

Level 2
12' - 0"

Level 1
0' - 0"

Figure 11-1.4 Partial South Elevation

TIP: You can switch to the Level 1 Floor Plan view while in the Toposurface tool, just click the Place Point tool again on the Ribbon.

9. Change the **Elevation** to **-0'-4"** (don't forget the minus sign) on the *Option Bar* and then pick all the inside and outside corners along the perimeter of the building which have not yet been selected.

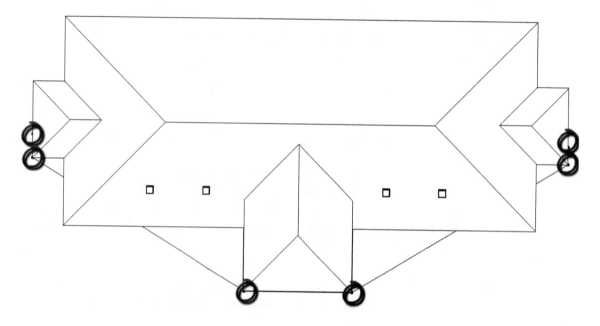

Figure 11-1.5 Site plan view – 6 points to be selected (elevation -0'-0")

10. Set the **Elevation** to **-2'-6"** and point to the ten points shown in Figure 11-1.6 which define the extents of the *Toposurface*.

   FYI: The elevations selected will generally provide a positive slope away from the building – this will be visible in elevations and sections.

Sketchy Lines
Within a view's Graphic Display Options you can turn on Sketchy Lines and adjust the sliders for two related settings; *Jitter* and *Extensions*. The first determines how wavy the lines are and the later controls how far the lines cross at corners.

This option is set per view. You will also want to turn on "smooth lines" for this view.

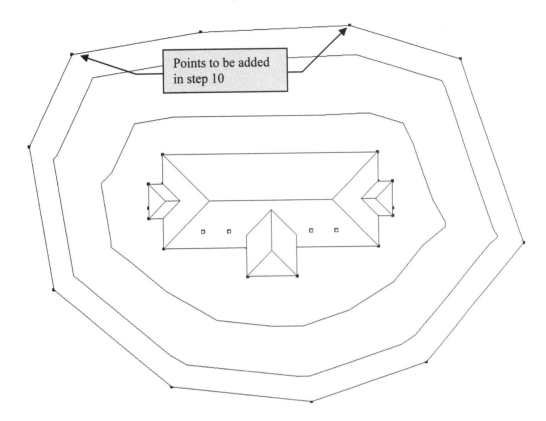

Points to be added in step 10

Figure 11-1.6 Site plan view – 10 points to be selected (elev – 2'-6")

11. Select the **green check mark** on the *Ribbon* to finish the *Toposurface*.

Revit has now created the *Toposurface* based on the points you specified. Again, the more points you add the more refined and accurate the surface will be.

Ideally you would use the *Toposurface* tool to create a surface from a surveyors' points file or contour lines drawn in an AutoCAD file – Revit can automatically generate surfaces from these sources, rather than you picking points. This process is beyond the scope of this tutorial.

12. Switch to the **3D view** to see your new ground surface (Figure 11-1.7).

Figure 11-1.7 Toposurface seen in 3D view

The toposurface is automatically added in sections and elevations (Figure 15-1.8). It may need to be turned off in other views.

Figure 11-1.8 Section with ground pattern added

If your building has a basement or space partially below grade you will need to add a **Building Pad** to "stamp" out an area of the *Toposurface*. To add one you select the tool, draw an outline in a plan view and then specify the depth, or height, of the pad. The *Toposurface* then removes, or adds, ground below the *Building Pad*. If you have a stepped basement you will need multiple Building Pads. Their edges can align but they cannot overlap.

Next you will quickly create a sidewalk to wrap up this lesson.

You can use the *Subregion* tool or the *Split Surface* tool to create the driveway and sidewalks. The *Subregion* tool defines an area that is still part of the main site object – the *Split Surface* tool literally breaks the *Toposurface* into separate elements. Splitting a surface can create problems when trying to move or edit the site so you will use the *Subregion* tool.

13. Switch back to the **Site** plan view.

14. Select **Massing & Site → Modify Site → Subregion** tool and sketch the lines for the sidewalk (Figure 11-1.9).

15. Click the **green check mark** on the *Ribbon* to finish the *Subregion*.

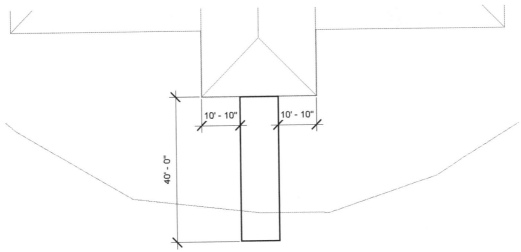

Figure 11-1.9 Partial site plan – closed sketch lines for subregion

16. Switch to 3D view to see your sidewalk (Figure 11-1.10). Notice the 2D lines sketched in the site plan view have been projected down onto the surface of the 3D site object!

Notice that the shade and render material is still the same as the main ground surface. You will learn how to change this in a moment.

When you select the *Toposurface* and click *Edit Surface* on the *Ribbon* you can select existing points and edit their elevation to refine the surface.

17. In the 3D view, select the sidewalk *Subregion*.

18. In the *Properties Palette*, set the *Material* to **Concrete – Cast-in-place concrete**.

19. Set the main site element's *Material* to **Site – Grass**.

20. Make sure the *Visual Style* for your 3D view is set to **Shaded** so you can see the "shaded" version of the materials.

   TIP: Set via View Control bar.

Figure 11-1.10 3D view with sidewalk added

That concludes this overview of the site tools provided within Revit. You now have everything modeled in your project so you can start to develop rendered images of your project for presentations.

Exercise 11-2:
Creating an Exterior Rendering

The first thing you will do to prepare a rendering is set up a view. You will use the *Camera* tool to do this. This becomes a saved view that can be opened at any time from the *Project Browser*. A *Camera* view differs from the default 3D view in that it is a perspective view.

Creating a Camera View:

1. Open file 11-1.rvt and *Save-As* to **11-2.rvt**.

2. Open the **Level 1** view and **Zoom to Fit**, so you can see the entire plan.

3. Select **View → Create → 3D Views → Camera**.

4. Click the mouse in the lower right corner of the screen to indicate the camera eye location.

   NOTE: Before you click, Revit tells you it wants the eye location first on the Status Bar.

5. Next click near the atrium curtain wall; see Figure 11-2.1.

FIGURE 11-2.1 Placing a Camera in Level 1 plan view

Revit will automatically open a view window for the new camera. Take a minute to look at the view and make a mental note of what you see and don't see in the view (Figure 11-2.2).

6. Switch back to the **Level 1** plan view.

7. Adjust the camera, using its grips, to look similar to Figure 11-2.3.

> *TIP:* *If the camera is not visible in plan view, right click on the 3D view name in the Project Browser (3D View 1) and select Show Camera.*

FIGURE 11-2.2 Initial Camera view

FIGURE 11-2.3 Revised camera – Level 1

8. Now switch to *3D View 1* and adjust the **Crop Region** to look similar to **Figure 11-2.4**.

This will be the view we render later in this exercise.

FIGURE 11-2.4 Revised camera – 3D View 1

Assigning Materials to Objects:

Materials are scanned images or computer generated representations of the materials your building will be made of.

Typically materials are added while the project is being modeled. For example, when you create a material (using the *Materials* command on the *Manage* tab), you can assign a material at that time. Of course, you can go back and add or change it later. Next you will change the material assigned for the exterior brick wall.

9. Switch to **Level 1** plan view.

10. Select an exterior wall somewhere in plan view.

11. Click **Edit Type** in the *Properties Palette* and then click **Edit** *structure*.

12. Notice the material selected for the exterior finish is **Brick; Common** click in that cell (Figure 11-2.5).

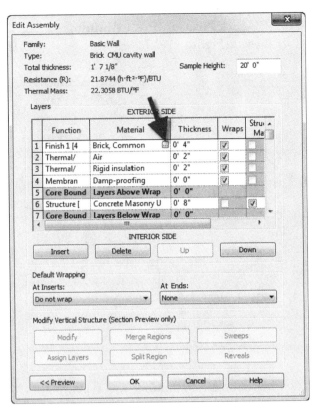

FIGURE 11-2.5 Exterior wall assembly

13. Click the "**…**" icon to the right of the label **Brick, Common**.

Now you will take a look that the definition of the material *Brick, Common*.

You are now in the *Materials* dialog. You should notice that a material is already selected on the left. Next you will select a different brick material.

14. Click on the **Replace Asset** icon (Step 1 in Figure 11-2.7).

You can browse through the list and select any material in the list to be assigned to the *Brick, Common* material in Revit. The material does not have to be brick but would be confusing if something else were assigned to the *Brick, Common* material.

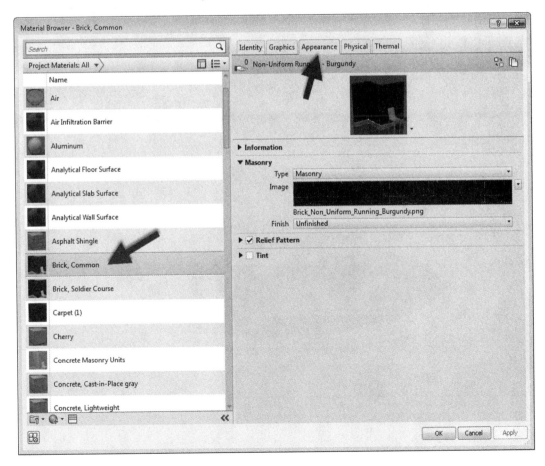

FIGURE 11-2.6 Materials dialog

15. Scroll down in the *Masonry* section and double-click **Non-uniform Running - Red**, and then click the red **X** to close the *Asset Browser* (Figure 11-2.7).

Notice the material listed is now updated.

16. Click **OK** to close *all open* dialog boxes.

Now, when you render, any element (wall, ceiling, etc.) that has the material *Brick, Common* associated with it, will have a red brick appearance.

FIGURE 11-2.7 Revit's Asset Library

If you need more than one brick color, you assign that material to another wall type.

Sun Path

It is possible to turn on a feature called *Sun Path*. This shows the path of the sun over a day and a year. This is accessed from the *View Control Bar* while in a 3D view.

Once on, you can click and drag the sun along its daily or yearly path!

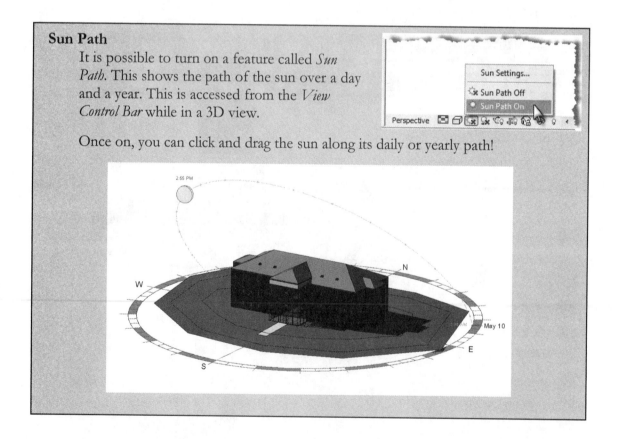

Project Location:

Next you will specify the project location on the earth. This will make the daylight accurate in your renderings.

17. Select **Manage → Project Location → Location** from the *Ribbon*.

Location

18. In the *Project Address* field enter **Minneapolis, MN**.

    a.   You may enter your location is you wish.

    b.   It is also possible to enter the actual street address.

19. Press **Enter**.

You should now see an internet based map as shown below, including latitude and longitude.

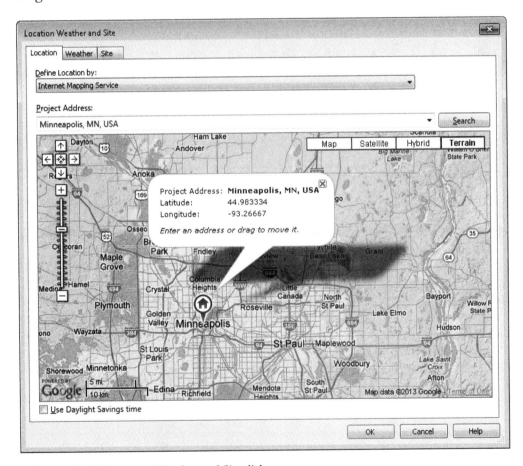

FIGURE 11-2.8 Location Weather and Site dialog

20. Click **OK** to save the location settings.

Sun Settings:

Next you will define the sun and shadow settings. You will explore the various options available.

21. Select **Manage → Settings → Additional Settings → Sun Settings** from the *Ribbon*.

22. Make the following changes. (Figure 11-2.9)

   a. *Solar Study:* **Still**.

   b. Uncheck *Ground Plane* at Level.

   c. Select **Summer Solstice** on the left.

   d. Change the year to 2013.

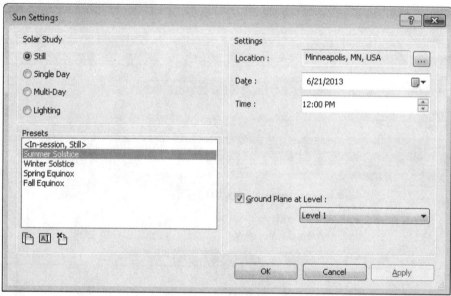

FIGURE 11-2.9 Sun Settings dialog

23. Click **OK** to close the dialog.

Setting Up the Environment:

You have limited options for setting up the building's environment. If you need more control than what is provided directly in Revit you will need to use another program like Autodesk 3DS Design 2015 which is designed to work with Revit and can create extremely high quality renderings and animations; it even has day lighting functionality that helps to validate LEED® (Leadership in Environmental and Energy Design) requirements. You can adjust the lighting and the background.

24. Switch to your camera view: **3D View 1**.

25. Select the **Show Rendering Dialog** icon on the *View Control Bar*, it looks like a teapot (Figure 11-2.10).

> *FYI: This icon is only visible when you are in a 3D view, the same as the Navigation Wheel and ViewCube.*

The *Rendering* dialog box is now open (Figure 11-2.11). This dialog box allows you to control the environmental settings you are about to explore and actually create the rendering (which you will do soon!).

FIGURE 11-2.11 Rendering dialog

FIGURE 11-2.10 Render dialog icon

26. In the *Lighting* section, click the down-arrow next to *Scheme* to see the options. Select **Exterior: Sun and Artificial** when finished (Figure 11-2.12).

FIGURE 11-2.12 Lighting options

The lighting options are very simple choices: is your rendering an interior or exterior rendering and is the light source Sun or Artificial – or both? You may have artificial lights (i.e., light fixtures like the ones you placed in the office) but still only desire a rendering solely based on the light provided by the sun.

27. In the *Lighting* section, set the *Sun* set to **Summer Solstice**. (This relates to the settings in Figure 11-2.9.)

FYI: In the Sun Settings dialog box, Revit lets you set up various "scenes" which control time of day. Two examples would be:

- *Daytime, summer*
- *Nighttime, window*

Looking back at Figure 11-2.9, you would click *Duplicate* and provide a name. This name would then be available from the *Sun* drop-down list in the *Render* dialog box.

28. Click on the **Artificial Lighting** button (Figure 11-2.13).

You will now see a dialog similar to the one shown to the right (Figure 11-2.13).

You will see several 2x4 light fixtures. The light fixtures relate to the fixtures you inserted in the reflected ceiling plans. It is very convenient that you can place lights in the ceiling plan and have them ready to render whenever you need to (i.e., render and cast light into the scene!). Here you can group lights together so you can control which ones are on (e.g., exterior and interior lights).

FIGURE 11-2.13 Scene Lighting dialog

29. Click **Cancel** to close the *Artificial Lighting* dialog.

30. Click the down-arrow next to *Style* in the *Background* area (Figure 11-2.14).

31. Select **Sky: Few Clouds**.

FIGURE 11-2.14 Background style

Notice that for the background, one option is Image. This allows you to specify a photograph of the site, or one similar. It can prove difficult getting the perspective just right but the end results can look as if you took a picture of the completed building.

32. Close the *Renderings* dialog by clicking the "X" in the upper right; all your render settings will be saved for this view.

Next you will place a few trees into your rendering. You will adjust their exact location so they are near the edge of the framed rendering, so as not to cover too much of the building.

33. Switch to **Site** plan view and select **Architecture → Build → Component → Place a Component** from the *Ribbon. (Close the Render dialog if it is still open.)*

34. Pick *RPC Tree – Deciduous:* **Largetooth Aspen 25′** from the *Type Selector* on the *Ribbon.*

> **FYI:** *If the tree is not listed in the* Type Selector, *click* Load Family *and load the deciduous tree family from the* Plantings *folder.*

35. Place three trees as shown in **Figure 11-2.15**. (You will make one smaller in a moment.)

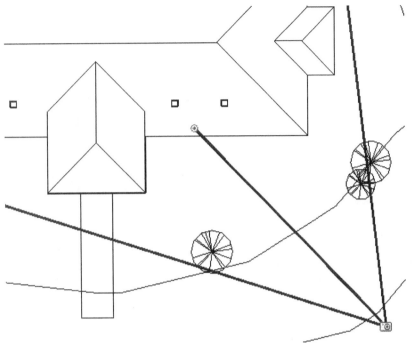

FIGURE 11-2.15 Level 1 with trees added

36. Adjust the trees in plan view, reviewing the effects in the 3D View 1 view, so your 3D view is similar to Figure 11-2.16.

37. In the Level 1 plan view, select the tree that is shown smaller in **Figure 11-2.14**.

38. Select **Edit Type** on the *Properties Palette*. Click **Duplicate** and enter the name: *RPC Tree – Deciduous:* **Largetooth Aspen 18′**.

Images courtesy of LHB (www.LHBcorp.com)

39. Change the *Height* to **18'** (from 25') and then click **OK** to close the open dialog box.

The previous three steps allow you to have a little more variety in the trees being placed. Otherwise, they would all be the same height, which is not very natural.

FIGURE 11-2.16 3D View 1 – with trees

40. Open the **3D View 1** camera view.

41. Open the **Rendering** dialog again.

42. Make sure the *Quality* is set to **Draft**.

> **FYI:** *The time to process the rendering increases significantly as the quality level is raised.*

43. Click **Render** from the *Rendering* dialog box.

You will see a progress bar while Revit is processing the rendering (Figure 11-2.17).

FIGURE 11-2.17 Rendering progress

After a few minutes, depending on the speed of your computer, you should have a rendered image similar to Figure 11-2.18 below. You can increase the quality of the image by adjusting the quality setting in the *Render* dialog. However, these higher settings require substantially more time to generate the rendering. The last step before saving the Revit project file is to save the rendered image to a file.

FYI: Each time you make changes to the model, you will have to re-render the view to get an updated image. Depending on exactly how your view was setup, you may be able to see light from one of the light figures in the office off the Atrium. Also, notice the railing through the curtain wall; Revit has the glass in the windows set to be transparent!

FIGURE 11-2.18 Rendered view

44. From the *Rendering* dialog select **Export**.

> *FYI: The "Save to Project" button saves the image within the Revit Project for placement on Sheets. This is convenient makes the project size larger, so you should delete old ones!*

45. Select a *location* and provide a *file name*.

Render Render Render
in Cloud Gallery

46. Set the *Save As* type: to **JPEG**.

47. Click **Save**.

48. If you are a student or work for a company who has Autodesk Subscription, try using the **Render in Cloud** tool on the *View* tab. Adjust the settings to the maximum resolution to see how fast it will render. Click the **Render Gallery** button to see the results! **Note:** You must log into *Autodesk 360* first.

The image file you just saved can now be inserted into MS Word or Adobe Photoshop for editing.

Exercise 11-3:
Rendering an Isometric in Section

This exercise will introduce you to a view tool called *Section Box*. This tool is not necessarily related to renderings, but the two tools together can produce some interesting results. The Section Box works in any 3D, even camera views. This can be used throughout the design process to better visualize your model.

Setting up the 3D View:

1. Open file ex11-2.rvt and **Save As ex11-3.rvt**.

2. Switch to the *Default* **3D** view via the 3D icon on the *QAT (not the 3D View 1 from Exercise 11-2)*.

3. Make sure nothing is selected so the *Properties Palette* is showing the **View Properties**.

4. Activate the **Section Box** parameter and then click **OK**.

You should see a box appear around your building, similar to Figure 11-3.1. When selected, you can adjust the size of the box with its grips. Anything outside the box is not visible. This is a great way to study a particular area of your building while in an isometric view. You will experiment with this feature next.

Section Box (shown selected)

6 grips to manipulate the *Section Box* – only visible while the *Section Box* is selected

FIGURE 11-3.1 3D view with Section Box activated

5. To practice using the **Section Box**, drag the grips around until your view looks similar to **Figure 11-3.2**.

    TIP: This will require the ViewCube tool as well.

FIGURE 11-3.2
3D view with adjusted Section Box

This creates a very interesting view of the Level 1 – West Wing. What client would have trouble understanding this drawing? Notice the ground in section as well.

6. Now re-adjust the **Section Box** to look similar to **Figure 11-3.3**. Notice toilet room is visible.

FIGURE 11-3.3
3D view

7. From the *Manage* tab, select *Additional Settings***Sun Settings** and change the following *Sun* settings (Figure 11-3.4):
    a. Click **Duplicate** (name: 28 February 8am)
        (Must select something other than <In-session> first)
    b. *Date:*   **2/28/2013**
    c. *Time:*   **8:00am**

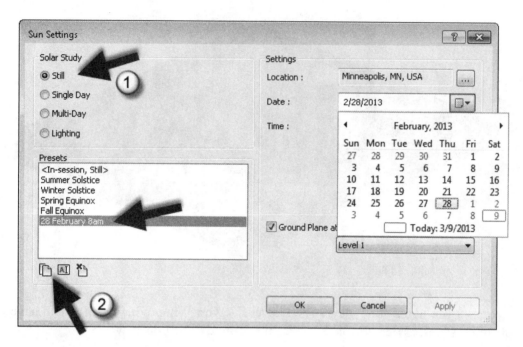

FIGURE 11-3.4 Modified Sun settings

8. Select the **Render** icon, select the *Scheme*: **Exterior: Sun only**, and then set *Sun* to: **23 February 8am**.

9. Set the *Background Style* to: **Color**. Leave the default color as is.

10. Select the **Region** option and then adjust the "render region crop" that appears to indicate the area to be rendered.

    TIP: *This tool is nice for checking a material before rendering the entire building, which takes longer.*

11. Click **Render** to generate a rendered image.

The image will take a few minutes to render (again, depending on the speed of your computer). When finished it should look similar to **Figure 11-3.5**. The image looks much better on the screen or printed in color.

FIGURE 11-3.5 Rendered isometric view

Adjusting an Element's Material:

As previously mentioned, most elements already have a material assigned to them. This is great because it allows you to quickly render your project to get some preliminary images. However, they usually need to be adjusted. You will do this next.

12. Switch to **Level 1** plan view and zoom in on the toilet rooms.

13. Select one of the toilet partitions.

14. Click the **Edit Type** button in the *Properties Palette*.

Notice the toilet partition material is set to *Toilet Partition*. This value is a material; you will change this next (Figure 11-3.6).

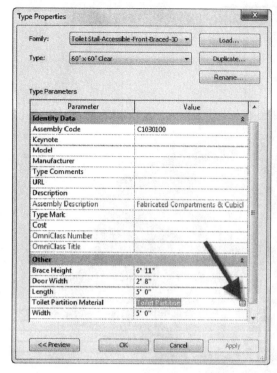

FIGURE 11-3.6 Toilet Partition properties

15. **Click** on the Toilet Partition value (which will cause a "..." icon to display to the right), click the icon.

You are now in the *Materials* dialog box, where you can create and edit *Materials*.

16. Select **Toilet Partition** (if not already selected on the left).

17. Change the *Render Appearance* to: *Stone - Granite*, **Polished - Black** (Figure 11-3.7).

    TIP: Try using the search box near the top, and type "Granite".

18. Close the open dialog boxes.

FIGURE 11-3.7 Material selector

19. You can now re-render the 3D view and see the results.

20. **Save** your project as ex **11-3.rvt**.

Duplicating a Material:

It is important to know how to properly duplicate a *Material* in your model so you do not unintentionally affect another *Material*. The information on this page is mainly for reference and does not need to be done in your model.

If you **Duplicate** a *Material* in your model, the **Appearance Asset** will be associated to the new *Material* AND the *Material* you copied it from! For example, in the first image (the right), we will right-click on Carpet (1) and duplicate it. Before we duplicate it, notice the *Appearance Asset* named "RED" is not shared (arrow #3).

Once you have duplicated a *Material*, notice the two carpet materials, in this example (second image), now indicate they both share the same *Appearance Asset*. Changing one will affect the other. Click the **Duplicate this asset** icon in the upper right (arrow #3).

Once the *Appearance Asset* has been duplicated (third image), you can expand the information section and rename the asset. You can now make changes to this material without affecting other materials.

Exercise 11-4:
Creating an Interior Rendering

Creating an interior rendering is very similar to an exterior rendering. This exercise will walk through the steps involved in creating a high quality interior rendering.

Setting up the Camera View:

1. Open ex11-3.rvt and **Save As ex11-4.rvt**.

2. Open **Level 2** view.

3. From the *QAT*, select **3D View → Camera**.

4. Place the *Camera* as shown in **Figure 11-4.1**.

Revit uses default heights for the camera and the target. These heights are based on the current level's floor elevation. These reference points can be edited via the camera properties.

FIGURE 11-4.1 Camera placed – Level 2 view

Revit will automatically open the newly generated camera view. Your view should look similar to **Figure 11-4.2**.

FYI: Make sure you created the camera on Level 2 and picked the points in the correct order.

FIGURE 11-4.2 Material selector

5. Using the **Crop Region** rectangle, modify the view to look like **Figure 11-4.3**.

> *TIP:* *You will have to switch to plan view to adjust the camera's depth of view to see the trees.*

> *REMEMBER:* *If the camera does not show in plan view, right-click on the camera view label in the project browser and select Show Camera. If you did not add a ceiling to the third floor lobby previously, you should do that now.*

> *FYI:* *A ceiling was added at the second and third levels in this image to "clean" things up for the rendering.*

FIGURE 11-4.3 Modified interior camera

6. Switch back to **Level 2** to see the revised *Camera* view settings; if you cannot see the camera, right-click on the camera view name in the *Project Browser* and select **Show Camera** from the pop-menu that appears.

Notice the field of view triangle is wider based on the changes to the Crop Region (Figure 11-4.4).

FIGURE 11-4.4 Modified camera – Level 2

7. Select the *Camera* in the level 2 plan view.

8. Change the **Eye Elevation** to **5'-6"** (Figure 11-4.5).

9. Click **Apply**.

Your interior camera view should now look similar to **Figure 11-4.6**. This would be a person standing on Level 1 looking up. The vertical lines are distorted due to the wide field of view (crop region). This is similar to what a camera with a 10-15mm lens would get in the finished building.

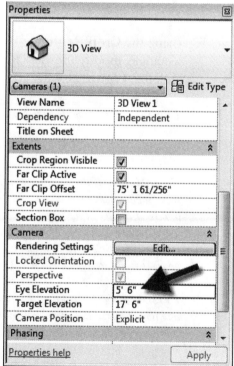

FIGURE 11-4.5 Camera properties

Creating the rendering:

Next you will render the view.

FIGURE 11-4.6 Interior camera view

10. Select **Show Render Dialog** from the *View Control Bar*.

11. Set the *Scheme* to **Interior: Sun only**.

12. Set the *Sun Setting* to **Lighting: Sunlight from Top Right**.

13. Click **Render** to being the rendering process.

This will take several minutes depending on the speed of your computer. When finished, the view should look similar to Figure 11-4.7.

14. Click **Export** from the *Rendering* dialog box to save the image to a file on your hard drive. Name the file **Atrium.jpg** (jpeg file format).

You can now open the *Atrium.jpg* file in Adobe Photoshop or insert into MS Word to manipulate or print.

To toggle back to the normal hidden view, click **Show the Model** from the *Rendering* dialog box.

There are many things you can do to make the rendering look even better. You can add interior light fixtures and props (e.g., pictures on the wall, items on the counter top, and lawn furniture). Once you add interior lights, you can adjust the Sun setting to nighttime and then render a night scene.

TIP: Setting the output to Printer rather than Screen allows you to generate a higher resolution image. Thus, between the Quality setting and the output setting you can create an extremely high quality rendering, but it might take hours, if not days, to process!

Revit also gives you the ability to set a material to be self-illuminating. This will allow you to make a button on the dishwasher look like it is lit up or, if applied to the glass on the ranger door, like the light in the oven is on! You can also set a lamp shade to glow when a light source has been defined under it so it looks more realistic.

FIGURE 11-4.7 Rendered view

Image courtesy of LHB (www.LHBcorp.com)

Rendering a Night Scene:

One more variation we will look at is rendering the interior atrium view at nighttime. This involves adjusting the sun settings so the Sun is not considered and making sure you have the correct number of light fixtures to light the space being rendered.

15. Add Ceilings and light fixtures to Levels 2 and 3 per steps covered in previous chapters.

16. Open the *Rendering* dialog box.

17. Make the adjustments shown in the image to the left. Make sure Scheme is set to **Interior: Artificial Only**.

18. While in the camera view for the Atrium, click on the **Render** button.

When the rendering is completed you will have a night view of your interior atrium. This clearly shows the effect the 2x4 light fixtures have on the rendering, as they are the primary light source for this rendering. Your image should look similar to **Figure 11-4.8**.

You can also try this (especially if you have placed light fixtures for the entire building) on your exterior camera view. Nighttime renderings can be very dramatic.

The image to the left is a pool created and rendered in Revit. The rendering is only using artificial lights and the "water" material is distorting the pool light and the striping on the bottom of the pool.

Image courtesy of LHB (www.LHBcorp.com)

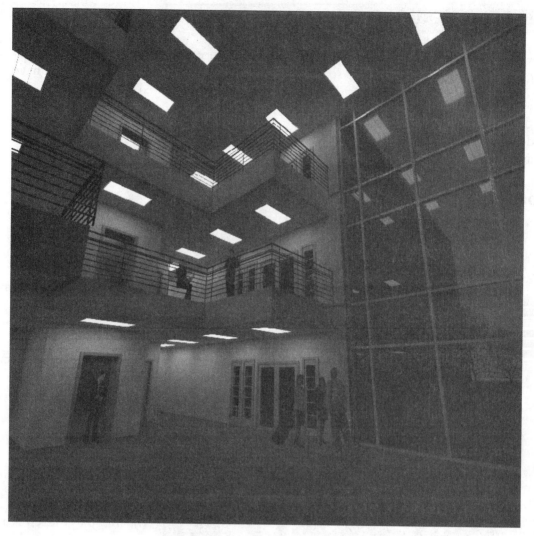

FIGURE 11-4.8 Rendered nighttime view

TIP: *Setting the Visual Style to realistic can produce nice results without doing a rendering. Clicking the Graphic Display Options, see image to the left, allows you to turn on a feature called Show Ambient Shadows and/or Cast Shadows. Both of these settings help to produce a more realistic look without doing a rendering. This can make the view slow, but not other views.*

You will learn how to add people in the next lesson!

Notice you can see reflections in the curtain wall glass. Revit accurately renders reflective surfaces like glass and shiny or polished metal (like the elevator doors). This creates a more realistic rendering.

19. **Save** your project as **11-4.rvt**.

Exercise 11-5:
Adding People to Rendering

Revit provides a few RPC (Rich Photorealistic Content) people to add to your renderings. These are files from a popular company that provides 3D photo content for use in renderings (http://www.archvision.com). You can buy this content in groupings (like college students) or per item. In addition to people, they offer items like cars, plants, trees, office equipment, etc.

Loading Content into Current Project

1. Open ex11-4.rvt and **Save As 11-5.rvt**.

2. Switch to **Level 2** view.

3. Select **Component** → **Place a Component**.

4. Click the **Load Family** button on the *Ribbon*.

5. Browse to the **Entourage** folder and select both the **RPC Male** and **RPC Female** files (using the *Ctrl* key to select both at once) and click **Open**.

6. Place one **Male** and one **Female** as shown in **Figure 11-5.1**.

FIGURE 11-5.1 Level 2 – RPC people added

The line in the circle (Figure 11-5.1) represents the direction a person is looking. You simply rotate the object to make adjustments.

7. Switch to **Level 1** view.

8. Place a few of the other people available (similar to Fig. 11-5.3)

FIGURE 11-5.2 Element Type Selector

FIGURE 11-5.3 Level 1 – people added

9. Switch to your interior atrium camera view.

10. Render the Atrium view with the daytime settings previously used.

Your rendering should now have people in it and look similar to **Figure 11-5.4**.

Adding people and other "props" gives your model a sense of scale and makes it look a little more realistic. After all, architecture is for people. These objects can be viewed from any angle. Try a new camera view from a different angle to see how the people adjust to match the view and perspective, maybe from the third floor looking down to Level 1.

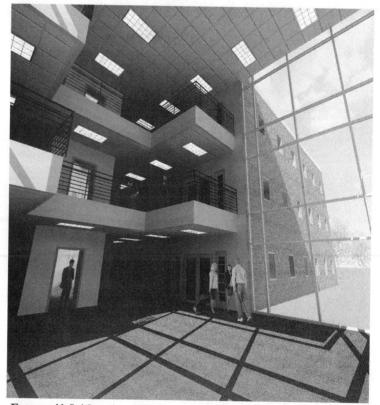

FIGURE 11-5.4 Interior Atrium view with people added; rendered view

11. **Save** your project as **ex11-5.rvt**.

Revit also has several settings which can make your camera view look more realistic without doing a rendering. The image below is an example. It has the *Visual Style* set to **Realistic** (notice even the RPC people are visible), which creates a nice bright image. The view also has **Ambient Shadows** and **Photographic Exposure** enabled in the view's *Graphic Display Options* dialog. Another option is to set the *Visual Style* to **Ray Trace**.

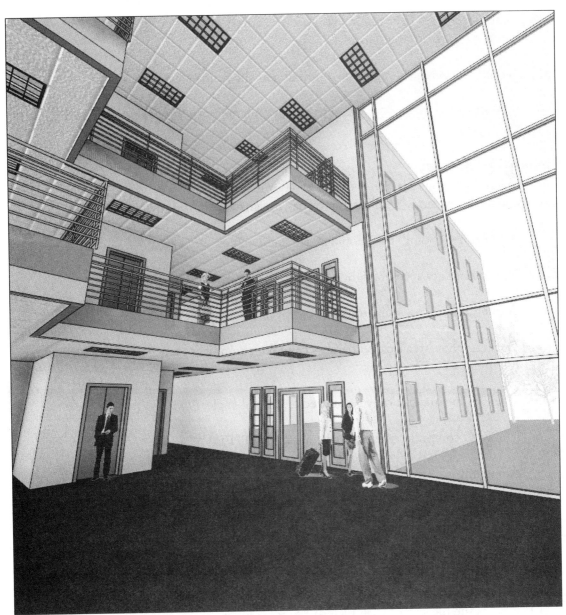

FIGURE 11-5.5 Interior Atrium view with people added; Revit camera view set to Realistic

FYI: *As with other families and components, the more you add to your project, the bigger your project file becomes. It is a good idea to load only the items you need and delete the unused items via the Project Browser. Your project should be about 8 to 9MB at this point in the tutorial.*

Self-Exam:

The following questions can be used as a way to check your knowledge of this lesson. The answers can be found at the bottom of this page.

1. Creating a camera adds a view to the *Project Browser* list. (T/F)

2. Materials are defined in Revit's *Materials* dialog box. (T/F)

3. After inserting a light fixture, you need to adjust several setting before rendering and getting light from the fixture. (T/F)

4. You cannot create a nighttime rendering as the sun is always on. (T/F)

5. Use the _____ _____ tool to remove a large portion of the model in 3D.

Review Questions:

The following questions may be assigned by your instructor as a way to assess your knowledge of this section. Your instructor has the answers to the review questions.

1. You cannot "point" the people in a specific direction. (T/F)

2. You cannot get accurate lighting based on day/month/location. (T/F)

3. Adding *Families* to your project does not make the project file bigger. (T/F)

4. Creating photo-realistic renderings can take a significant amount of time for your computer to process. (T/F)

5. The RPC people can only be viewed from one angle. (T/F)

6. The RPC components do not cast shadows (T/F).

7. Adjust the _____ _____ to make more of a perspective view visible.

8. You use the _____ tool to load and insert RPC people.

9. You can adjust the *Eye Elevation* parameter of the camera via the camera's

   _____.

10. What is the file size of (completed) Exercise 11-5? _____ MB

Lesson 12
Office Building: CONSTRUCTION DOCUMENTS SET:

This lesson will look at bringing everything you have drawn thus far together onto sheets. The sheets, once set up, are ready for plotting. Basically, you place the various views you have created on sheets. The scale for each view is based on the scale you set while drawing that view, which is important to have set correctly because it affects the text and symbol sizes. When finished setting up the sheets, you will have a set of drawings ready to print, individually or all at once. See the view on sheets for additional information.

Exercise 12-1:
Setting Up a Sheet

Creating a Sheet View:

1. Open ex11-5.rvt and **Save As** 12-1.rvt.

2. Select **View →** **Sheet Composition →** **New Sheet**.

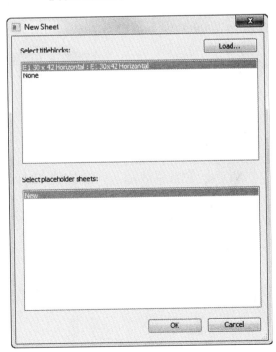

Next Revit will prompt you for a Titleblock to use. The template file you started with only has one; that's the one you will use (Figure 12-1.1).

3. Click **OK** to select the **E1 30x42 Horizontal** titleblock.

NOTE: A new item shows up in the Project Browser under the heading: Sheets. Once you get an entire drawing set ready, this list can be very long.

FIGURE 12-1.1 Select a Titleblock

FIGURE 12-1.2 Initial Titleblock view

4. **Zoom** into the sheet number area (lower right corner).

5. Adjust the text to look similar to **Figure 12-1.3**.

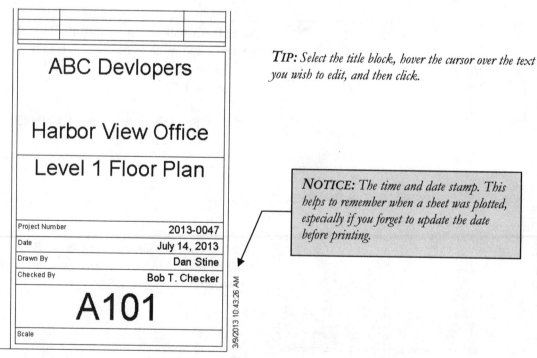

TIP: *Select the title block, hover the cursor over the text you wish to edit, and then click.*

NOTICE: *The time and date stamp. This helps to remember when a sheet was plotted, especially if you forget to update the date before printing.*

FIGURE 12-1.3 Revised Titleblock data

6. **Zoom out** so you can see the entire sheet.

7. With the sheet fully visible, click and drag the **Level 1** label (under floor plans) from the *Project Browser* onto the sheet view.

You will see a box that represents the extents of the view you are placing on the current sheet.

8. Move the cursor around until the box is somewhat centered on the sheet (this can be adjusted later at any time).

Your view should look similar to **Figure 12-1.4**.

FIGURE 12-1.4 Sheet view with Level 1 added

9. Click the mouse in a "white" area (not on any lines) to deselect the Level 1 view. Notice the box goes away (unless the Crop Region is set to display in the view being placed).

10. **Zoom In** on the lower left corner to view the drawing identification symbol that Revit automatically added. (Figure 12-1.5)

(1) **Level 1**
1/8" = 1'-0"

FIGURE 12-1.5 Drawing title

NOTE: The drawing number for this sheet is added automatically. The next view you add will be number 2. The view name is listed. This is another reason to rename the elevation and section views as you create them. Also notice that the drawing scale is listed. Again, this comes from the scale setting for the Level 1 view.

11. **Zoom Out** to see the entire sheet again.

12. Add two more sheets and set up Levels 2 and 3 on them:

    a. Sheet A102 → Level 2 Floor Plan

    b. Sheet A103 → Level 3 Floor Plan

NOTE: When you create a new sheet, most of the titleblock is filled in and the number has increased by 1. This information can be changed if needed.

TIP: Back in the view, if you select the Crop Region, you can select Edit Crop to adjust the perimeter to be L-shaped if needed. This also works with the Callout tool on the View tab.

Setting Up Exterior Elevations:

Next you will set up the exterior elevations on the A200 series sheets.

13. Create a new Sheet and adjust the title block data:

    a. Sheet Title: Exterior Elevations

    b. Sheet Number: A200

14. Drag the **South** elevation view onto the sheet. Place the drawing near the lower right.

15. Drag the **North** elevation view onto the same sheet. Place the drawing so that the drawing title tag is aligned. (Revit will snap to this position vertically.)

    TIP: When placing a view on a sheet, Revit will display a dashed reference line when the model portion of the view aligns with an adjacent model view. This allows you to ensure views align with each other on a sheet.

Your drawing should look similar to Figure 12-1.6. These same steps can be applied to the floor plan views to hide the trees if desired.

FIGURE 12-1.6 North and South exterior elevations

Next you will turn off the trees in the south view. Normally you would turn them off in all views. However, you will only turn them off in the south view to show that you can control visibility per view on a sheet.

16. Click anywhere on the South elevation view to select it.

17. Now **Right-Click** and select **Activate View** from the pop-up menu (see image to right). *TIP: you can also double-click within the view.*

At this point you are in the viewport and can make changes to the project model to control visibility, which is what you will do next.

18. Type **VV** on the keyboard (do not press **Enter**).

19. In the visibility dialog **Uncheck Planting**.

20. Close the open dialog box.

21. Right-click anywhere in the drawing area and select **Deactivate View** from the pop-up menu. *TIP: you can also double-click outside of the viewport to deactivate.*

Now the trees are turned off for the South Elevation but not the North.

FIGURE 12-1.7 North & South exterior (trees removed from south view)

22. Create another sheet for the other two exterior elevations (East and West); the sheet should be number **A201**.

Now you will stop for a moment and notice that Revit is automatically referencing the drawings as you place them on sheets.

23. Switch to **Level 1** (see Figure 12-1.8).

Notice in Figure 12-1.8 that the number A200 represents the sheet number that the drawing can be found on. The number one (1) is the drawing number to look for on sheet A200.

FIGURE 12-1.8 Level 1 – elev. Reference tag filled-in

Setting Up Sections:

24. Create a sheet numbered **A300** and titled **Building Sections**.

25. Add a cross section, in plan view, through the atrium area.

26. Add the three building sections as shown in **Figure 12-1.9**.

FIGURE 12-1.9 Sheet A300 building sections

27. Switch to _Level 1_ plan view and zoom into the area shown in Figure 12-1.10.

Notice, again, that the reference bubbles are automatically filled in when the referenced view is placed on a sheet. If the drawing is moved to another sheet, the reference bubbles are automatically updated.

You can also see in Figure 12-1.9 (above) that the reference bubbles on the building sections are filled in.

Keep in mind that the _View Scale_ for each view controls the size of the text, dimensions and symbols. This ensures all the annotation is the same size on the printed sheet no matter what the scale of the drawing/view is. So if you added a 3″=1′-0″ detail in the open space, in the lower left, on sheet A300 above; the annotation would be the same size as the adjacent building section views.

FIGURE 12-1.10 Level 1 – Section ref's filled in

Setting Up Remaining Sheets:

Next you set up sheets for the remaining views that have yet to be placed on a sheet (except for the 3D views).

Create the following sheets and place the appropriate views on them:

- A111   Level 1 Reflected Ceiling Plan
- A112   Level 2 Reflected Ceiling Plan
- A113   Level 3 Reflected Ceiling Plan
- A400   Wall Sections
- A500   Interior Elevations
- A600   Details (see Figure 12-1.13)
- A800   Schedules

Notice that the new sheets, just created, can be found under *Sheets (all)* on the *Project Browser* (Figure 12-1.11).

FIGURE 12-1.11
Project Browser; Sheets (all)

Question: On a large project with hundreds of views, how do I know for sure if I have placed every view on a sheet?

Answer: Revit has a feature called *Browser Organization* that can hide all the views that have been placed on a sheet. You will try this next.

28. Take a general look at the *Project Browser* to see how many views are listed. (See Figure 12-1.13 on page 12-10.)

29. Select **Views (all)** at the top of the *Project Browser* (Figure 12-1.12).

30. In the *Type Selector*, pick **not on sheets** (Figure 12-1.12).

31. Notice the list in the *Project Browser* now has fewer views listed. (See Figure 12-1.15 on page 12-10.)

The *Project Browser* now only shows views which have not been placed onto a sheet. Of course, you could have a few views that do not need to be placed on a sheet, but this feature will help eliminate errors.

Next you will reset the *Project Browser*.

32. Using the process just described, set the *Project Browser* back to **All** (Figure 12-1.12).

The image to the right, Figure 12-1.13, shows the details created in Chapter 8. If you recall, these are 2D Drafting Views not directly tied to the 3D model.

FIGURE 12-1.12 Project Browser and Type Selector

FIGURE 12-1.13 Drafting Views placed on sheet

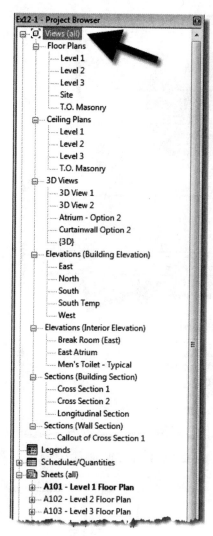

FIGURE 12-1.14
Project Browser; Views (all)

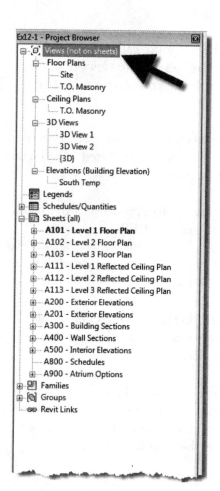

FIGURE 12-1.15
Project Browser; Views (not on sheets)

Sheets with Design Options:

Finally, you will setup a sheet to show two of the atrium *Design Options*.

33. Create a *Sheet* named **Atrium Options** and number it **A900**.

34. Open both *Atrium – Option 2* and *Curtainwall Option 2 views* and change the scale to **⅛" = 1'-0"**.

35. Place the two views, mentioned above, on sheet A900. (See Figure 12-1.16.)

FIGURE 12-1.16 Atrium Options Sheet; two views with Design Options added

Design Options can be used to present alternates to the client or the contractor.

36. **Save** your project as **ex12-1.rvt**.

The sheet border can be modified to match the design firms sheet design, including adding a scanned logo; however creating the logo in a native Revit format would be better. As you saw, the default sheet size in the Revit template is 30"x42". However, most design firms have standardized on 22"x34" as half size sets can easily be printed on 11"x17" paper. Half size sets are a nice size for a reference set at ones desk. Plus it is one-fourth the paper of a full size set.

FIGURE 12-1.17 Standard sheet size of 22″x34″ can be printed to 11″x17″ at half scale

Exercise 12-2:
Sheet Index

Revit has the ability to create a sheet index automatically. The sheet index is placed on the first sheet in the set of drawings to help the contractor find specific information when it is needed. Some drawing sets can have hundreds of sheets. You will study this now.

Creating a Sheet List View:

1. Open ex12-1.rvt and **Save As** ex12-2.

2. Select **View → Create → Schedule → Sheet List**.   Sheet List

You are now in the *Sheet List* dialog box. Here you specify which fields you want in the sheet index and how to sort the list. (Figure 12-2.1) This process is identical to the steps required to setup a schedule.

3. Add **Sheet Number** and **Sheet Name** to the right *(click Add →)*.

4. On the *Sorting* tab, sort by **Sheet Number**.

5. Click **OK**.

FIGURE 12-2.1
Sheet List Properties Dialog; sheet number and name "added"

Now you should notice that the *Sheet Names* are cut off because the column is not wide enough. You will adjust this next.

6. Move your cursor over the right edge of the *Drawing List* table and click-and-drag to the right until you can see the entire name (Figure 12-2.2).

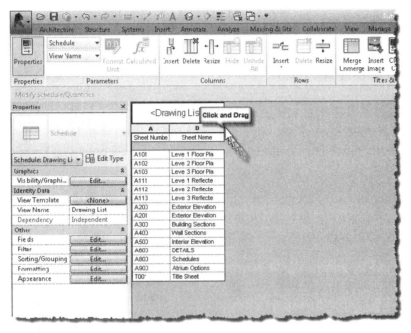

FIGURE 12-2.2
Sheet List view; notice sheet names are cut off in the right column

TIP: Via the Properties palette you can adjust the settings on the Sorting/Grouping tab to sort the sheets by sheet number.

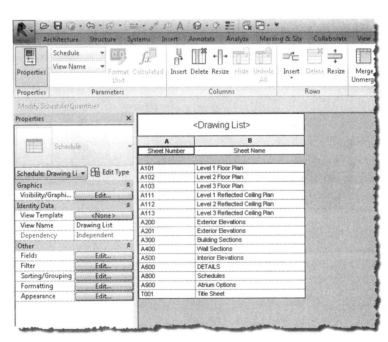

FIGURE 12-2.3
Sheet List view; sheet names are now visible

Setting Up a Title Sheet:

Now you will create a title sheet to place your sheet index on.

7. Create a new Sheet:
   a. *Number:* **T001**
   b. *Name:* **Title Sheet**

8. From the *Schedules/Quantities* category of the *Project Browser*, place the view named **Sheet List** on the *Title Sheet*. Once on the sheet, drag the "triangle" grip to adjust the column width (Figure 12-2.4).

Next you will place one of your rendered images that you saved to file (raster image). If you have not created a raster image, you should refer back to Lesson 11 and create one now (otherwise you can use any BMP or JPG file on your hard drive if necessary).

9. Select **Insert → Import → Image**.

Image

10. Browse to your JPG or BMP raster image file, select it and click **Open** to place the Image.

11. Click on your title sheet to locate the image.

Your sheet should look similar to Figure 12-2.5.

Sheet List	
Sheet Number	Sheet Name
A101	Level 1 Floor Plan
A102	Level 2 Floor Plan
A103	Level 3 Floor Plan
A111	Level 1 Reflected Ceiling Plan
A112	Level 2 Reflected Ceiling Plan
A113	Level 3 Reflected Ceiling Plan
A200	Exterior Elevations
A201	Exterior Elevations
A300	Building Sections
A400	Wall Sections
A500	Interior Elevations
A600	DETAILS
A800	Schedules
A900	Atrium Options

FIGURE 12-2.4
Sheet list on a sheet

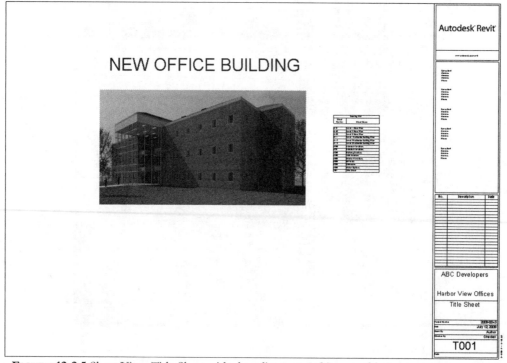

FIGURE 12-2.5 Sheet View: Title Sheet with sheet list, text and image added

12. Use the **Text** command to add the title shown in Figure 12-2.5.

    a. Create a new text style named **1″ Arial**.

When you have raster images in your project, you can manage them via the *Raster Images* dialog.

13. Select **Insert → Import → Manage Images**.   🖼 Manage Images

You are now in the *Raster Image* dialog which gives you a little information about the image and allows you to delete it from the project (Figure 12-2.6). You can also "swap" the image out with another image by using the *Reload From…* button.

FIGURE 12-2.6 Raster Image dialog

14. Click **OK** to close the *Raster Images* dialog.

15. **Save** your project as **ex12-2.rvt**.

Exercise 12-3:
Printing a Set of Drawings

Revit has the ability to print an entire set of drawings, in addition to printing individual sheets. You will study this now.

Printing a Set of Drawings

1. **Open ex12-2.rvt.**

2. Select **Application Menu → Print.**

3. In the *Print range* area, click the option **Selected views/sheets** (Figure 12-3.1).

4. Click the **Select...** button within the *Print range* area.

FIGURE 12-3.1 Print dialog box

You should now see a listing of all views and sheets (Figure 12-3.2).

FIGURE 12-3.2 Selecting tool for printing

Notice at the bottom you can **Show** both **Sheets** and **Views**, or each separately. Because you are printing a set of drawings you will want to see only the sheets.

5. **Uncheck** the **Views** option.

The list is now limited to just sheets set up in your project.

6. Select all the drawing Sheets.

7. Click **OK** to close the **View/ Sheet Set** dialog.

FYI: Once you have selected the sheets to be plotted you can click Save. This will save the list of selected drawings to a name you choose. Then, the next time you need to print those sheets, you can select the name from the drop-down list at the top (Figure 12-3.2). On very large projects (e.g., with 20 floor plan sheets) you could have a "Plans" list saved, a "Laboratory Interior Elevations" list saved, etc.

8. IF YOU ACTUALLY WANT TO PRINT A FULL SET OF DRAWINGS, you can do so now by clicking OK. Otherwise click **Cancel**.

9. You do not need to save the file at this time.

[End of Exercise 12-3]

You should now have a basic understanding of the Autodesk Revit Architecture software. **Gook luck with your future Revit projects!**

If you want to continue your studies, be sure to check out these other books by this author:
- Residential Design Using Autodesk Revit
- Design Integration Using Autodesk Revit
- Interior Design Using Autodesk Revit

Self-Exam:

The following questions can be used as a way to check your knowledge of this lesson. The answers can be found at the bottom of this page.

1. You have to manually fill in the reference bubbles after setting up the sheets. (T/F)

2. You cannot control the visibility of objects per viewport. (T/F)

3. It is possible to see a listing of only the views that have not been placed on a sheet via the *Project Browser*. (T/F)

4. You only have to enter your name on one titleblock, not all. (T/F)

5. Use the _____ tool to create another drawing sheet.

Review Questions:

The following questions may be assigned by your instructor as a way to assess your knowledge of this section. Your instructor has the answers to the review questions.

1. You need to use a special command to edit text in the titleblock. (T/F)

2. The template you started with has several titleblocks to choose from. (T/F)

3. You only have to enter the project name on one sheet, not all. (T/F)

4. The scale of a drawing placed on a sheet is determined by the scale set in that view's properties. (T/F)

5. You can save a list of drawing sheets to be plotted. (T/F)

6. Use the _____ _____ tool to edit the model from a sheet view.

7. The reference bubbles will not automatically update if a drawing is moved to another sheet. (T/F)

8. On new sheets, the sheet number on the titleblock will increase by one from the previous sheet number. (T/F)

Lesson 13
Introduction to Revit Content Creation:

This chapter will introduce you to many of the basic concepts which relate to using and creating families. The reader will benefit from learning to create custom content as the need often arises. An entire book could be written just on creating *Families*. This chapter is intended to provide a very basic introduction to help get you started.

Exercise 13-1:
Basic Family Concepts

Kinds of Families:

Autodesk Revit has three primary types of *Families*; they are
- *System Families*
- *Loadable Families*
- *In-Place Families*.

This book will mainly focus on the first, that being loadable families. Below is a brief explanation of each, followed by a graphic to help tell the story.

<u>System Families:</u>
Autodesk describes *System Families* generally as the portion of the building that is **constructed on site**. Things like walls, floors, ceilings, roofs, stairs, wiring, ductwork and piping are system families. These families can only be defined and exist within the *Project Environment*.

Unlike loadable families (doors, windows, furniture), System families cannot exist separately outside the project environment. This image shows a wall in plan with its various layers of material.

System Families have the ability to **host** *Loadable Families*. The concept of *Hosted Families* will be covered in more detail later in this section, but here is a simplified explanation: a wall hosted *Family*, such as a window, can only exist within a wall, it automatically moves with the wall and is deleted when the wall is deleted.

It is too bad that *System Families* cannot exist outside the project in individual files as it would be helpful to have several construction types predefined and load them when needed. As opposed to having them predefined within the Revit project template. Therefore, your options are to have the *System Family* predefined in a template file or Copy/Paste them between projects. This author prefers to load relevant content and not have extraneous items cluttering the selection lists. There are always tricks and workarounds to facilitating this concept but it is not as simple as *Loadable Families* which are described next.

Loadable Families:

Building components which are **constructed in a factory** and shipped to the project site are what mainly makeup *Loadable Families*. These are typically just referred to as *Families* rather than "Loadable" Families; this book will mainly use the term *Family* and mean "*Loadable*" *Family*. Building elements such as doors, windows, furniture, casework, columns, beams, appliances, electrical devices (i.e., outlets and switches), electrical panels, mechanical equipment (i.e., VAV boxes, air handling units and water heaters), duct fittings and plumbing fixtures (i.e., toilets and sinks) constitute *Loadable Families*.

Plumbing fixtures, such as this toilet, are "loadable", that is, they can exist in a file outside of the project environment.

Image credit: Stabs, Wingate

As the name implies, these *Families* can be stored outside of the *Project Environment* within individual files (*.rfa is the family extension, versus *rvt which is the project file extension). Using a "Load Family" command (found on the Insert tab), one is able to bring one or more Families into the Project Environment for placement.

In-Place Families:

Using a special command (*Architecture* → *Build* → *Component* → *Model In-Place*) within the *Project Environment* it is possible to create what is called an *In-Place Family*. This feature allows you to create a *Family* within the context of your project.

The *In-Place Family* has a couple of rather significant warnings that go along with it. <u>First</u>, it is meant for one-off items like a reception desk or a unique built in cabinet. If you copy an *In-Place Family* it is really just making another independent instance of the family – which makes the Revit project file grow in size. If you know something will occur more than once it should be created as a *Loadable Family*, not

Stone trimmed opening created as an in-place family to interface with project conditions.
Image courtesy of LHB, Inc.

an *In-Place Family*. <u>Second</u>, *In-Place* families cannot ever exist outside the *Project Environment*, similar to System Families, so the item may not be added to your firm's library for use on another project. One last point is from Autodesk's "Revit Platform Performance Document"; *In-Place Families* tend to reduce system performance within the Project Environment, especially on larger projects.

So with these points in mind it is best to use *Loadable Families* whenever possible. However, they are still acceptable in some situations.

Creating *In-Place Families* will not specifically be covered in this book. However, the process is almost identical in several ways to creating *Loadable Families* so you should be able to create them without too much trouble when needed.

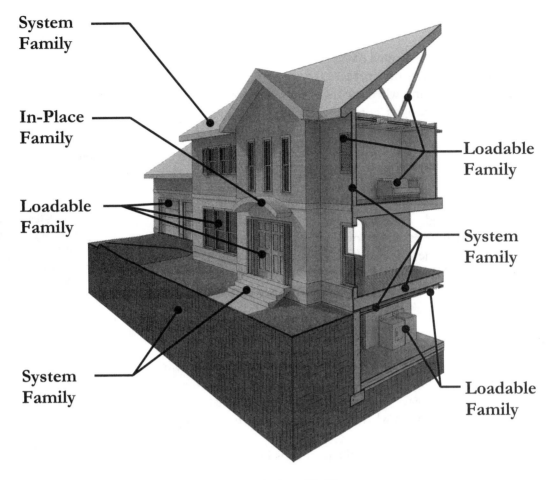

System
Family

In-Place
Family

Loadable
Family

Loadable
Family

System
Family

System
Family

Loadable
Family

FIGURE 13-1.1 Types of Families; System, Loadable and In-Place

Nested Families:

It is possible to insert one or more *Families* into another *Family*; this is called nesting a family. One way in which this is useful might be two double-hung windows, as shown in the image above. Although it is possible to simply place the two windows close to each other in the project, this does not represent the reality of how the window will need to be documented in the project and how it will be delivered to the job site. The two windows would typically be mulled together by the window manufacturer and shipped and installed as one unit. By nesting one family into another, and then copying it you can quickly create a two window unit, which can also be tagged as one window. Lastly, nested families can typically have their position controlled more easily by parameters because it acts as one element rather than several, or even hundreds.

Hosted Families:

Loadable Families can be created to be Hosted or Non-hosted. As briefly mentioned above, the host is a *System Family* (e.g., a wall, floor, ceiling or roof) and when the host is moved, copied or deleted the Hosted Family is moved, copied or deleted.

Wall hosted family - Window.
Image credit: Stabs, Wingate

This feature helps solve some coordination problems but also creates a few new problems.

Problems solved:
When a wall is moved, things like cabinets, toilet fixtures, windows, specialty equipment (e.g., paper towel dispensers, grab bars, mirrors, etc.), doors and electrical devices (e.g., light switches and outlets) all move with the wall. This significantly helps with last minute coordination.

Roof hosted family – Solar
Conforms to slope of roof.
Image credit: Stabs, Wingate

Problems created:
A few problems have surfaced when using hosted content. For example, when designing a kitchen the wall cabinets are hosted. It is difficult to quickly mirror one's kitchen design. Also, when a supply air diffuser is hosted by a ceiling there is occasionally a problem with the ductwork when the ceiling is moved vertically.

Ceiling hosted family – Light Fixture
Image credit: Stabs, Wingate

Oftentimes the benefits outweigh the problems created.

> **TIP:** *One technique is creating your content initially as non-hosted and then nest that family into a hosted family, giving you access to both types; which is convenient as it is not possible to convert from one type to the other. Quick examples of why you would want to do this: wall cabinets in a kitchen are sometimes hung from rods above a peninsula countertop. Also, light fixtures which are attached to a ceiling are sometimes suspended within mechanical rooms or basements which do not have ceilings.*

Face based family – FE Cabinet
Image courtesy of LHB, Inc.

Family Types:

Revit *Families* have the ability to hold information in placeholders called parameters. These parameters are defined, when created, to hold a specific kind of information; for example, text, integer, number, length, currency, yes/no, etc. This helps to validate data when it is entered. You cannot type text into a parameter that is set to currency. Finally, some of the parameters, such as lengths, can be associated with actual dimensions in the *Family*. Adjusting a length parameter value actually changes the size of the *Family*.

Wall Cabinet:
With the information from the previous paragraph in mind, it is time to discuss how slight variations are dealt with for content that is geometrically the same; that is for example, a wall cabinet is a rectangular box that has four different heights, two different depths and several widths.

It is possible to create 100 individual *Families*, each of which represents one wall cabinet. However, this would be very cumbersome to manage; if one change was required you would have to open 100 files and make the same change 100 times. This is where *Family Types* are employed.

A single *Family* can have several *Types* defined. A *Type* is simply a saved state of all the parameter settings. For example, the wall cabinet may have two *Types* defined as follows:

Type A		Type B	
Parameter	*Value*	*Parameter*	*Value*
Width	**24"**	Width	**27"**
Depth	14"	Depth	14"
Height	24"	Height	24"
Model	**W241424**	Model	**W271424**
Manufacturer	Merillat	Manufacturer	Merillat
LEED – 500mi	Yes/No	LEED – 500mi	Yes/No

Normally the *Type* name would be more meaningful than Type A and Type B. As you can see, the various parameters can be edited within each type. Therefore, one wall cabinet Family can represent 100 different sizes.

Some of the information in the table above has a direct impact on the 3D geometry; the Width, Depth and Height parameters can be associated with dimensions in the *Family*. When the parameter is changed the size of the *Family* actually changes. So one only has to change the *Family* type in a *Project Environment* to change the size of the placed *Family*. And, of course, some of the information has no effect on the 3D geometry. Rather it is used to track design decisions and for scheduling purposes. Shared parameters can show up in schedules.

There are always exceptions to the rule, but generally speaking, anytime the geometry changes you need to create a new *Family*. For instance, one Family can represent all the wall cabinets with a single door. But when the cabinet width dictates two doors a new *Family* is required. This change in geometry cannot easily be managed within a single *Family*.

When the geometry changes a new Family is typically required.
The example above has different handle, door and drawer locations.

Family Types within the Project Environment.
When utilizing content within the *Project Environment* the *Family* and *Types* are presented as shown in the image below (Figure 13-1.2). Notice *Chair-Desk* only has one *Type* defined within that *Family* whereas *Cook Top-2 Unit* has three. Within the project anyone on the design team can manually add or delete *Types* associated with any *Family*.

FIGURE 13-1.2 Family Types within the Project Environment

Type Catalog:

There is one last concept to point out about *Family Types* before moving on. When a *Family* is loaded into a project all of its *Types* are automatically loaded. Sometimes this is good and other times it is not. The image on the previous page (Figure 13-1.2) shows manageable lists of *Families*. However, you can imagine how this list would get rather long if you loaded the wall cabinet *Family*, described on the previous pages, that had 100 types. Not only would the list be long, but you are likely only using one depth and two heights.

To better manage this situation Revit has a feature for *Families* called a *Type Catalog*. Rather than loading all of the *Types* into the project with the *Family*, the user is prompted to select the *Types* desired. This process could be repeated until all of the *Types* are ultimately loaded for a specific *Family*.

The image below (Figure 13-1.3) shows the dialog box the user is presented with when loading the steel wide flange beam *Family*.

Specify Types

Family:	Types:						
W-Wide Flange.rfa	Type	W	A	d	bf	tw	tf
		(all)	(all)	(all)	(all)	(all)	(all)
	W44X335	335	0.68 SF	3' 8"	1' 3 115/128"	0' 1 1/32"	0' 1 197/256"	0'
	W44X290	290	0.59 SF	3' 7 77/128"	1' 3 205/256"	0' 0 221/256"	0' 1 37/64"	0'
	W44X262	262	0.53 SF	3' 7 77/256"	1' 3 205/256"	0' 0 201/256"	0' 1 27/64"	0'
	W44X230	230	0.47 SF	3' 6 115/128"	1' 3 205/256"	0' 0 91/128"	0' 1 7/32"	0'
	W40X593	593	1.21 SF	3' 7"	1' 4 179/256"	0' 1 101/128"	0' 3 59/256"	0'
	W40X503	503	1.03 SF	3' 6 13/128"	1' 4 51/128"	0' 1 69/128"	0' 2 195/256"	0'
	W40X431	431	0.88 SF	3' 5 77/256"	1' 4 51/256"	0' 1 87/256"	0' 2 23/64"	0'
	W40X397	397	0.81 SF	3' 5"	1' 4 13/128"	0' 1 7/32"	0' 2 51/256"	0'
	W40X372	372	0.76 SF	3' 4 77/128"	1' 4 13/128"	0' 1 41/256"	0' 2 13/256"	0'
	W40X362	362	0.74 SF	3' 4 77/128"	1' 4"	0' 1 31/256"	0' 2 3/256"	0'
	W40X324	324	0.66 SF	3' 4 51/256"	1' 3 115/128"	0' 1"	0' 1 207/256"	0'

Select one or more types on the right for each family listed on the left   OK   Cancel   Help

FIGURE 13-1.3 Selecting specific *Types* when loading a *Family* via the *Type Catalog*

The implementation and use of *Type Catalogs* will be covered later in the book.

The first *Family* you create, in the next lesson, will not even have a *Type* as they are optional.

Instance and Type Parameters:

When creating *Parameters* for use in a *Family* you need to decide if it is an *Instance* or a *Type* parameter. Remember, parameters are placeholders for information in which some of them can be linked to geometry size and visibility.

An **Instance Parameter** only impacts the one or more *Families* that are selected, or about to be created within the *Project Environment*, whereas the **Type** parameter affects all instances of the *Family* within the project.

A good example to describe how Instance/Type parameters are used in a project is to consider a window. Looking at the image below you can see this window *Family* has been set up so that the width and height parameters are *Type* and the <u>Sill Height</u> is an *Instance* parameter. *FYI: You only know this here by the labels and arrows provided in the image (Figure 13-1.4).*

This works with the standard industry convention where all windows that are the same size (i.e., width and height) are labeled with a common mark or tag. For example, the 2'x4' window below might be referred to as "W1" in a project. Thus, if it was determined that all W1 window types need to increase in size to let in more natural light, changing one window's *Type Properties* would change the size of all "W1" windows in the project. On the other hand, the <u>Sill Height</u> dimension needs to be an *Instance* parameter. The "W1" windows might be 2'-4" above the first floor and 2'-8" above the second.

It is possible to edit a family and change a parameter from a *Type* to an *Instance*, with one exception; some parameters that are predefined in the template files are not editable. You cannot even change the name.

Final thought: a table *Family* might have its width and depth parameters set as *Type* or as *Instance* depending on how the design team wanted to use it in the project.

FIGURE 13-1.4 Exterior view of a window in the Family Editor

Family Templates:

When starting a new *Family* you need to know what it is and how it will be used in a project. With this information you can then select a *Family Template* from which to begin the content creation process.

Selecting the correct template saves time setting up the most basic parameters and in some cases is critical to the *Family* working. For example, the door and the window templates have the following parameters setup:

Door Template			Window Template	
Parameter	*Value*		*Parameter*	*Value*
Width	3'-0"		Width	3'-0"
Height	7'-0"		Height	4'-0"
Frame Width	3"		**Sill Height**	3'-0"
Model	*blank*		Model	*blank*
Manufacturer	*blank*		Manufacturer	*blank*

Other templates, such as **Generic Model**, do not have a <u>Width</u> and <u>Height</u> parameter predefined. Additionally, the door and window templates are wall hosted whereas the *Generic Model* is not.

Revit Architecture comes with over 70 template files. This book will only provide a discussion on a handful of them, but many are self-explanatory and it should be possible to discern what most of them are for after completing this book.

Family Categories:

Another item that needs to be covered at an overview level is the concept of a *Family Category*. Each *Revit Family* needs to be assigned to a specific category. This is done automatically by way of the template files for most *Families*. For example, starting a new *Family* from the window template file, the category has been set to window as shown in Figure 13-1.5 shows.

The category setting does two basic things: it controls which command is used to place the *Family* and it relates directly to manipulating visibility within the project; turning off the window category for a specific view makes all the windows disappear in that view.

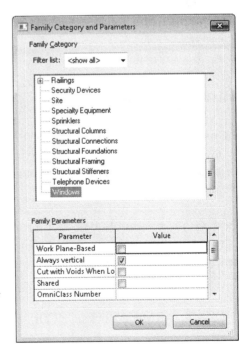

FIGURE 13-1.5 Family categories

Custom Family Libraries:

Whether you are creating content for personal use or for a large firm, you should have a plan on how and where to store your custom content. There are probably an infinate number of solutions to this problem, but a relativly simple one will be suggested here.

It is best to store your custom Revit content in a separate folder and not in the folders that contain the Revit OOTB content (OOTB = out of the box, meaning the content that comes with the software). It is best to segregate the content that has been created or edited to comply with your firms graphic or design standards. Additionally, each year, when a new version of Revit is released you wold need to sift through all the OOTB content folders to find your custom content.

Revit has a specific set of folders created to house the OOTB content (see Figure 13-1.6). One suggestion is to create those same folders in a parallel folder and place your content there. Then, when content is needed, a user might first look through the OOTB location and then the firm location. At some point your custom content may be sufficient enough to reverse the order in which you look for content (i.e., Firm folder and then OOTB folder).

Of course, in a firm setting, the content should be located on a server so everyone has access to the same content, and so it gets backed up!

Naming Families:

The name of the *Family* file (.rfa files) on your hard drive, or server, is also the name the users see in Revit. The following information is offered as a suggestion, as there is no hard-fast rule on *Family* naming.

The *Family* name should be concise and as short as possible, and is should not contain information that will appear in the *Type* name, or vice versa. For example:

Family name	*Type name*
Metal Locker – **Tall**	**Tall** 18″ x 18″

Annotations
Boundary Conditions
Cable Tray
Casework
Columns
Conduit
Curtain Panel By Pattern
Curtain Wall Panels
Detail Items
Doors
Duct
Electrical
Entourage
Fire Protection
Furniture
Furniture System
Lighting
Mass
Mechanical
Openings
Pipe
Planting
Plumbing
Profiles
Railings
Site
Specialty Equipment
Structural Columns
Structural Connections
Structural Foundations
Structural Framing
Structural Rebar Shapes
Structural Retaining Walls
Structural Stiffeners
Structural Trusses
Sustainable Design
Titleblocks

FIGURE 13-1.6
OOTB Family Folders

The *Family* name should be as generic as possible so others on the design team, or in the firm, can quickly ascertain what the various *Families* are. If only one type of locker is used then the *Family* name can be more generic. Similarly, the *Type* name within the *Family* should be easy to understand if possible; show the size of the locker rather than the model number. For example:

Generic naming convention:

Family name   *Type name*

Metal Locker – Tall   18″ x 18″

Detailed naming convention:

Family name   *Type name*

Arrow Locker – Tall   ALT181860

Locker family shown in perspective.

Remember, a *Family* often has several types defined within it. Thus, the example above would have several similarly named types which define several locker sizes.

The detailed naming convention above would be appropriate if a design firm used several locker manufacturers depending on the project type; maybe they specialize in sports facilities and design various types of locker rooms.

Another option, based on the example above, is to have a detailed *Family* name and a generic *Type* name:

Family name   *Type name*

Arrow Locker – Tall   18″ x 18″

A good naming convention will help promote efficiency in the project environment. Many of the *Families* are added to the Revit model via the catch-all tool: **Component: Place a Component** (on the *Architecture* tab). When the *Component* tool is active, the *Element Type Selector* lists all the *Families* that are loaded into the project; that is, all the *Families* that do not have their own insertion tool, as windows and doors do.

These *Families* are listed in alphabetical order in the *Element Type Selector,* within the project environment. Therefore, if the *Families* are not named properly, you might have a toilet at the bottom of the list, a Bathtub near the top and many other types of content sprinkled in between.

One solution to this problem would be to implement some sort of abbreviation or prefix naming system.

Families
- Annotation Symbols
- Casework
- Ceilings
- Columns
- Curtain Panels
- Curtain Systems
- Curtain Wall Mullions
- Detail Items
- Doors
- Floors
- Furniture
- Lighting Fixtures
- Parking
- Pattern
- Planting
- Plumbing Fixtures
- Profiles
- Railings
- Ramps
- Roofs
- Site
- Specialty Equipment
- Stairs
- Structural Beam Systems
- Structural Columns
- Structural Foundations
- Structural Framing
- Walls
- Windows

FIGURE 13-1.7 Project Browser within the Project Environment showing Family Categories

Each *Family* falls within a *Family Category* as previously discussed. These categories are listed within the *Project Browser*, note the list varies depending on the content currently loaded into the project. Creating a two letter prefix would sort the content by category within the *Element Type Selector*. For example:

CW	= Casework
FN	= Furniture
PF	= Plumbing Fixtures
SE	= Specialty Equipment

This naming convention would cause all the related content to be grouped together within the *Element Type Selector*.

FIGURE 13-1.8 Element Type Selector within the Project Environment showing loaded Families available for placement via the Component tool. **Left**, default naming; **right**, prefix added to control sort order.

Utilizing a naming convention like this means a firm's name or initials cannot appear at the beginning of the name.

Family and Type naming is highly subjective so one firm's solution may be completely different from another's. But, in any case, some sort of standard should be developed and agreed upon within each design firm.

Exercise 13-2:
The Box: Creating the Geometry

The emphasis will be placed on Revit features and techniques related to *Families* and not so much on geometry. A simple box will be created and then utilized to show many of the things that can be done with, and within, a *Family*. So, to keep things simple early on, a basic box will be used.

This exercise demonstrates how to start a *Family* and develop a 3D box that can be adjusted in size; i.e., a **parametric box**. Note that more detailed steps and graphics will be provided the first time a subject is covered. The subsequent steps for the same subject will be less detailed and may not contain graphics. It is therefore beneficial to work though the lessons in order.

Creating a New Family:

1. Open Revit Architecture 2015.

   a. Revit, Revit Structure or Revit MEP may also be used.

   b. There is no difference to the user between 32bit and 64bit versions of the software. Therefore it does not matter which one is used with this book.

2. **Application Menu → New → Family** (Figure 13-2.1)

Assuming Revit was installed properly you should see a large list of files from which to choose. If not, you may download the *Family* template files from Autodesk's website.

The template names make it rather obvious as to what each template file is intended to be used for. When a template is selected, Revit makes a copy of the file and then opens it as an unnamed *Family*; called **Famly1** until saved.

FIGURE 13-2.1 Starting a new Family

3. Select **Generic Model.rft** and then click **OK** (Figure 13-2.2).

FIGURE 13-2.2 Selecting a Family template file

The initial view is a plan view from the top (Figure 13-2.3). As seen in the *Project Browser*, the following views have been established, via the template file:

- Floor Plan
- Ceiling Plan
- 3D View
- Elevations
  - Back
  - Front
  - Left
  - Right

FIGURE 13-2.3 Initial view shown reference planes

In the initial plan view, Figure 13-2.3, are two *Reference Planes*; one horizontal and one vertical. These two *Reference Planes* define the center of the content about to be created, in each direction. The intersection of the two also defines the origin. The origin is the insertion point, relative to your cursor, when placing the *Family* in a project. Ultimately the box to be created needs to be centered on the intersection of the reference planes.

The *Reference Planes* do not appear in the *Project Environment*. However, Revit is aware of them and can use them when dimensioning and aligning to other elements; this depends on how a few properties for the *Reference Planes* are set, but in any case the *Reference Planes* are never visible.

Creating the Framework for a New Family:

A common method used when creating Revit content is to first add *Reference Planes*, make them parametric and then create the 3D geometry and lock its edges to the *Reference Planes*. This allows complex *Families* to be broken down into more manageable elements and makes controlling multiple 3D objects easier (i.e., moving one reference plane moves several 3D objects).

In the next few steps you will create *Reference Planes* that ultimately will control the size and location of a 3D box.

4. Select **Create → Datum → Reference Plane**.

To add a *Reference Plane* one simply picks two points in a view. A *Reference Plane* is a 3D plane that will appear in all views which cut through it, on end (or perpendicular to), or are within the Select/Elevation/Plan "view range". The edges of the *Reference Planes* are typically only visible unless "show" is toggled on under the *Create* tab on the *Ribbon*, and then, only the current *Work Plane* is shown.

5. Add a horizontal *Reference Plane* as shown in Figure 13-2.4.

   a. The exact location and length does not matter at this time, it will be adjusted later.
   b. Make sure the *Reference Plane* is snapped to the horizontal plane before picking the second point. Watch for the cyan-colored dashed line and a *tooltip* which displays the word horizontal.

   FYI: The use of the word "horizontal" above is in reference to the computer screen.

The first *Reference Plane* has now been added to the new *Family*. Later in the book, a dimension will be added between the two parallel *Reference Planes* shown in Figure 13-2.4. This dimension can be locked so it does not move, or made to be parametric in which case the end user in the project environment can edit a value in the properties of a selected element; causing the *Reference Plane* to move accordingly.

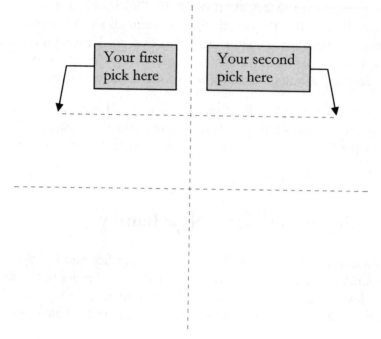

FIGURE 13-2.4 Adding a "horizontal" reference plane

6. Switch to the **Right** elevation view by double-clicking on it in the *Project Browser*.

Notice that the newly added *Reference Plane* is visible in this view, as well as the <u>Left</u> view. Again, this is because the *Reference Plane* is a 3D element.

FIGURE 13-2.5 Newly created *Reference Plane* visible in the "side" views

7. Close the **Right** elevation view and switch back to the **Plan** view.

8. Draw three more *Reference Planes* approximately as shown in Figure 13-2.6.

9. Select **Modify**, on the *Ribbon*, to finish the *Reference Plane* command.

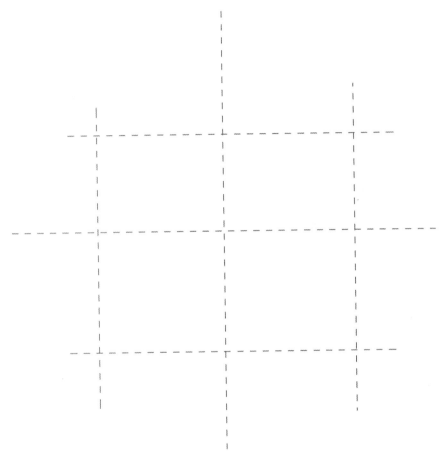

FIGURE 13-2.6 Three more reference planes added

The four *Reference Planes* just drawn will ultimately serve as the guides for the edge of the 3D box. The top and bottom edges of the box will be controled by *Reference Planes* not visible in the current view.

Next, the newly added *Reference Planes* position will be adjusted relative to the center or origin *Reference Planes* that came with the template file. This can be done simply by selecting one *Reference Plane* at a time and editing the on-screen temporary dimension which appears.

10. Select the top horizontal *Reference Plane* (Figure 13-2.7).

11. Edit the *Temporary Dimension* to be **2'-0"** (Figure 13-2.7).

   a. If needed, adjust the ends of the *Reference Planes* so they cross each other and form a corner as shown below. Procedure: select a *Reference Plane* and then click and drag on the visible endpoint grip.

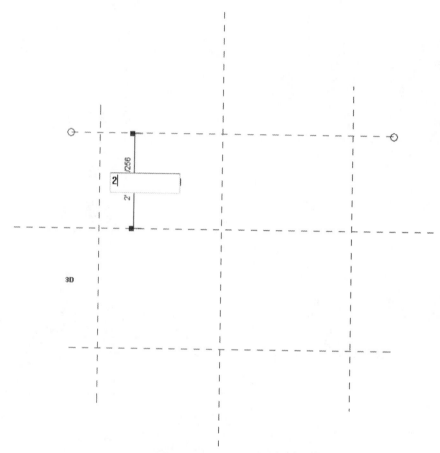

FIGURE 13-2.7 Top "horizontal" reference plane selected

12. Modify the remaining three *Reference Planes* to have the same **2'-0"** dimension off of the original centerline/origin *Reference Planes* that came with the template

The four *Reference Planes* now define the extents of a 4'-0" x 4'-0" box. This only defines the sides of the box. Next the top and bottom of the box will be defined.

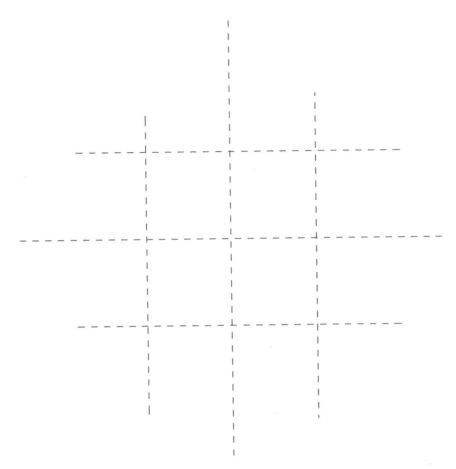

FIGURE 13-2.8 Four reference planes with position adjusted

13. In the *Project Browser*, double-click **Front** under *Elevations*.

The <u>Front</u> (or South elevation) shows two of the four *Reference Planes* created in this exercise. All *Reference Planes* that are perpendicular to the view are visible, as long as they are within view range. Additionally, the center (left/right) *Reference Plane* and one in line with the **Ref. Level** is visible; both of which came from the template.

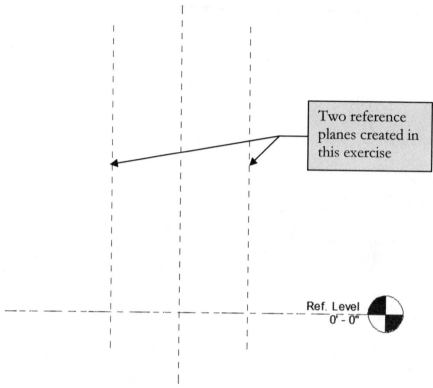

FIGURE 13-2.9 Front view

Next, a *Reference Plane* will be drawn as a guideline for the top of the 3D box. A *Reference Plane* is always drawn perpendicular to the "plane" that is being defined.

14. Draw a *Reference Plane* **2'-0"** above the Ref. Level (Figure 13-2.10).

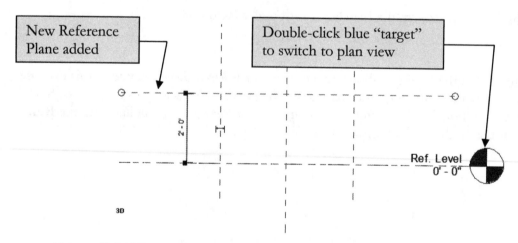

FIGURE 13-2.10 Front view; relocated ref. level

15. Switch back to the plan view, double-click **Ref. Level** under *Floor Plans* in the *Project Browser*, or Double-click the blue target, see Figure 13-2.10.

Creating the 3D Geometry:

Now that the framework, or guidelines, have been established using Reference Planes, the 3D geometry can be created. A simple box will be created.

16. Select **Create → Forms → Extrusion** from the *Ribbon*.

17. Draw a square within the outer *Reference Planes*, Figure 13-2.11.

   a. Select "rectangle" on the *Ribbon*, in the *Draw* panel.

   b. Notice the depth is set to 1'-0" on the *Options Bar*, this is fine.

   c. The exact size does not matter here.

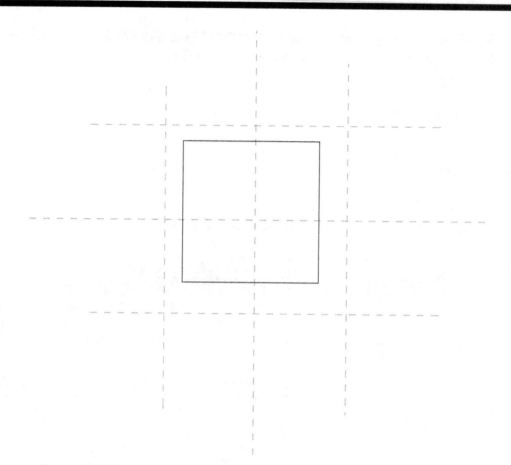

FIGURE 13-2.11 Sketch lines for 3D extrusion

When creating a *Solid Extrusion*, a simple 2D outline is sketched as in Figure 13-2.11. This defines the perimeter of the extrusion. When "finish extrusion" is selected, the 2D outline is extruded perpendicular to the sketch lines to a thickness (or depth) specified on the *Options Bar*.

The 2D sketch must be "clean"; meaning no gaps or overlaps occur at the corners. Because the rectangle option was selected the outline will automatically be "clean".

18. Select the **green check mark** on the *Ribbon*.

With the previous three simple steps a 3D box was created. This box will now serve as our "test subject" for an introduction on many of the basic options and settings that can be done with a *Family*.

The last step, in this exercise, is to align and lock the 3D geometry to the *Reference Planes*. Thus, whenever the *Reference Planes* move, so will the geometry. Revit provides a tool to easily do this; it is called **Align**. The tool brings two lines and/or surfaces into alignment. Once the *Align* tool has been employed, the opportunity to "lock" the relationship is available. This lock creates a parametric relationship within the *Family*. This is just one of the tools in which a *Family* can be made parametric.

19. Select **Modify** → **Align** on the *Ribbon*.

20. Select the vertical *Reference Plane* on the right (Figure 13-2.12).

21. Select the right-hand side of the box.

The right side of the box should now be aligned with the *Reference Plane* (Figure 13-2.12). If the *Reference Plane* moved rather than the edge of the box, click **Undo**. When using the *Align* tool, the element that does not move is selected first.

22. Click the **Padlock** icon that appears, to lock the relationship between the edge of the box and the *Reference Plan*.

    a. Figure 13-2.12 shows the icon in its initial position, unlocked.

    b. Clicking the "unlocked" icon will change it to a "locked" icon.

    c. When a *Reference Plane* is selected the "locked" icon will appear.

        i. This lets the users know a "lock" exists.

        ii. Clicking the "locked" icon will unlock the relationship.

    d. Selecting the 3D box does not reveal the locked icon (except when in "edit sketch" mode).

Select this ref plane – Step 20

FIGURE 13-2.12 Aligning 3D geometry to reference planes

23. **Align** and **Lock** the other three sides of the box (Figure 13-2.13).

    a.   Remember to select the *Reference Plane* first.

    b.   Select *Undo* on the *Quick Access Toolbar* if you select things in the wrong order.

The four sides of the 3D box now have a parametric relationship to the four *Reference Planes* created in the plan view.

Next, the top and bottom of the 3D box will be *Aligned* and *Locked* to *Reference Planes*.

24. Switch to the **Front view** via the *Project Browser*.

FIGURE 13-2.13 Side of 3D box aligned with *Reference Planes*

25. **Align** and **Lock** the top of the box, which is 1'-0" high, to the top *Reference Plane* (Figure 13-2.14).

FIGURE 13-2.14 Aligning 3D geometry to reference planes

26. **Select the 3D box** to reveal the edit grips (Figure 13-2.15).

Notice the four triangle shaped grips on each side of the box. These grips can be dragged, which repositions the selected side. The one limitation with editing geometry with these grips is that there is no way to control the distance in which the edge is moved.

FIGURE 13-2.15 3D geometry selected, edit grips revealed

In the next step, the bottom of the box will be raised to make it easier to *Align* and *Lock* it to the bottom *Reference Plane*. It is not required that this be done. However, it is easier to select things in the correct order and assure the desired things are selected; which can be challenging when several things overlap.

27. Click and drag the bottom grip up as show in Figure 13-2.16, the exact position does not matter.

FIGURE 13-2.16 Bottom of 3D box repositioned

28. *Align* and *Lock* the bottom edge of the 3D box with the bottom *Reference Plane*.

29. Switch back to the **Plan View**.

Flexing the Family:

Now that the 3D box has been tied to the *Reference Planes*, anytime the *Reference Planes* are moved the 3D box will move with it. This will be tested next.

30. Select the *Reference Plane* on the right and use the **Move** tool to move it **1'-0"** more to the right (Figure 13-2.17).

   a. The *Move* tool is only visible when something is selected.
   b. The exact distance here does not matter.

31. Notice the 3D box moves with the *Reference Plane* (Figure 13-2.17).

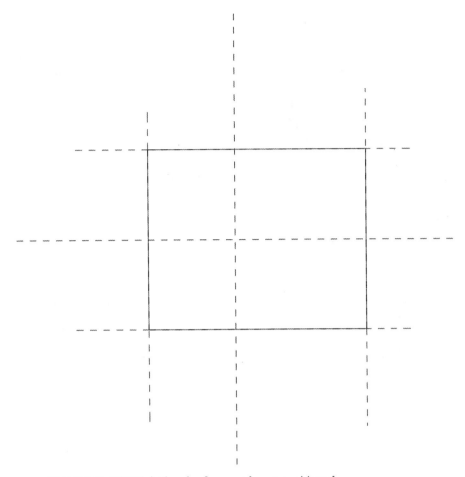

FIGURE 13-2.17 Right-hand reference plane repositioned

32. Click **Undo** on the *Quick Access Toolbar* to undo the previous step.

Now the *Family* will be loaded into a project to show how that process works. Once in the project, the content does not have any direct connection to the external *Family* created in this lesson.

33. Open a **new project**; see chapter one if needed.

    a. Use the default template.

34. Switch back to the **Family Editor**, by pressing **Ctrl + Tab**.

    a. Ctrl+Tab cycles through open projects and views.

Before loading the *Family* into a project it should first be saved to a file. The main reason is to establish the *Family's* name. The *Family's* file name becomes the name of the content within a Revit project.

35. Save the *Family* to your hard drive as **Box.rfa**.

    a. The location where the file is saved does not matter, however it would be a good idea to create a folder in which all the files created in this text are stored.

    b. It is highly recommended that all data files be backed up regularly. If a Revit file becomes corrupt a backup may be the only solution; another option would be to send the file to Autodesk support and they may be able to salvage it.

36. Click the **Load into Project** button on the *Ribbon*.

Revit automatically switched back to the Revit Project.

Load into Project

37. *In the project:* Select **Architecture → Build → Component**.

38. With the *Box* family current in the *Element Type Selector*, click somewhere within the floor plan view to place an instance of the box.

39. Click the **3D** icon on the *Quick Access Toolbar* to see the 3D box.

40. **Save** the *Family* as **Box**, and the *Project* as **Box Project**.

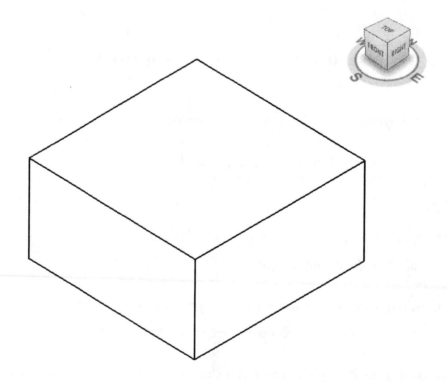

Exercise 13-3:
The Box: Adding Parameters

In this exercise the steps required to make the box parametric will be covered. Parametric, in this case, means that certain parameters control the size of the box. Thus, in the project environment it is possible to select the box, go to its properties, edit a few parameters (e.g., width and height) and then the box will change size accordingly. This is a very powerful feature and can save time crating content, as a *Family* is not required for every size.

All parameters are either a ***Type*** parameter or an ***Instance*** parameter. An introduction to this concept was presented on page 13-8 of this chapter. This exercise will help to better explain the differences and how to implement them.

1. Open the ***Box*** *Family* created in the previous exercise.

   a. It is recommended that a copy of the "Box" *Family* be saved for each exercise in case problems arise and an older file is needed to revert back to. Maybe copy the "Box" *Family* file and rename it to Box 13-2 to save a copy of the *Family* from the previous exercise.

Adding Dimensions:

The first step in making 3D geometry parametric is to add dimensions in a view. Two dimensions will be added in plan view, which will eventually be tied to parameters to control the width and depth of the 3D box.

2. In the *Ref. Level* plan view, select **Annotate → Dimension → Aligned**.

3. Click the vertical left and right *Reference Planes*, and then click a third point to position the dimension line (Figure 13-3.1).

   TIP: The third click needs to be in a blank area, as clicking on something will add another segment to the dimension string.

   TIP: Be careful to select the reference plane and not the 3D box.

4. Similar to the two previous steps, add another dimension for the other side of the box (Figure 13-3.2).

FIGURE 13-3.1 Dimension added to reference planes

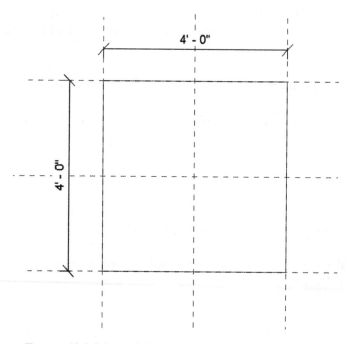

FIGURE 13-3.2 Second dimension added

Creating Parameters:

Now that the dimensions are placed, they can be tied to parameters. The dimensions can be tied to previously created parameters or a new parameter can be created based on the selected dimension. The later will be employed, that is: selecting a dimension and then creating a parameter for it.

When defining a parameter, the user must specify the following:

- Name
- Parameter Type
  - o Family Parameter
  - o Shared Parameter
- Group parameter under
- Instance or Type
- Discipline
- Type of Parameter

You will gain a better understanding of how these various settings work once you start using them, but the following descriptions are offered as a primer for what is about to be covered in the next few steps.

Name: The *Parameter Name* should be descriptive. It can have spaces and symbols. However, dashes and other mathematical formula symbols should be avoided as they will confuse Revit when using them to do calculations. The name IS case sensitive. One common naming convention is to name all custom parameters with all uppercase letters to distinguish the Revit default parameters from the custom ones. The name can be changed at any time.

Parameter Type: The *Parameter Type* concept takes a little time to fully understand. A simple explanation will be provided here so as not to get too bogged down in the details early on.

Family parameters: cannot appear in schedules (e.g., a door schedule or a furniture schedule) or be used in tags (e.g., a door tag or a furniture tag). Thus, if one were to create a *Family Parameter* to keep track of the recycled content, that value (e.g., 80%) could not appear in a schedule, nor could it appear in a tag (e.g., a tag that listed the item number and directly below it the 80% value). This is the option that will be used initially in this book.

Shared parameters: can be shared by multiple projects and families, and appear in schedules and tags. This method requires the use of an external text file to manage the parameters.

Group parameter under: The *Group parameter under* setting simply specifies which section to place the parameter in when displayed in the properties dialogs in the project (see Figure 13-3.3). This setting can be changed at any time after the parameter has been created.

Instance vs. Type: The *Instance* vs. *Type* parameter has already been discussed; see page 13-8. This setting can be changed at any time after the parameter has been created.

Discipline: This setting is simply a way to manage the large number of value types as can be seen in the information below.

FIGURE 13-3.3 Instance Propertied dialog for box family (in a project environment)

Type of Parameter: The *Type of Parameter* is how Revit knows what type of information will be stored in a specific placeholder, or parameter.

Looking at the images to the left, one can see the various disciplines and parameter types that can be used.

Setting this properly has the following benefits:

- *Input validation*: when a *Parameter* is set to the type *Integer*, a user working with the family in a project cannot enter a decimal number.

- *Proper formatting*:
    o Common, Currency = 1.50
    o Electrical, Wattage = 60 W
    o Structural, Force = 2.45 kip

FYI: *Additional formatting can be done in the project via Project Units and also within the scheduling functionally.*

This setting cannot be changed once the parameter has been created; it would have to be deleted and recreated.

Revit MEP and Revit Structure both have additional parameter types.

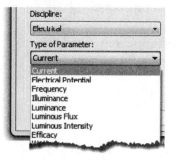

5. Select the horizontal dimension (see Figure 13-3.4).

Notice one of the options, on the *Option Bar*, is **Label**; and it has a drop-down list next to it. This might better be titled "Parameter", because the drop-down list presents *Parameters* that can be tied into the selected dimension, and ultimately used to drive the dimensions from the *Properties* dialog from within a project. However, once a parameter has been tied into a dimension a *Label* does show up next to the dimension text as will be seen in a moment; so the *Label* title is not totally inappropriate.

6. From the **Label** drop-down list, on the *Options Bar*, select **<Add parameter>** (see Figure 13-3.4).

FIGURE 13-3.4 Adding a parameter to a previously drawn dimension

The information on creating parameters, covered on the previous two pages, can now be put to use. Notice, in Figure 13-3.5, that the *Discipline* and *Type* of *Parameter* have been automatically selected because there are no other options when tying a parameter into a dimension. Therefore, creating a parameter for a dimension using this method saves a little time.

7. Enter the following in the *Parameter Properties* dialog (Figure 13-3.5):

    a. *Parameter Type:*   **Family parameter**
    b. *Name:*   **Width**
    c. *Group under:*   **Dimensions**
    d. *Instance vs. Type:*   **Type**

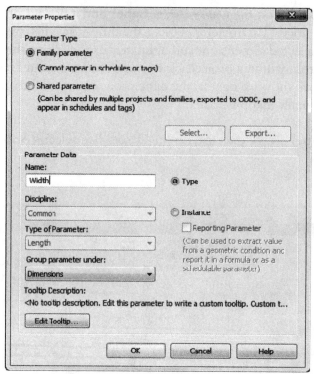

FIGURE 13-3.5 Creating the *Width* parameter

8. Repeat the previous steps to add a **Depth** parameter or label to the vertical dimension in the *Ref. Level* view.

Notice, on the *Options Bar*, that previously created parameters are listed in the *Label* drop-down list. If the Width parameter were selected for the vertical dimension, one parameter would drive both the width and height of the box.

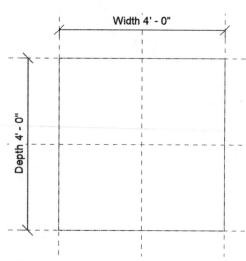

Looking at Figure 13-3.6, notice both dimensions have a *Label* associated with the dimension. This *Label* helps keep track of which dimensions are parametric. Another use for dimensions in a family is to "lock" it in order to maintain a relationship or spacing.

Even though the *Reference Planes* show up in the elevation views (front, left, etc.), the dimensions do not. So it is not visually obvious in the Left view that the *Depth* parameter has been created.

FIGURE 13-3.6 *Depth* parameter added

Next, an *Instance Parameter* will be created for the height of the box. Once the box family is loaded into a project, the height can vary from box to box (i.e., per instance). However, if the width (or depth) is changed, all boxes in the project will change. You will test this in a project momentarily.

9. Switch to the **Front** view.

Notice the *Width* dimension is not visible in this view.

10. Add a **dimension** from the *Reference Level* to the *Reference Plane* at the top of the box.

11. Add a **Height** parameter to the dimension (see Figure 13-3.7 and 13-3.8).

    a. Be sure to select the **Instance** option.

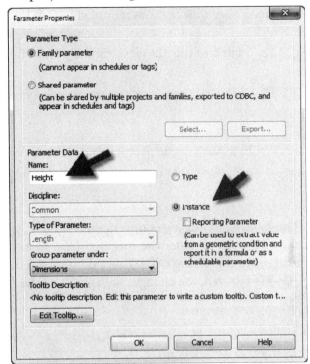

FIGURE 13-3.7 Creating the *Height* parameter

As can be seen in Figure 13-3.8, the Height parameter has been successfully added. This dimension can be seen in opposite views, the <u>Back</u> view in this case, but it cannot be seen in the side views, Left and Right in this case.

FIGURE 13-3.8 Front view; *Height* parameter added

Flexing the Family:

Now that parametric dimensions have been added to the *Family* it is necessary to flex them and make sure they work as intended before loading into a project.

12. Switch to the **3D view** via the *Quick Access Toolbar*.

13. Click the **Types** tool on the *Ribbon*

> *FYI: Notice the last three tools on the* Ribbon *are repeated for each tab; this is for convenience within the Family Editor.*

The *Family Types* dialog is now open (Figure 13-3.9). Notice the three parameters created are showing up; and under the specified *Dimensions* heading. The easiest way to "flex" the *Family* is to move this dialog off to one side, adjust the dimension(s) and then press *Apply*. When *Apply* is selected, the changes are applies to the *Family* without the need to close the dialog box.

Also, notice the Height parameter has "(default)" next to its name. This is because it is an Instance parameter. The Height can vary, but when the Family is initially placed, the "default" value will be used.

FIGURE 13-3.9 Family Types dialog

14. In the *Family Types* dialog, make the following adjustments:

    a. Height: **6"**

    b. Width: **1'-0"**

    c. See Figure 13-3.10.

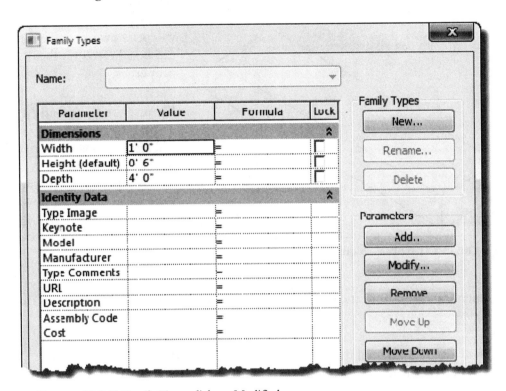

FIGURE 13-3.10 Family Types dialog - Modified

15. Move the dialog box off to one side, so the 3D view of the box can be seen, drag on the dialog title bar; this will allow the changes to the box to be seen.

16. Click **Apply**.

TIP: Clicking Apply *within a dialog box commits the changes to the model. This allows the user to see if the modification looks correct before closing the dialog box and possibly needing to reopen it. If the changes do not need to be visually inspected first, the* OK *button can simply be selected – it is not necessary to click* Apply *first.*

The size of the box should now be modified as shown in Figure 13-3.11 below. When flexing the family, the size was changed by a large enough amount to make it unmistakable that a change occurred. Just changing the numbers by an inch or two might make it hard to notice the adjustment visually.

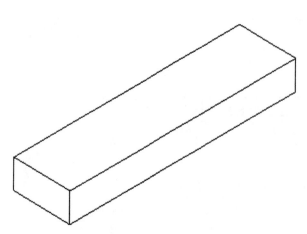

Next the box will be loaded into the Project environment; there it will be shown how the family can be adjusted via the properties.

Because the *Width* and *Depth* are **Type Parameters**, any change will affect all instances of the box. On the other hand, with the *Height* being an **Instance Parameter** – one change will only affect the selected objects.

FIGURE 13-3.11 3D Box - Modified

17. Open the *Project* from the previous exercise: **Box Project**. Do <u>not</u> close the **Box Family**.

18. Press **Ctrl + Tab** until the **Box** *Family* is current (Ctrl + Tab switches between the currently open views).

19. Click the **Load into Project** button on the *Ribbon*.

Load into Project

The **Box Project** is a Revit *Project* that already contains a *Family* named **Box**, which was loaded at the end of the previous exercise. When Revit notices that a *Family* is being loaded with the same name as one previously loaded, it will present the user with the **Family Already Loaded** dialog, see Figure 13-3.12, which provides a few options in which to choose from. Revit will not assume that the file being loaded is a replacement for the previously loaded *Family*. Rather, the user must decide by selecting one of two overwrite options or clicking *Cancel* to not load the *Family* at all. It could be that a totally different box was created or downloaded and should not replace the currently loaded box, in this case you would click *Cancel* and rename the *Family* so it does not conflict with the previously loaded one.

Most of the time the first overwrite option should be selected, as the second may overwrite project specific changes to the *Family*; such as the **Cost** parameter.

20. Click **Overwrite the existing version**.

FIGURE 13-3.12 Family Already Exists prompt

TIP: Revit will only display the "Family Already Exists" prompt if the Family file being loaded has been modified as compared to the version already in the Project file.

If the user has more than one Revit project open, a dialog displays in which the user selects which project(s) to load the *Family* into.

The **Box Project** file becomes the current view on the computer screen and the **Box** *Family* changes size to match the values of the newly added *Parameters*.

21. In any view (i.e., Level 1, Elevations, 3D), **select** the previously placed **Box** within the *Drawing Window*.

Notice the selected element temporarily turns blue and the *Modify Generic Models* contextual tab is displayed on the Ribbon.

22. With the Box selected, notice the *Properties Palette*.

Of the three parameters created in this exercise, only one shows up under the *Instance Parameters* (see Figure 13-3.13). The other two parameters, <u>Width</u> and <u>Depth</u>, will be visible in the *Type Parameters* dialog which will be explored next.

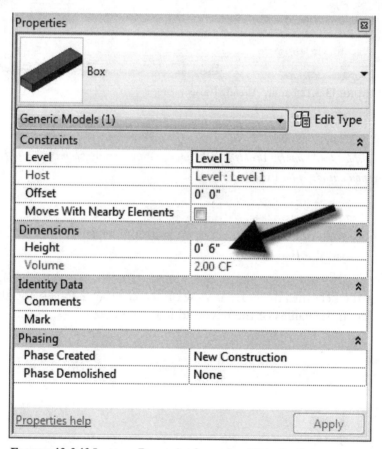

FIGURE 13-3.13 Instance Properties for updated Box family

23. In the *Properties Palette* dialog box, click **Edit Type**.

The two *Type Parameters* show up here in the *Type Properties* dialog, see Figure 13-3.14. An example will be shown next on exactly what the difference is between an *Instance Parameter* and a *Type Parameter*. However, it may be helpful the go back, at this time, and review the **Instance and Type Parameters** discussion earlier in this chapter (see page 13-8) before proceeding.

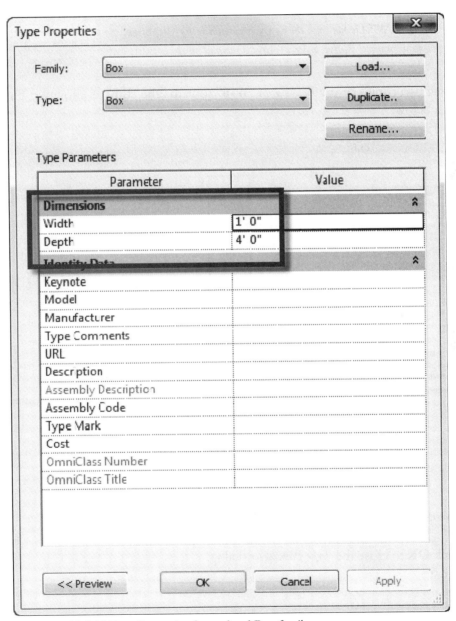

FIGURE 13-3.14 Type Properties for updated Box family

24. Close the dialog box by selecting **Cancel**.

Next, two additional boxes will be placed to show the different between *Instance and Type Parameters*. This can be accomplished by clicking the *Place a Component* button on the *Architecture* tab, as was done to place the first box, or by simply copying the existing box.

25. Select the box, if not already selected, and then click **Copy** on the *Ribbon*.

> **WARNING:** *Do not click the* Copy *command in the* Clipboard *panel, this is for copies between views or projects! Rather, use the* Copy *command on the* Modify *panel.*

26. Make two copies of the *Box Family*, **6'-0"** towards the **right** as shown in Figure 13-3.15 below.

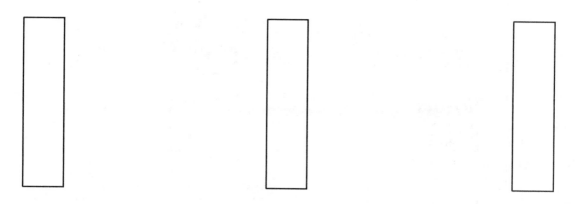

FIGURE 13-3.15 Box family copied for *Type* versus *Instant* study

27. Select the *Box* instance on the far left, and then view its *Type Parameters*; click **Edit Type** on the *Properties Palette*.

28. Change the **Width** *Parameter* from 1'-0" to **4'-0"**.

29. Click **OK** to close the *Type Parameter* dialog.

Because the <u>Width</u> *Parameter* is a *Type Parameter*, all instances of the type <u>Box</u> are updated instantly, see Figure 13-3.16 below. The <u>Depth</u> and <u>Height</u> for each remain unchanged. It makes no difference which box is selected anywhere in the *Project*. If this box existed on 20 different floors and in multiple phases, they would all have been updated. This is an important concept to understand because, just as it is easy to make several corrections or revisions with this technique, it is just as easy to make several errors in the design.

If additional widths are needed, either an additional *Type* would need to be added to the *Family* or a totally new *Family* would need to be created. *FYI: If the geometry is the same, and just the dimensions need to change, one would typically make a new* Type, *within an existing* Family, *rather than a new* Family.

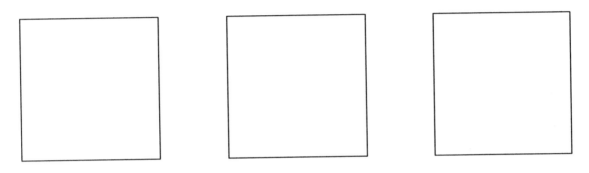

FIGURE 13-3.16 Type parameter <u>Width</u> changed

Next, the *Instant Parameter* <u>Height</u> will be studied. To see this change a vertical (i.e., elevation) or 3D view needs to be opened.

30. Switch to the **South** exterior elevation via the *Project Browser*.

FIGURE 13-3.17 South exterior elevation

Notice the Boxes are all **6″** tall (Figure 13-3.17) which was set previously in the *Family Editor*, prior to being loaded into the current *Project*.

31. Select the box in the middle and view its *Instance Properties* via the *Properties Palette.*

32. Change the **Height** from 6″ to **2′-3½″**.

Notice that just the selected instance was changed.

FIGURE 13-3.18 South exterior elevation middle box modified

TIP: It is possible to change multiple instances at once if they are all selected prior to editing the Properties Palette *dialog. Additionally, if EVERY instance in the entire Project needs to be modified, simply select one and then right-click and pick the "Select all instances" option. Caution should be used when employing the second tip as things change in ALL views and on ALL levels, and in ALL phases of the current Project, when the "entire Project" options is selected.*

33. **Save** both the *Project* and the *Family* as they will be further developed in the next exercise.

Revit Model Content Style Guide

Autodesk has recently released a document intended to help standardize how Revit content is made. This will help when sharing projects between offices and when downloading content from manufacturer's websites. Specifically, adding tags and scheduling will be greatly streamlined. This new document may be viewed and downloaded from the following location:

http://seek.autodesk.com/manufacturer.htm

Look for a link on the right-hand side called *Revit Model Content Style Guide.*

Exercise 13-4:
The Box: Formulas and Materials

The ability to add formulas and materials will be covered in this exercise.

The ability to add **formulas** means that the <u>Width</u> *Parameter* could be "programmed" such that it is always half the size of the depth *Parameter*; this is the example that will be explored in this exercise. Additionally, one could control the spacing of shelving brackets based on the length of the shelf, or the size of a lintel based on the width of the window below it, the lintel would need to be in the window family in this case. As should be obvious, the possibilities are many.

Defining **materials** in the *Family Editor* means that the component is ready to be rendered the moment it is placed in the project. It may not always be possible to anticipate what the material should be, but it is often more convenient to have something selected rather than nothing, which renders a flat gray color.

Cabinets with different materials applied (same family)

Adding a formula:

The following steps show how to add a formula to a parameter.

1. Open the **Box** *Family* created in the previous exercise.

    a. It is recommended that a copy of the **Box** *Family* be saved for each exercise in case problems arise and an older file is needed to revert back to. Maybe copy the **Box** *Family* file and rename it to **Box 13-3** to save a copy of the *Family* from the previous exercise.

2. Click the **Types** button on the *Ribbon* (see image to right).

Notice in the *Family Types* dialog below that a column named *"Formula"* exists. *Whenever* something is entered in this column the *Value* is grayed out for that *Parameter* (i.e., row); the result of the formula becomes the *Value* for that *Parameter*. A preliminary example is shown below.

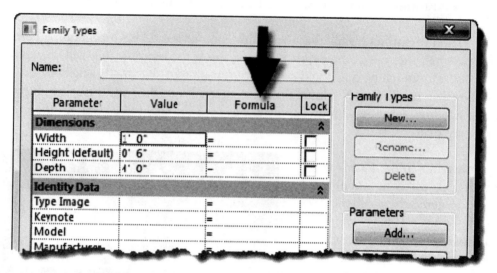

FIGURE 13-4.1 Family Types dialog

It is often helpful to open and explore the various *Families* that come with Revit; this can provide much insight on how to do certain things. The image below shows several formulas used to define a pipe elbow *Family* that comes with Revit MEP. The values next to the formulas are the result of the adjacent formula; it is not possible to manually enter a value in this case, when a formula is present. Notice how other parameters can be used in formulas; this is case sensitive.

Parameter	Value	Formula
Dimensions		
Tick Size (default)	115/256"	= Fitting Outside Diameter * 0.4 * tan(Angle / 2)
Nominal Radius (default)	1/2"	=
Nominal Diameter (default)	1"	= Nominal Radius * 2
Insulation Radius (default)	9/16"	= Fitting Outside Radius + Insulation Thickness
Fitting Outside Diameter (default)	1 1/8"	= text_file_lookup(Lookup Table Name, "FOD", Nominal Dia
Center to End (default)	13/16"	= Center Radius * tan(Angle / 2)
Angle (default)	90.000°	=

FIGURE 13-4.2 Sample Family showing complex formulas

3. For the *Width* parameter, in the *Formula* column, enter the following: **Depth/2** (see Figure 13-4.3).

4. Click into a different cell within the *Family Types* dialog to see the *Value* update.

Notice the <u>Width</u> Value is now half of the <u>Depth</u>; i.e., 2'-0" (see Figure 13-4.3).

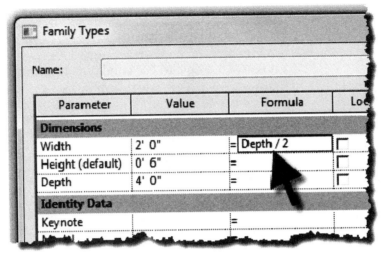

FIGURE 13-4.3 Adding formula to control the width

TIP: When using parameters in a formula, keep the following in mind:

- *Parameters in formulas must match the case (i.e., uppercase, lowercase, mixed) of the Parameters being referenced. Typing "depth" rather than "Depth" in the example above would not work – Revit would show an error message.*
- *A Parameter used in a formula must exist in the Family before it can be used.*
- *If a Parameter is deleted, any formulas that use that Parameter will also be deleted. Revit will present a warning first.*
- *If a Parameter is renamed, Revit will automatically rename the Parameter in all formulas in which it is used.*

Below are a few of the basic symbols Revit can use in formulas. See Revit's *Help System* for a full list:

- *Addition*: **+**
- *Subtraction*: **-**
- *Multiplication*: *****
- *Division*: **/**
- *Tangent*: **Tan**
- *Cosine*: **Cos**
- *Sine*: **Sin**

Conditional Formatting

It is also possible to use conditional statements in a formula such as IF, AND, OR, <, >, =

Here are a few examples:

- if(Depth > 3', 2', 1')
- if(and(Depth > 3', Height = 1'), 2', 1')
- See Revit's *Help* for more info.

Next the *Family* will be loaded into the *Project Environment* to see the formula in action.

5. Open the project file **Box Project**, and then switch to the **3D view**.

6. Press **Ctrl + Tab** until the **Box Family** file is current.

7. Click the **Load into Project** button on the *Ribbon*.

Notice the size of the box changes. When the <u>Depth</u> is now changed, the <u>Width</u> will automatically be updated. This will be tested next.

8. Select one of the boxes and, via its *Type Properties*, change the **Depth** to **6'-0"** and then.

   a. Click in an adjacent cell.

   b. Notice the <u>Width</u> instantly updates.

9. Click **OK** to close the dialog and accept the changes.

All three boxes change size; 6'-0" depth and 3'-0" width. The height is still an *Instance Parameter* so it remained unchanged.

10. Switch back to the box family.

Next, a brief look at a few variations.

The following revisions will not be saved; the Cancel button will be selected to discard the next two steps.

11. Change the formula for *Width* to simply read **Depth** (see Figure 13-4.4).

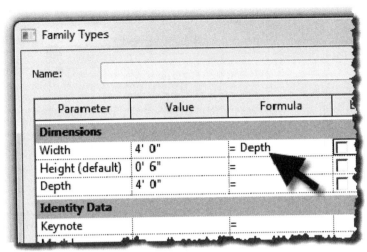

FIGURE 13-4.4 Modifying formula to control the width

Thus, it is possible to have one *Parameter* simply equal another one.

12. Click **Cancel** to discard the formula change.

Another way to achieve the results shown in the previous image and steps is to have one *Parameter* control two dimensions. This would reduce the number of *Parameters* from three to two as the *Family* currently stands. The image on the next page (see Figure 13-4.5) shows an example of this. Simply select a previously drawn dimension and then select the desired *Parameter* from the *Label* drop-down list on the *Options Bar*. This is only visible when a dimension is selected.

One *Parameter* could control several dimensions. A *Parameter* has to be of type *Length* (versus *Text, Currency, Volume, Yes/No,* Etc.) to work with a *Dimension*. The *Label* drop-down list will automatically filter the list.

It is best if the dimensions reference the *Reference Planes* rather than the 3D geometry.

FIGURE 13-4.5 One Parameter controlling multiple dimensions

This concludes the brief introduction to adding formulas to a *Family*. The remainder of this exercise will shift gears a bit and look at adding materials to the box family.

Adding a Material:

Adding a *Material* in the *Family* can save time for the design teams using the content when it comes to creating renderings.

13. Select the 3D extrusion that represents the box in the *Family Editor*.

14. View the *Properties Palette* dialog box.

Notice, in Figure 13-4.6, that the *Material* is set to *By Category*. This will be changed to something specific to this *Family*.

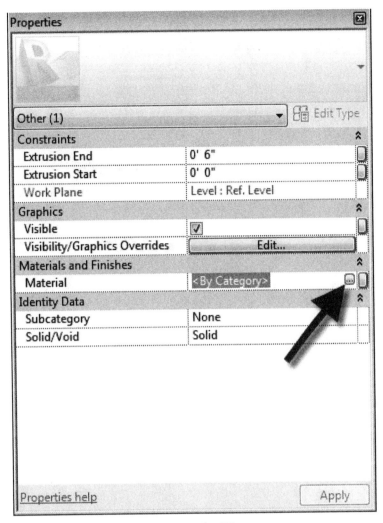

FIGURE 13-4.6 Instance Parameters for 3D geometry

15. Click in the cell with *<By Category>* to reveal the small link button to the right, see Figure 13-4.6.

16. Click the **link-button** to open the *Materials* dialog.

Notice the *Family* has a limited number of *Materials* loaded, see Figure 13-4.7. The following sequence of steps will show how to create a new *Material* and define it.

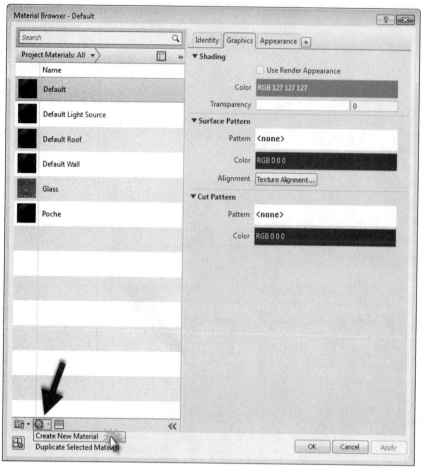

FIGURE 13-4.7 Materials for the Box Family, not the Box Project

17. Click the **Create New Material** icon in the lower left corner; see arrow in Figure 13-4.7.

18. Right-click the new *Material* and **Rename** it to **Box Material** see Figure 13-4.8.

19. Click the **Surface Pattern** preview area (currently set to "none"); see Figure 13-4.9.

> *TIP: Make sure the* Graphics *tab is selected to see the* Surface Pattern *area.*

FIGURE 13-4.8 Naming new material

FIGURE 13-4.9 Setting surface pattern

A new "Model" *Surface Pattern* will be created. A "Model" pattern will not change scale with the *View Scale* in the *Project Environment*; this is meant for real-world items like siding, title, CMU, etc. as seen in elevation. Conversely, the "Drafting" patterns do change scale with the *View Scale* and is meant for representative patterns typically used in sections to imply a certain material.

20. Select **Model** for *Pattern Type* and then follow the steps shown in Figure 13-4.10 to create a new "Model" based *Fill Pattern* named **3″ Tile**.

FIGURE 13-4.10 Creating a new model based surface pattern

21. Click **OK** to close the *Fill Patterns* dialog, but not the *Materials* dialogs!

Next you will add an *Appearance* asset so you can control how the material will appear in a rendering.

22. Click to add an **Appearance** asset (Figure 13-4.11).

23. Set the *Render Appearance* to **3in Square - Terra Cotta** (from the *Appearance Library*).

FIGURE 13-4.11 Selecting rendering appearance

24. Click **OK** to close the *Materials* dialog box.

The fill pattern is now visible, Figure 13-4.12. However, the render appearance is not visible until loaded and rendered in a project. Per steps previously covered in the textbook, load the family into the project and do a rendering in a 3D view.

TIP: When loading a Family, if the project already has a material named "box material", per the above example, the material definition in the project will take precedence if the two are not identical.

25. **Save** the Box *Family*.

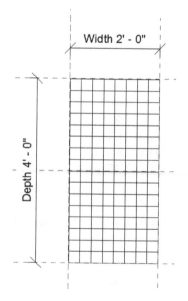

FIGURE 13-4.12 Family Editor

26. Load the updated *Family* into the **Box Project** (*Project* file).

When the newly updated *Family* is loaded into the project, the **Fill Pattern** shows up right away (Figure 13-4.13). The fill pattern can be selected on each face of each box and be rotated and reposition as desired, in the *Project Environment*.

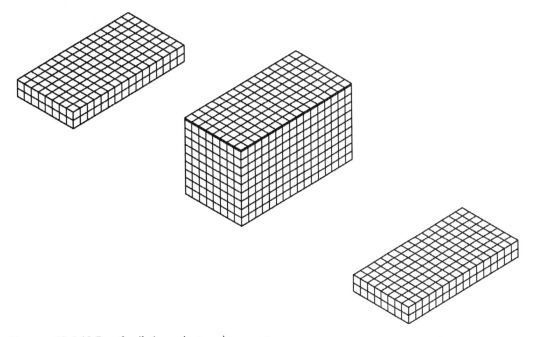

FIGURE 13-4.13 Box family in project environment

27. Switch to a 3D or Camera view and create a **rendering** to see the *Render Appearance* material.

    a. Adding a floor below the boxes will allow the shadows to show up as in the image to the right.

28. **Save** the *Project*.

FIGURE 13-4.14 Rendered in project environment

Changing the Material in the Project Environment:

So far, the *Material* for the Box has been "hard wired" within the *Family* and cannot be changed once in the *Project Environment*. In this last set of steps, the techniques required to achieve this goal will be covered.

Just to make things more clear: it is possible to create several 2D shapes in a single *Family*. For example, a door has a solid for the frame, the door panel and a vision panel; see the image to the right (Figure 13-4.15).

Therefore, it would not make sense for Revit to provide one built-in parameter that controls the *Material* for everything in the *Family*.

FIGURE 13-4.15 Door family with multiple materials defined

In the door example, a parameter is created for each *Material* needed in the *Family*. Next, each solid in the *Family* is mapped to one of the three *Parameters*. It is possible for one *Parameter* to control the *Material* of several 3D elements; e.g., a "glass material" *Parameter* controls the *Material* for all seven pieces of glass in Figure 13-4.15.

29. In the Box *Family* click the **Types** button.

30. Click the **Add...** button to make a new *Parameter*.

31. Modify the *Parameter Properties* dialog as shown in Figure 13-4.16.

    a. *Name*:
       Finish Material

    b. *Group*:
       Graphics

    c. *Type*:
       Material

32. Click **OK**.

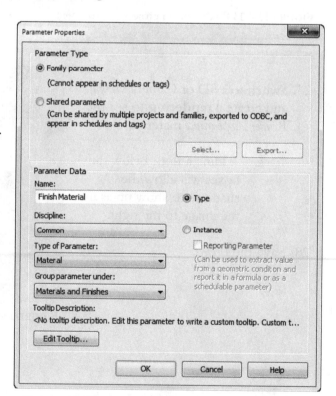

FIGURE 13-4.16 Creating a new parameter

33. In the *Family Types* dialog, change the "value" for **Finish Material** to **Box Material**. (See Figure 13-4.17.)

FIGURE 13-4.17 Setting material for new parameter

At this point, a new *Parameter* has been created but does not control anything yet. In the next few steps you will map the *Material* for the 3D box to the *Material* parameter just created in the previous steps. After this, the *Family Types* parameter will be the only way to change the *Material* for the box.

34. Click **OK** to close the *Family Types* dialog box.

35. Select the box and then look at the **Properties Palette**.

36. Click the small mapping icon to the far right of the **Material** *Parameter* (see Figure 13-4.18).

FIGURE 13-4.18 Mapping material to parameter

FIGURE 13-4.19 Mapping material to parameter

The *Associate Family Parameter* dialog is now displayed. Revit presents the user with a list of *Parameters* that are of the *Type* "material" (versus text, currency, etc.). At this point, the only option is the *Parameter* just created.

37. Select **Finish Material** from the list and then click **OK** (see Figure 13-4.19).

FIGURE 13-4.20 Mapped material

Now that the *Material* is mapped to a *Parameter*, notice that the mapping icon now has an **equal** sign in it and the rest of the row is grayed out, see Figure 13-4.20. The grayed out *Material* means that the *Family Type Parameter* is now controlling this *Instance Parameter*.

38. **Save** the **Box** *Family* again.

39. **Load** the *Family* into the box Project.

40. Select the one of the boxes and view its **Type Parameters**.

41. Notice **Finish Material** is now an option.

42. **Save** the **Box Project** file.

Exercise 13-5:
The Box: Family Types and Categories

This exercise will study *Family Types*. A *Type* is simply the ability to save various parameter settings in a *Family* so they do not need to be entered manually within each Project.

Thus far, in this chapter, a *Family* with just a single *Type* has been created. Any new *Family* automatically has one *Type* if none are specifically created; the *Type* name is the same as the *Family* name once loaded into the *Project Environment*. This exercise will look at how to create several predefined *Types* within the *Family Editor* and how to create additional *Types* on the fly within the *Project Environment*.

Why use Types? Let us say a "Box" manufacturer offers several standard sizes. When creating the *Family* for the "Box", it would be most expedient to create a *Type* for each standard option. This would save the end-user(s) time in more ways than one. If a design firm had trusted custom Revit content, an end-user could load the "Box" *Family* and pick a size from the predefined *Types*; knowing that they are real options. Maybe some rarely used or over priced options are intentionally omitted. However, just not having to enter the data manually can be a great benefit.

The reader may wish to turn back to the first exercise in this chapter and review the information initially presented on this topic, see page 13-5.

Finally, the use of **Categories** will be studied. Revit uses *Categories* to control visibility and to determine which command will be used to place a *Family* (e.g., Door tool, Window tool, Mechanical Equipment tool, Component tool).

1. **Open** the *Family* named **Box**.

2. Click the **Types** button on the *Ribbon*.

Notice, in Figure 13-5.1, that the *Name* drop-down at the top is blank. Clicking the *New* button on the right allows one or more named *Types* to be created.

Once *Types* exist, all the *Parameter* **Values** below relate specifically to the selected named *Type*.

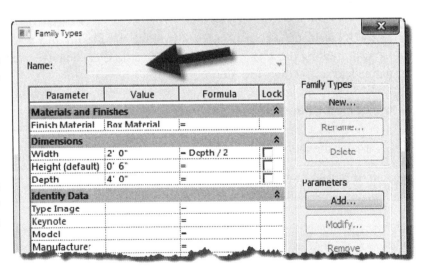

FIGURE 13-5.1 Family Types – no types created yet

Next, four *Types* will be created in the <u>Box</u> *Family*. Each *Type* will have a different <u>Depth</u> assigned to it.

3. In the *Family Types* dialog, click the **New...** button.

4. Enter **2'-0" x 4'-0"** for the name of the first *Type* (Figure 13-5.2).

FIGURE 13-5.2 Naming the family type

Type names should be descriptive and not duplicate any part of the *Family* name (i.e., the name of the file on the hard drive). In this example the exact size will be used as the *Type* name. In other cases it might be more useful to list the model number or some other descriptive wording.

5. Click **OK**.

Now, one *Type* exists in the *Name* drop-down list. Note that the *Type* name matches the values below, this was intentional. However, it should be stated that the name and values could be inconsistent. The name has no direct control over any of the *Parameter* values; i.e., the

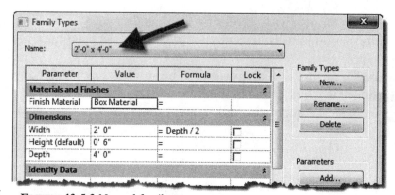

FIGURE 13-5.3 Named family type

name 2'-0" x 4'-0" does not automatically make the <u>Depth</u> and <u>Width</u> *Values* match. Thus, the person creating the *Family* needs to does some QA (quality assurance) checking. This will be made clear in the next few steps.

6. Click the **New...** button again.

7. Enter the name **3'-0" x 6'-0"**.

   a. Remember, because of the formula added in the previous exercise, the <u>Width</u> is always half the <u>Depth</u>.

The **Box** *Family* now has two *Types* created; each can be easily selected within the *Project Environment*.

Revit is now managing two complete lists of *Parameters*; one for each *Type*. As will be proven momentarily, the *Values* (i.e., <u>Width</u> and <u>Depth</u>) can vary from one list to the other.

As seen in Figure 13-5.4, the new *Type* did not change the *Parameter Values* below. Next this will be changed.

FIGURE 13-5.4 Second named family type

8. With the *Type* 3'-0" x 6'-0" current, change the <u>Depth</u> to **6'-0"**.

FIGURE 13-5.5A First type settings

FIGURE 13-5.5B Second type settings

9. Using the *Name* drop-down list, switch back and forth between the two options; notice the *Parameter Values* change (Figures 13-5.5A and B).

10. Create two more *Type* per the information below:
    a. *Name*: **4'-0" x 8'-0"**   **5'-6" x 11'-0"**
    b. *Depth*: **8'-0"**   **11'-0"**

Now that several *Types* have been defined in the **Box** *Family* it will be loaded into the *Project Environment* to see how they work.

11. **Open** the **Box Project** file, if not already open.

12. In the <u>Box</u> *Family* file, click the **Load into Project** button.

13. Select **Overwrite the existing version**.

14. Select the **Component** tool from the *Architecture* tab on the *Ribbon*.

15. Select the **Type Selector** (Figure 13-5.6).

FIGURE 13-5.6 *Type Selector* in the project environment

Looking at Figure 13-5.6, notice all the *Types* created in the *Family Editor* are now available under the *Family* name **Box**. A *Type* named **Box** is also listed because the *Family* was previously loaded without any specific *Types* created; and as mentioned previously, when no *Types* exist Revit will create one with the same name as the *Family*. This can be deleted for renamed in the *Project Browser*, within the *Families* section.

Selecting a Category

Selecting a *Category* is actually one of the first things typically done when starting a new *Family*. However, this change was left until now to make it perfectly clear what this setting does.

NOTE: Some Family *templates will already have the correct* Category *selected (e.g., door, window, casework templates). However, the* **Box** *Family was started with the* **Generic Model** *template, so the* Category *needs to be set manually; as this template can be used for many things.*

16. **Open** the **Box** *Family* (if not already open).

17. On the *Create* tab, click **Category and Parameters**.

This list represents all the *Categories* used by Revit to control visibility and determine which tool inserts any given *Family*. *Categories* are also used by *Filters* and for scheduling. This list is "hard wired" and cannot be modified in any way.

This list is for Revit Architecture; the initial list is different for each flavor of Revit. However, clicking the "Show categories from all disciplines" option will show the same list in all three flavors of Revit.

At this point we will pretend that our **Box** *Family* is *Furniture*. Once set to be "furniture", the **Box** will show up in the *Furniture* schedule(s) and be visible (or not visible) based on the visibility and filter settings for any given view.

18. Click **Furniture** and then click **OK.**

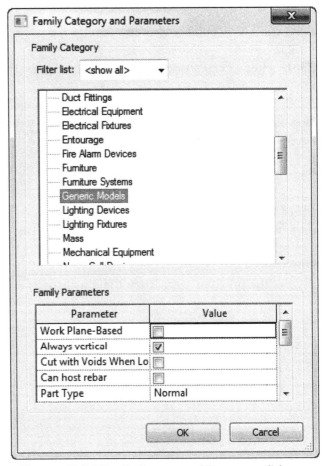

FIGURE 13-5.7 Family Category and Parameters dialog

TIP:

The **Furniture** *category is generally for freestanding items that are not fastened to the building. Examples might be chairs, tables, desks, beds, etc.*

*The **Furniture Systems** category is for modular desks, often called cubicles. These can be fastened to the wall and/or have power and data hardwired to them. Thus they are different enough from regular furniture to warrant a separate section.*

19. **Save** the **Box** *Family*.

Next the modified *Family* will be loaded into the project and tested.

20. Load the *Family* into the **Box Project** file per steps previously covered.

21. In the **Box Project**, switch to the default **3D view**.

The next few steps will show how the visibility of the furniture category now affects the <u>Box</u> family.

22. Type **VV** to control visibility settings for the current view.

23. Uncheck *Furniture* on the *Model Categories* tab (Figure 13-5.8).

Notice there is a category for "Generic Models" as well. This would have allowed control of the **Box** *Family* previously. However, this category should be used sparingly due to its ambiguity.

24. Click **OK**.

The three boxes should have been hidden from the 3D view. They should still be visible in other views as long as the view's *Visibility Graphics Override* dialog did not have the *Furniture Category* turned off.

25. Per the previous steps, **turn the Furniture Category back on** in the *3D view*.

26. **Save** the **Box Project** file.

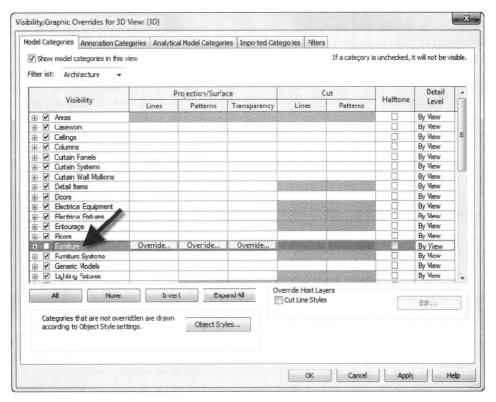

FIGURE 13-5.8 VISIBILITY control in the project

Revit does not have a specific *Furniture* tool on the *Ribbon* so new instances of the **Box** *Family* would still be placed using the *Component* tool.

Care should be taken to select the correct *Category* for Revit *Families*. If someone is in a hurry they may hastily select a wrong *Category* which could have a huge negative impact on a project in terms of budget and completion time.

For example, a "smart board" for a classroom might be placed on the *Furniture Category* when it should have been placed on *Electrical Equipment*. Near the end of the project the design team decides to turn off all the *Furniture* for the construction documents set, as it was laid out for design only and is not part of the bid set. Now, the final set is missing all of the "smart boards" in the floor plans, ceiling plans and interior elevations.

Much more could be said and taught about *Family* creation but is beyond the introductory scope of this text.

Smart board family with materials

Self-Exam:

The following questions can be used as a way to check your knowledge of this lesson. The answers can be found at the bottom of this page.

1.   *Loadable Families* can be imported into a project as needed. (T/F)

2.   How a *Family* is named is not important. (T/F)

3.   The <u>sill height</u> of a window is usually an *Instance* parameter. (T/F)

4.   Use the _____ _____ tool to create the framework for a new *Family*.

5.   The solid tool, used in this chapter, to create the 3D box: _____.

Review Questions:

The following questions may be assigned by your instructor as a way to assess your knowledge of this section. Your instructor has the answers to the review questions.

1.   The 3D box, drawn in this chapter, was aligned and then locked to the reference planes as part of the process of creating parametric content. (T/F)

2.   *Loadable Families* are typically preferred over in-place *Families*. (T/F)

3.   A <u>family name</u> and a *Family's* <u>type name(s)</u> should not have redundant information. (T/F)

4.   It is possible to specify if a parameter is an <u>instance</u> or <u>type</u> while in the process of creating it. (T/F)

5.   When the geometry changes, a new *Family* is typically required, rather than being able to use named *Types*. (T/F)

6.   The tool used to get a completed family into a project (while in the family editor environment): _____.

7.   Of the two types of *Fill Patterns*, only the _____ type patterns do not change size when the view scale changes.

8.   A *Family's* _____ setting controls/determines its visibility and which tool is used to place the item in the project environment.

9.   When a *Parameter* is associated to one or more dimensions, the *Parameter's* value controls the length of the dimension (and object being dimensioned) (T/F).

10. It is not possible to make one parameter to always be one half the size of another. (T/F)

Appendix A
Autodesk® Revit® Architecture Certification Exam:

This appendix will cover the certification exam that is offered by Autodesk to help users prove their level of knowledge. This can be helpful when seeking an increase in salary from your current employer or to be listed on your resume.

Appendix A-1:
Introduction and Overview

In the competitive world in which we live it is important to stand out to potential employers and prove your capabilities. One way to do this is by passing one of the Autodesk Certification Exams. A candidate who passes an exam has credentials from the makers of the software that you know how to use their software. This can help employers narrow down the list of potential interviewees when looking for candidates.

When the exam is successfully passed a certificate signed by the CEO of Autodesk, Carl Bass, can be printed out and displayed at your desk or included with your resume; see example below. You also have access to an Autodesk logo for use on business cards or on flyers promoting your work; two examples are shown below as well. This author uses the professional logo in the front of books and in presentations.

Autodesk offers two exams for Autodesk Revit Architecture; **Certified User** and **Certified Professional**.

- *Certified User:* This is an entry level exam to verify you have a basic understanding of the Revit user interface and functionality. The exam consists of 30 questions, many of which are multiple choice and some are matching or point and click (hotspot). The test is taken on a computer at any Autodesk Certification Center. The test must be completed in less than 60 minutes.

- *Certified Professional:* This is an intermediate level exam to prove you have a firm understanding of Revit Architecture's features. Before taking this exam, the *Certified User* exam must have been taken and successfully passed. Not only is this exam computer based, but it is also a hands-on Revit test. That is, you actually use the Revit Architecture software. There are 35 questions which have to be answered in 120 minutes.

Before taking the *Certified User* exam, you can prepare by working through this textbook and taking the assessment test online from home, work or school. The practice exam costs $48 and will give you an idea about how you will do on the exam.

Autodesk recommends how much time you should study and practice before taking each exam, the following highlights their recommendations:

- *Certified User Exam:* 50 hours of hands on experience. Much of this requirement can be achieved by working through this book.

- *Professional Exam:* 400 hours of hands on experience.

FYI: This textbook may not cover every Revit concept or feature that could be asked on the exam. See the exam objectives on Autodesk's website.

Be sure to manage your time while taking the test. Quickly go through the test and answer the questions that are easy to you, skipping the ones you are not immediately sure of. The exam software allows you to view a list of questions you have not answered or have marked. Once you have answered all the easy questions you can, then go back and think through those which remain. Do not exit the exam until you are completely finished, as you will not be able to re-enter the exam after that point.

Once the exam is finished you will immediately see your score. If you failed, you should note the objective areas where you missed questions and study those areas more before taking the test again. Be sure to print your score report and take it with you to study.

Resources:
- http://www.certiport.com/autodesk
- Autodesk Certification Site: www.autodesk.com/certification
- Autodesk Authorized Training Center (ATC): www.autodesk.com/atc
- Online Testing Service: http://autodesk.starttest.com

Exercise A-2:
Certification Exam Sample Test

This section is provided to help you test your Revit knowledge before paying to take the associates assessment test or the certification exam. The answers to the questions will be on the last page. Keep in mind these questions are meant to aid in preparing to take the associates exam and not the professional exam, as the latter is a hands-on software exam.

The questions are made up by the author and should not be memorized, thinking the same questions might be asked on the exam. These questions are similar in that they relate to the exam objectives listed on the previous page and are in the format described on the Autodesk website; multiple choice. You are provided 30 questions, equal to the actual exam. It is recommended that you time yourself so that you only have one hour.

It is recommended that you wait to take this sample test until you have completed all the tutorials in this book and on the CD.

Directions: Answer the following questions in 60 minutes or less:

TIP: The software helps you answer the question in the correct way. That is, if you are expected to select only one answer you can only select one; this looks like a circle. If you are expected to select all that apply, you select one or more square boxes:

        O = Select only one answer
        □ = Select all that apply

1. Which of the following is NOT a valid *Model Graphics Style*?
    - □ Shading with Edges
    - □ Realistic
    - □ Cartoon
    - □ Consistent Colors

2. How do you sort a schedule?
    - o Cut and Paste the rows
    - o Fields tab > Add Parameter
    - o Sorting/Grouping tab > Sort By
    - o Appearance tab > Sorting

3. What can you send a client or contractor that does not require them to have Revit and is a much smaller file; but only requires a free download to view?
    - o DXF file
    - o Word file (DOCx)
    - o DWF or DWFx file
    - o Excel file (XLSx)

4. Which are TRUE about a titleblock in Revit?
   - ☐ "Sheet number" must be unique
   - ☐ Are found on sheets
   - ☐ Project title automatically appears on all sheets
   - ☐ "Drawn by" field must be unique

5. Which TWO things are true about renderings?
   - ☐ Renderings never take more than 5 minutes
   - ☐ Shadows are always created
   - ☐ The sun always casts light
   - ☐ The final rendering is not saved automatically

6. A *Room* has to be created in each level 1 plan you which to see a room tag in. For example: Level 1 Floor Plan, Level 1 Ceiling Plan, Level 1 Finish Plan.
   - ○ True
   - ○ False

7. What is NOT possible with the *Text* tool?
   - ○ Add a leader with no text
   - ○ Center justify the text
   - ○ Change the style
   - ○ Add multiple leaders

8. Which are true about *Detail Views*?
   - ☐ The *View Scale* can be adjusted
   - ☐ They update geometry when the model updates
   - ☐ They are 2D drawings
   - ☐ A different text tool is needed to add notes, compared to a model view

9. While sketching a stair, you can:
   - ○ not adjust the stair width
   - ○ stop the sketch short of the specific level
   - ○ end up with various size risers
   - ○ not use snaps

10. Which are true about railings?
    - ☐ Added automatically with stairs
    - ☐ Can adjust height on options bar while sketching path
    - ☐ Automatically added to edge of interior floor openings
    - ☐ style can be changed, when selected, via the *Type Selector*

11. Select the item that can be loaded into the project from a file:
    - ○ Wall
    - ○ Door
    - ○ Floor
    - ○ Roof

12. Which TWO views are automatically created when a level is added to a project?
   ☐ Floor plan
   ☐ Detail view
   ☐ 3D view
   ☐ Ceiling plan

13. It is not possible to adjust the location of a ceiling grid once it is placed in the model.
   ☐ True
   ☐ False

14. Rows can be manually added to a schedule for items not found in the model.
   o True
   o False

15. Curtain walls can only have a consistent grid pattern.
   o True
   o False

16. Which are true statements about walls?
   ☐ Tops can conform to underside of roof above
   ☐ Corners and intersections automatically clean up with others of same type
   ☐ Most detail shown while in *Coarse* detail level setting
   ☐ Show heaver when they pass through the cut plane

17. Select the statements that are true about doors.
   ☐ Doors may be placed in an elevation view
   ☐ Doors can only be deleted in plan views
   ☐ Doors are floor hosted
   ☐ Doors can be deleted from the schedule

18. When a ceiling is added, the top of the ceiling is placed a distance from the floor that is specified in the *Properties Palette*.
   o True
   o False

19. Select the various constraints:
   ☐ Equality
   ☐ Alignment
   ☐ Pin
   ☐ Length
   ☐ Shared Parameter
   ☐ Locked Dimension

20. Which statement is true about camera views?
   ☐ The eye elevation cannot be adjusted
   ☐ The target elevation can be adjusted
   ☐ You cannot adjust how far into the model you see
   ☐ Camera views can only be created form the *Ribbon*

21. If you delete a locked dimension you have the option to keep the constraint.
    - ○ True
    - ○ False

22. Which key do you use to be able to select elements which are overlapped?
    - ☐ Caps Lock
    - ☐ Alt
    - ☐ Tab
    - ☐ F6

23. Which are window family *Type Parameters*?
    - ☐ Window Sill
    - ☐ Width
    - ☐ Height
    - ☐ Type Mark

24. Where are newly created views listed?
    - ○ Options Bar
    - ○ Application Menu
    - ○ Ribbon
    - ○ Project Browser

25. You need to change the *Type Selector* to get different line options while using the *Detail Line* tool.
    - ○ True
    - ○ False

26. Which are components of the User Interface?
    - ☐ Options Bar
    - ☐ Application Menu
    - ☐ View Control Bar
    - ☐ Project Browser
    - ☐ Door Family

27. Which Statements are true about grid lines?
    - ☐ Two grids can have the same number
    - ☐ Show up automatically in elevation and section views
    - ☐ Start and end points will automatically align if drawn correctly
    - ☐ Grid heads and display on either end or both

28. Which statements are true about the rendering dialog?
    - ☐ The quality can be adjusted
    - ☐ Render time and quality are directly proportional
    - ☐ An image can be selected for the background
    - ☐ You can specify the season, summer, sprint, winter or fall.

29. A callout can be added in a plan, elevation or section view.
    ☐ True
    ☐ False

30. The default template is the preferred starting point for most projects.
    ☐ True
    ☐ False

ANSWERS:

1. Which of the following is NOT a valid *Model Graphics Style*?
   o Shading with Edges
   o Realistic
   o Cartoon
   o Consistent Colors

2. How do you sort a schedule?
   o Cut and Paste the rows
   o Fields tab > Add Parameter
   o Sorting/Grouping tab > Sort By
   o Appearance tab > Sorting

3. What can you send a client or contractor that does not require them to have Revit and is a much smaller file; but only requires a free download to view?
   o DXF file
   o Word file (DOCx)
   o DWF or DWFx file
   o Excel file (XLSx)

4. Which are TRUE about a titleblock in Revit?
   ☐ "Sheet number" must be unique
   ☐ Are found on sheets
   ☐ Project title automatically appears on all sheets
   ☐ "Drawn by" field must be unique

5. Which TWO things are true about renderings
   o Renderings never take more than 5 minutes
   o Shadows are always created
   o The sun always casts light
   o The final rendering is not saved automatically

6. A *Room* has to be created in each level 1 plan you which to see a room tag in. For example: Level 1 Floor Plan, Level 1 Ceiling Plan, Level 1 Finish Plan.
   o True
   o False

7. What is NOT possible with the *Text* tool?
   o Add a leader with no text
   o Center justify the text
   o Change the style
   o Add multiple leaders

8. Which are true about *Detail Views*?
   ☐ The View Scale can be adjusted
   ☐ They update geometry when the model updates
   ☐ They are 2D drawings
   ☐ A different text tool is needed to add notes, compared to a model view

9. While sketching a stair, you can
   o not adjust the stair width
   o stop the sketch short of the specific level
   o end up with various size risers
   o not use snaps

10. Which are true about railings?
    o Added automatically with stairs
    o Can adjust height on options bar while sketching path
    o Automatically added to edge of interior floor openings
    o style can be changed, when selected, via the *Type Selector*

11. Select the item that can be loaded into the project from a file
    o Wall
    o Door
    o Floor
    o Roof

12. Which TWO views are automatically created when a level is added to a project
    ☐ Floor plan
    ☐ Detail view
    ☐ 3D view
    ☐ Ceiling plan

13. It is not possible to adjust the location of a ceiling grid once it is placed in the model.
    o True
    o False

14. Rows can be manually added to a schedule for items not found in the model.
    o True
    o False

15. Curtain walls can only have a consistent grid pattern.
    o True
    o False

16. Which are true statements about walls?
    ☐ Tops can conform to underside of roof above
    ☐ Corners and intersections automatically clean up with others of same type
    ☐ Most detail shown while in *Course* detail level setting
    ☐ Show heaver when they pass through the cut plane

17. Select the statements that are true about doors.
    - ☐ Doors may be placed in an elevation view
    - ☐ Doors can only be deleted in plan views
    - ☐ Doors are floor hosted
    - ☐ Doors can be deleted from the schedule

18. When a ceiling is added, the top of the ceiling is placed a distance from the floor that is specified in the *Properties Palette*.
    - o True
    - o False

19. Select the various constraints
    - ☐ Equality
    - ☐ Alignment
    - ☐ Pin
    - ☐ Length
    - ☐ Shared Parameter
    - ☐ Locked Dimension

20. Which statement is true about camera views?
    - o The eye elevation cannot be adjusted
    - o The target elevation can be adjusted
    - o You cannot adjust how far into the model you see
    - o Camera views can only be created form the *Ribbon*

21. If you delete a locked dimension you have the option to keep the constraint.
    - o True
    - o False

22. Which key do you use to be able to select elements which are overlapped?
    - o Caps Lock
    - o Alt
    - o Tab
    - o F6

23. Which are window family *Type Parameters*?
    - ☐ Window Sill
    - ☐ Width
    - ☐ Height
    - ☐ Type Mark

24. Where are newly created views listed?
    - o Options Bar
    - o Application Menu
    - o Ribbon
    - o Project Browser

25. You need to change the *Type Selector* to get different line options while using the *Detail Line* tool.
    - o True
    - o False

26. Which are components of the User Interface?
    - ☐ Options Bar
    - ☐ Application Menu
    - ☐ View Control Bar
    - ☐ Project Browser
    - ☐ Door Family

27. Which statements are true about grid lines?
    - ☐ Two grids can have the same number
    - ☐ Show up automatically in elevation and section views
    - ☐ Start and end points will automatically align if drawn correctly
    - ☐ Grid heads and display on either end or both

28. Which statements are true about the rendering dialog?
    - ☐ The quality can be adjusted
    - ☐ Render time and quality are directly proportional
    - ☐ An image can be selected for the background
    - ☐ You can specify the season, summer, sprint, winter or fall.

29. A callout can be added in a plan, elevation or section view.
    - o True
    - o False

30. The default template is the preferred starting point for most projects.
    - o True
    - o False

Notes:

Appendix V
Introduction to Autodesk Vasari:

This appendix will take a look at Autodesk® Vasari®, a new derivative of Autodesk® Revit® which is in a public beta cycle at the time this book was published (Spring 2013). Autodesk® Vasari® is a conceptual design and analysis application, built on the Revit platform, which can be used for complex organic modeling, preliminary energy modeling, and micro-climate site studies.

Vasari started in Autodesk Labs, which is a division of Autodesk. They develop new technologies and allow the general public to freely test them. Some of these technologies are eventually incorporated into other programs such as AutoCAD or Revit. Other developments are stuck back on the shelf because the concept did not gain any traction.

Hopefully this brief introduction will spark your interest and you will research this tool in more depth on your own!

Appendix V-1:
Introduction

Accessing the Application

The software can be downloaded by anyone at **http://autodeskvasari.com**. You will be required to provide your name and a few other details before downloading the program. Once downloaded, the software will work for a fixed amount of time and then becomes non-functional. This "time-bomb" protects Autodesk's investment should they decide to begin selling the program. It also forces users to upgrade to the latest version and thereby continue to help through testing the latest version of the software.

The entire program exists in a single EXE file which can be placed on your desktop for easy access. There is no software to install; you just run the EXE file. Once the application is started, you immediately see a resemblance to the Revit *User Interface*, Figure V-1.1. In the lower right corner you can see a separate *Video Skills Learning* panel. This can be closed and accessed again later via the *Help* menu. You are encouraged to watch these videos to learn more about Vasari.

As you explore the Vasari *User Interface*, you will quickly notice many of the general Revit tools have been removed. Vasari is in no way intended to replace Revit, but many of these features may end up in a future version of Revit or a compatible related application. Right now, Vasari can open Revit files and vice versa. So you can get Revit walls, doors, windows, etc. in Vasari by opening a Revit model, but you cannot create them directly in Vasari.

The application is named after **Giorgio Vasari** (1511 - 1574), an Italian painter, writer, historian, and architect.

FIGURE V-1.1 Vasari user interface

To investigate some of the features of Vasari, you will open a Revit sample file found on the CD (Figure V-1.2). This model has sun shades at the windows and PV panels on the roof.

1. Select: **Application Menu → Open → Project**

2. Browse to the **Vasari Sample Files** folder on the CD.

3. Open file **Office Building.RVT**.

FIGURE V-1.2 Office Building sample model

You should now be viewing a 3D view similar to Figure V-1.2. Notice the *Project Browser* and *Properties Palette* are exactly like they are in Revit.

Project Location

The first thing you need to do before any analysis can be performed is specify where the project is on Earth. This includes location, true north angle and month and day. This information must be known for valid solar, wind and energy modeling studies. You learned how to set some of these options in the rendering chapter. You will set these values next.

4. On the *Analyze* tab, select **Location** (Figure V-1.3).

You must be signed in to **Autodesk 360** to use the various *Autodesk Cloud Services* associated with Vasari. A *Cloud Service* is where the primary computing for something is accomplished online rather than on your computer. This allows extremely large computer server farms to process the information in a fraction of the time.

5. If you are not already logged in, do so.

FIGURE V-1.3 Location tool on Analyze tab

You should now see the dialog shown in Figure V-1.5. Notice all the nearby weather stations are listed and identified on the map.

The closest weather station is selected by default and it is typically the best one to use. Sometimes it is more appropriate to select a weather station farther away. For example, there might be a large elevation difference or a large body of water with buoy-based weather stations.

6. Type in **Minneapolis, MN** and then press **Enter**.

    FYI: You can enter a full address as well. Enter your city or home address.

7. With the proper location defined, click **OK**.

FIGURE V-1.4 Sign in prompt

Once the location is set, the **ViewCube** shows the specified location below it as seen in the image to the right.

Next you want to make sure that **True North** has been properly defined. Sometimes **Plan North**, or *Project North*, is the same; however, most of the time this is not the case. The model is always drawn relative to the computer screen (Plan North). But the actual position on a site relative to *True North* being straight up typically needs to be adjusted.

Minneapolis, MN, USA

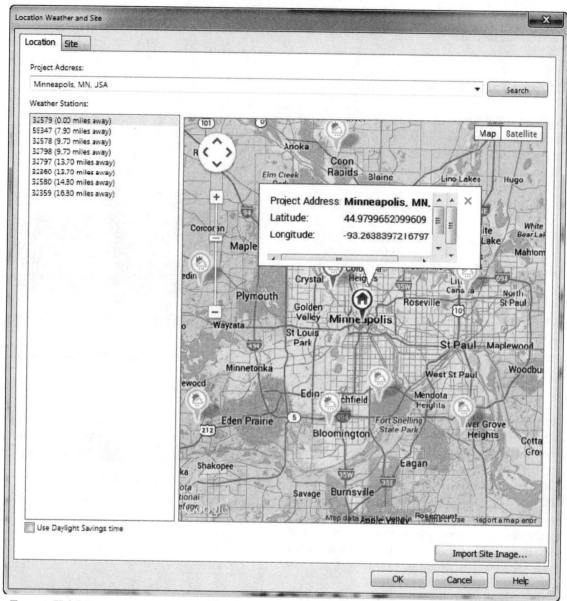

FIGURE V-1.5 Location Weather and Site dialog

> *TIP:* *Notice the Import Site Image in the dialog above!*

Setting True North

Before you can adjust *True North* you need to be in a plan view. It is best to duplicate the *Site Plan* view for this step.

8. Right-click on the **Site Plan** view in the *Project Browser*.

9. Select **Duplicate View → Duplicate**.

10. Rename the new view: **Site Plan – True North**.

11. With the new Site Plan view active, and nothing in the view selected, set the following in the *Project Browser*:

    a. *Orientation*: **True North** (Figure V-1.6).

Nothing should have changed as *True North* and *Project North* are the same. You will change this now.

12. On the *Ribbon* select **Analysis → Position → Rotate True North**.

13. Click the two points shown in Figure V-1.7.

    a. The first point is straight up and vertical from the default rotation point.

    b. The second point is 45 degrees off of the first point.

The site plan should now be rotated as shown in Figure V1-8. This angle would match the civil engineer's site plan orientation. The best part about this is that the rest of the Revit project has not changed.

FIGURE V-1.6 View orientation

FIGURE V-1.7 Rotate True North

FIGURE V-1.8 True North Rotated

14. Switch to the **Site Plan** view (not the *True North* version, but the original view).

Notice that *Project North* has not changed. The floor plan still aligns with the computer screen making it easier to select and edit the model.

With the position and True North set, you are ready to try a few of the analysis tools in Vasari.

Wind Rose

Autodesk makes another separate analysis application called **Autodesk Ecotect**. This program is more advanced but is not based on the Revit platform. Thus, it is more difficult for Revit users to model in, or get their Revit model into this program. To help with this hurdle, Autodesk has ported a few features into Vasari. That is the case for the first feature we will be looking at, called Wind Rose.

The *Wind Rose* tool allows you to consider the speed and direction of prevailing winds at different times of year based on the site location and orientation you chose.

15. Switch to the default **Perspective** view, named **Vasari 3D**.

16. Select the **Ecotect Wind Rose** tool from the *Ribbon*.

You should see the *Ecotect Wind Rose* dialog as shown in Figure V-1.9. There are two main things you should notice here. First, at the bottom of the screen you can adjust the wind rose graphic to only consider a specific time of year and/or time of day. This is useful if you are designing a baseball field and want to exclude the off-season times of year.

The second point of interest is the ability to push this wind rose graphic back into your Vasari model. You will do that next.

17. Click the **Send Wind Rose to BIM project** button – which is pointed out in Figure V-1.9.

18. Select the **Inner Radius Around Model** option (Figure V-1.10).

19. Close the *Wind Rose* dialog, and change the *Visual Style* to **Consistent Colors** in order to visualize the *Wind Rose* better.

Your perspective view should now look similar to Figure V-1.11. This is a great image to print out and study how the building will be impacted by prevailing winds. This might cause you to rotate the building, change the location of an employee patio, or add a row of trees.

Of course, it is important to study this early in the design process so the design can still be easily changed.

This view can be shared with the client as well.

The *Wind Rose* graphic is in the *Mass* category. To turn off the visibility of the *Wind Rose* you need to select **Show Mass by View** on the *Analyze* tab. You can also select the *Window Rose*, right-click and select **Hide Element in View**.

If you switch to any other view you will notice the *Wind Rose* appears as it is considered a 3D element.

FIGURE V-1.9 Ecotect Wind Rose dialog

FIGURE V-1.10 Wind Rose display type

FIGURE V-1.11 Wind Rose added to model

Wind Tunnel

This tool allows the designer to actually see the wind engage the proposed building design. Adding adjacent buildings and trees will give a more accurate picture. On the screen you will actually see animated colors representing wind at various speeds. This is not easily depicted in a book, so you will have to try it to see the full effect.

20. Select the *Wind Rose* and delete it.

> **FYI:** *If you don't delete it, the extents will be larger than they need to be for the wind tunnel study.*

21. While in the *Perspective* view, select **Wind Tunnel** from the *Ribbon*.

Similar to the *Wind Rose* tool, a separate application opens to show the *Wind Tunnel* analysis. The next three figures (12, 13 and 14) show snapshots in time from the animation. Notice how the trees and the main entry way are affected by the wind patterns.

22. If needed, use the icons across the top to zoom in and view the model better.

23. Try adjusting the **Position** slider to change the height at which the wind is calculated within the model.

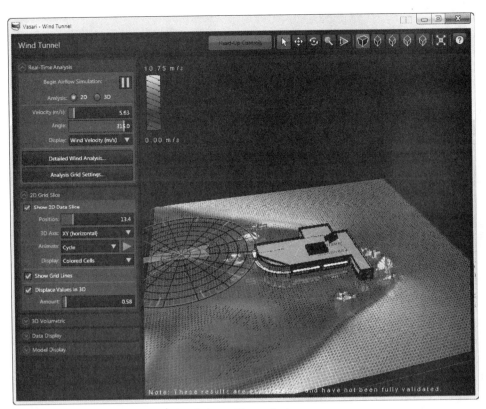

FIGURE V-1.12 2D Airflow simulation – Example 1

FIGURE V-1.13 2D Airflow simulation – Example 2

FIGURE V-1.14 3D Airflow simulation – Example 3

Solar Radiation

The last two features you will look at only work with *Mass* elements rather than Revit walls, doors and windows. *Masses* are created in Revit or from the *Model* tab in Vasari. To save time, you will open another file which has nothing but a *Mass* element in it. However, creating a *Mass* is very easy. The following lists a basic overview on how to create a simple *Mass*:

- Select **Model → Create Mass**.

- Select one of the *Draw* tools (i.e., Line, Rectangle, Arc, etc.).

- Create a closed footprint.

- Select the lines just drawn and then drag the **up arrow** to extrude a solid (see image to the right).

- Click the **Finish Mass** button when done

These are the most basic steps for creating *Mass* elements. Vasari can do so much more! Unfortunately, there is not enough room in this introductory appendix to cover more.

24. Open the Revit sample file named **Office Building Mass Study.RVT** from the CD.

You should see the massing model shown in Figure V-1.15. This model is based on the author's *Commercial Design Using Autodesk Revit* textbook.

FIGURE V-1.15 Massing model sample file

The *Location* has already been set. First you will try the solar radiation at the current *True North* and then rotate the model to see how the analysis changes.

25. Switch to the **Default 3D View** via the *Quick Access Toolbar* (Figure V-1.16).

    FYI: This will also work in the perspective view.

FIGURE V-1.16 Default 3D view icon

26. Select the **Solar Radiation** icon from the *Analysis* tab.

27. Accept the default settings and click the **Analyze** button (Figure V-1.17).

28. Select **Analyze all mass faces in view**.

29. Click **Close** when done.

30. Switch to the **Floor Plan: 2D Site** view and rotate *True North* **45 degrees** per the steps covered at the beginning of this appendix.

31. Run the *Solar Analysis* tool again.

32. Click **Edit** next to *Analysis Display Settings* and uncheck the **Visible** option.

Figures V-1.18 and V-1.19 show the sun being more intense when the entry faces due South.

FIGURE V-1.17 Settings dialog

FIGURE V-1.18 Solar radiation study – original orientation

FIGURE V-1.19 Solar radiation study – building rotated on site

You could *Duplicate* this 3D view and leave the graphics and legend on. Or you can click the *Edit* button next to **Analysis Display** in the *Properties Palette* and turn it off.

Energy Analysis

The last feature you will look at is preliminary energy modeling based on overall volume and selected construction systems. Vasari offers lists from which to choose the major building elements to be used; such as walls, doors, windows, glass type, HVAC systems, and more. This is selected from standard lists because the building has not even been modeled yet. We are still just looking at massing elements. If we find the shape or orientation of the building needs to change, it is easier to do it now when we are just dealing with a *Mass* rather than later when there are potentially thousands of elements in the Revit model. Remember, Vasari is for preliminary design and Revit is for the design development and construction document phases.

We will take a quick look at the options for systems, but ultimately will just be accepting the defaults.

33. Click the **Energy Settings** tool on the *Ribbon.*

You now see the *Energy Settings* dialog.

34. Click the **Edit** button next to the *Conceptual Constructions* parameter.

FIGURE V-1.20   Energy settings dialog and Conceptual constructions dialog

Click on one of the constructions and then click the down-arrow which appears. This will reveal the various options within that category. Take a few minutes to explore all the options in each of these dialogs. Do not make any changes at this time.

FYI: The Mass *needs to have* **Mass Floors** *assigned to it for all this to work properly.*

35. Click **OK** to close the open dialog boxes.

36. Click the **Enable Energy Model** tool on the *Analyze* tab.

Your model should now look similar to Figure V-1.21. Vasari automatically added windows, or **Mass Glazing**, which fill 40% of the exterior walls, and zones for the HVAC system. The windows may not match the intended design but for a preliminary analysis this is typically fine as long as the overall percentage is close. It is possible to model your own *Mass Glazing* if you want to be more specific.

FIGURE V-1.21 Energy settings dialog and Conceptual constructions dialog

Your model is now ready to calculate its energy consumption.

37. Click the click **Run Energy Simulation** button.

38. Accept the suggested *Run Name* by clicking **Continue** (see image at right).

Your model is now being sent to the *Cloud* for analysis via the Autodesk's **Green Building Studio** engine. This type of analysis can be calculated in a fraction of the time in the *Cloud* versus on your computer.

39. When finished, click the **Results & Compare** button on the *Ribbon*.

When finished you will see the dialog shown in Figure V-1.22, which lists the annual and life cycle costs for the building. This is all based on the building construction, location, True North, and local utility rates! You can try changing the shape and/or site orientation and then compare the results side-by-side in this dialog. Click **Open → Green Building Studio** for more detailed analysis options (see images on the next page).

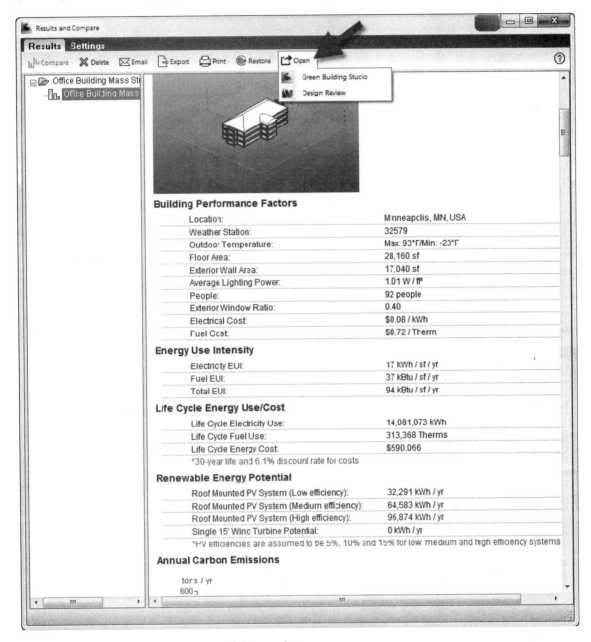

FIGURE V-1.22 Preliminary energy modeling results

This concludes the introduction to Vasari. There is much more to this application and hopefully you will be motivated to dig in more so you can leverage this exciting technology.

FIGURE V-1.23 Project opened in Autodesk Green Building Studio (cloud service)

FIGURE V-1.24 Autodesk Green Building Studio – automatic alternative runs showing potential savings

Index